The Frangipani is Dead:
Contemporary Pacific Art in New Zealand, 1985–2000

The Frangipani is Dead: Contemporary Pacific Art in New Zealand, 1985–2000

Karen Stevenson

HUIA

First published in 2008 by Huia Publishers,
39 Pipitea Street, PO Box 17–335,
Wellington, Aotearoa New Zealand.

www.huia.co.nz

ISBN 978-1-86969-325-1

Cover design: Tim Hansen

National Library of New Zealand Cataloguing-in-Publication Data

Stevenson, Karen.

The frangipani is dead : contemporary Pacific art in New Zealand, 1985–2000 / Karen Stevenson.

Includes bibliographical references and index.

ISBN 978-1-86969-325-1

1. Arts, Pacific Island—20th century. 2. Art, Modern—20th century —New Zealand. I. Title.

700.899—dc 22

Published with the support of the Pacific Arts Committee of Creative New Zealand

creative nz
ARTS COUNCIL OF NEW ZEALAND TOI AOTEAROA

For Mom and Kelsey

Table of Contents

Acknowledgements

My interest in Pacific arts is longstanding. My life with tifaifai on the bed, carved wooden bowls (often used for potato chips) scattered in the lounge, and a father in a pareu getting the morning paper was unique in Los Angeles. Regular visits from family and friends from Tahiti filled our house with music and laughter. One song I recall was 'Boîte de la Hellaby'—a jingle about corned beef. These experiences inspired a continuing investigation into Pacific arts, history and culture. Then, shortly after my arrival in Christchurch, I was shown a photograph of a bull made of corned beef tins, and my past and present lives merged. My academic interests in the assertion of identity through art came full circle as I gazed upon a bull that touched on the foundations of my own identity. It also established an identity for a new art movement in New Zealand—contemporary Pacific art.

Within two months of taking up my position at the University of Canterbury in 1995, three non-related activities took place: *Bottled Ocean* opened at the Robert McDougall Contemporary Art Annex; a selection panel was gathering to decide who would be the first Macmillan Brown Artist in Residence at the Centre for Pacific Studies at the University of Canterbury; and Jonathan Mane-Wheoki (a colleague in the School of Fine Arts) offered me a large box of newspaper clippings, invitations and fliers, and suggested that there just might be something there to work with. My introduction to contemporary Pacific art was complete.

I begin my acknowledgements with the *Bottled Ocean* exhibition and its curator, Jim Vivieaere. I not only acknowledge the importance of this exhibition, but also want to thank Jim Vivieaere for taking the time to respond to my questions and to offer insights, which I have drawn upon in this work. I must also thank Fatu Feu'u, the first Macmillan Brown Artist in Residence, who spent many an afternoon talking to me, explaining how to look at contemporary art and teaching me how to ask questions of artists. I was exposed to a new direction that I found exhilarating—one that would continue to challenge and excite me over the following decade. The nudge to follow this movement, to be a spokesperson for it, was gently provided by Jonathan Mane-Wheoki, and I thank him for that.

The understanding that I have acquired about contemporary Pacific art has been gained through investigation and conversation—a lot of conversation. I want to express my gratitude to the artists who over the last decade have taken the time not only to answer questions, but also to teach me what questions to ask. This give and take has provided me with a better understanding of their work. They have given freely of their time, their hearts and their perspectives regarding their own practice and, further, regarding contemporary Pacific art and its place in New Zealand, the Pacific and the world. Without those artists this book would not be possible.

I would also like to acknowledge the artists who delved into their archives to find images that have not been published before. Their time and effort for doing so is much appreciated. Thanks go to Richard Shortland Cooper, Dagmar Dyck, Graham Fletcher, Ian George, Niki Hastings-McFall, Ioane Ioane, Nanette Lela'ulu, Andy Leleisi'uao, Iosefa Leo, Ani O'Neill, Lyle Penisula, Johnny Penisula, Rosanna Raymond, Evotia Tamua, Filipe Tohi, Michel Tuffery, Sheyne Tuffery and Veronica Vaevae for providing images for this book.

In addition I want to acknowledge the aid given by friends, institutions and galleries in the provision of images for the book. I thank Julie Fua'i, Roger Fyfe of the Canterbury Museum, Geoffrey Heath of the Auckland Art Gallery Toi o Tāmaki, Danny Leaosavai'i, Andy Murnane and Paul Jeffcoat of Dawn Raid Entertainment, Tanya Muagututi'a of Pacific Underground, Marion McGuire of PaperGraphica, Joanna Moore of Te Papa Tongarewa, Rangihiroa Panoho, Giles Petersen, Hilary Scothorn, Duncan Shaw-Brown, Michael Tucker and Sarah Crowe of Loop, Tory Whanau of the New Zealand Film Commission, Deborah White of Whitespace, Nicola Woodhouse of City Gallery Wellington, Richard Wooten of the Sarjeant Gallery, and Fuli Pereira of the Auckland Museum.

I must also acknowledge Ron Brownson of the Auckland Art Gallery Toi o Tāmaki, Sean Mallon of Te Papa Tongarewa, the Pacific Business Trust, Lonnie Hutchinson, Shigeyuki Kihara, Lily Laita, John Pule, Greg Semu, Misa Tupou and Sima Urale. This list represents many emails and conversations that have led to the acquisition and publication of the images in this book.

I would, too, like to acknowledge the many other people without whose help I could not have completed this project. They include Douglas Horrell, Matt Roland and Devon Sinclair for their help creating the image files; Belinda Grigg and Gina Irish, who both assisted in the creation and compilation of artist files; my colleagues at the School of Fine Arts who have supported this project; Maria Ifopo and Stephanie Oberg for many conversations; and Anton Carter, Phyllis Herda, Jessica Johnston, Andy Leleisi'uao and Fuli Pereira for comments on this manuscript. A special thank you goes to Brian Bargh and others at Huia for bringing this project to press.

I end as I began, with thanks to my family. Tahiti's arts and cultures are my foundations, my connection to the islands, my introduction to the link between past and present, to the importance of tradition in the contemporary. Thank you for your support. Mom and Kelsey this is for you.

List of Illustrations

INTRODUCTION

CHAPTER 01

CHAPTER 02

CHAPTER 03

Introduction

As a stereotype, the Pacific is embedded in the discourse on colonisation, representation and gender. The Pacific and its traditions are seen as "other", as exotic—a tourist experience, a souvenir. The clichés of the happy islander, sun-drenched beaches and beautiful maidens perpetuate the myth—a myth based, of course, in the real world experiences of both artists and their audiences. The Pacific has also become a key player in New Zealand's popular culture. In the late 1990s, barkcloth was used to wallpaper the sets of Shortland Street, tivaevae were incorporated into advertising campaigns and the brown-eyed girl still smiles from the CD art of Annie Crummer, Sulata and Lole.[1]

Key to understanding this artistic movement is the fact that most of the artists involved were born in New Zealand and most were under thirty. They are from a generation not unlike previous generations, yet one that has a foot in two cultures. As Pacific scholar Jemaima Tiatia (1998) suggests, they are caught between cultures. This notion has been taken up by many artists, but was exemplified by Misa Tupou's *A Choice of a New Generation* **[figure In.1]**. By placing a Coca-Cola can within a coconut, he draws upon the advertiser's slogan. With humour, he addresses a key issue in New Zealand: a generation gap, a rift between the island and the urban. In so doing, the suggestion is posited that this generation's heart is not in the islands. Except for the umu in the back garden, their urban reality is far removed from their ancestral home. For many, the islands are as much a dream as they are to the tourists that flock there annually. It is their geographic reality that enables these artistic expressions. As Jonathan Mane-Wheoki stated:

> Certainly, the challenge of reconciling where they have come from with where they now find themselves infuses the work of contemporary Pacific Island artists in New Zealand with a distinctive radiance. (Mane-Wheoki 1996c: 29)

As a reflection of one of the Pacific diaspora destinations, contemporary Pacific art is unique to the social, economic and political realities of New Zealand. Laugutu Poloai commented on this in her *Economical Resources*, which weaves together plastic shopping bags in a downward spiral. Understanding the social, economic and political realities of Pacific Islanders is essential for an appreciation of this artistic practice. Referencing issues of identity, of (re-)presentation, of the acquisition of knowledge and of the urban landscape, contemporary Pacific art is integrally woven into their New Zealand reality. These strands form the basis of contemporary Pacific art practice. These are the issues that drive this movement, the issues that are discussed in this work.

In the 1990s, Pacific art became a flourishing and vital style within New Zealand art practice. Labelling the movement "Pacific" demonstrates that ethnicity was a key factor in recognising the artists involved with this contemporary practice. Clearly, ethnicity has to do with identity, offering statements of exclusion and/or inclusion, defining oneself vis-à-vis another. Most of the artists that fit the Pacific label detest the stereotype that the term conjures up. Frequently it is this stereotype or, more specifically, the renegotiation or destruction of it that plays a large role in Pacific art practice. This is not unique to New Zealand. Issues of identity and the finding of an ethnic voice were also very much a part of a global academic and artistic debate that started in the 1970s, a debate that structures a broader framework of contemporary indigenous art.[2] Many of the issues are similar for indigenous art and for Pacific art — they focus on identity, hybridity and place. As Nicholas Thomas (1996a: 314) noted, Pacific art 'privileges diasporic creativity and speaks across the racial divisions'. The debate has, in fact, forced the issue of identity, which seems now to be 'above all about belonging to a culture: it ain't where you're at, it's where you're from' (Thomas 1996b: 340). This concept is integral to the work of Pacific artists as they strive to find a place to stand and, in consequence, identity and politics become entangled.

Indigenous politics in the Pacific were influenced by a political activism that began shortly after World War II. Samoa was first to gain independence — in 1962; between then and 1980, when Vanuatu became independent, much of the Pacific became self-governing.[3] As the Pacific Islands became independent nations, identity became marked by cultural difference. Seeking symbols that could be representative of their fledgling nation states, Pacific Islanders looked to the arts as symbols of their Pacific identity (Keesing & Tonkinson 1982, Nero 1992, and Stevenson 1990). Independence and the well-received exhibitions of their artistic heritage spurred a cultural renaissance that had an enormous effect throughout the Pacific.

In New Zealand the politics of sovereignty played itself out, with issues of identity coming to a head in the mass protests of the 1981 Springbok Tour.[4] For Māori, two key results of this political activity were the creation of the Waitangi Tribunal and the positioning of New Zealand as a bicultural nation. Inevitably, these political endeavours and achievements were reflected in Māori artwork. As Jonathan Mane-Wheoki noted:

> So powerfully engaged with these political and cultural matters are most contemporary Māori artists that to seek mere aesthetic or intellectual gratification from their art is almost unthinkable. (Mane-Wheoki 1995b: 5)

With New Zealand positioned as a bicultural nation, supported by a treaty, Māori were acquiring an equal voice. The strength of this position is reflected in a strong artistic practice based on cultural heritage and identity. The prominence of Māori art afforded, in turn, a platform for Pacific Islanders as they, too, critiqued their social reality. This has led to a synergy of social and political concerns expressed through the arts. Creating a cultural foundation supported by a traditional past and invigorated by the present, the island and the urban were combined in the creation of a vital art movement.

In New Zealand's post-colonial era Pacific Islanders began to pick and choose which aspects of their traditional past they would put out for public scrutiny. How they would represent not only themselves but also the cultures they wished to emulate became the underlying issue of each individual agenda. However, key to this discourse is the reality of migration and the social context of Pacific Islanders

Figure In.1 › Misa Tupou, *A Choice of a New Generation*, coconut, printed aluminium and straws. Image provided by Pacific Business Trust.

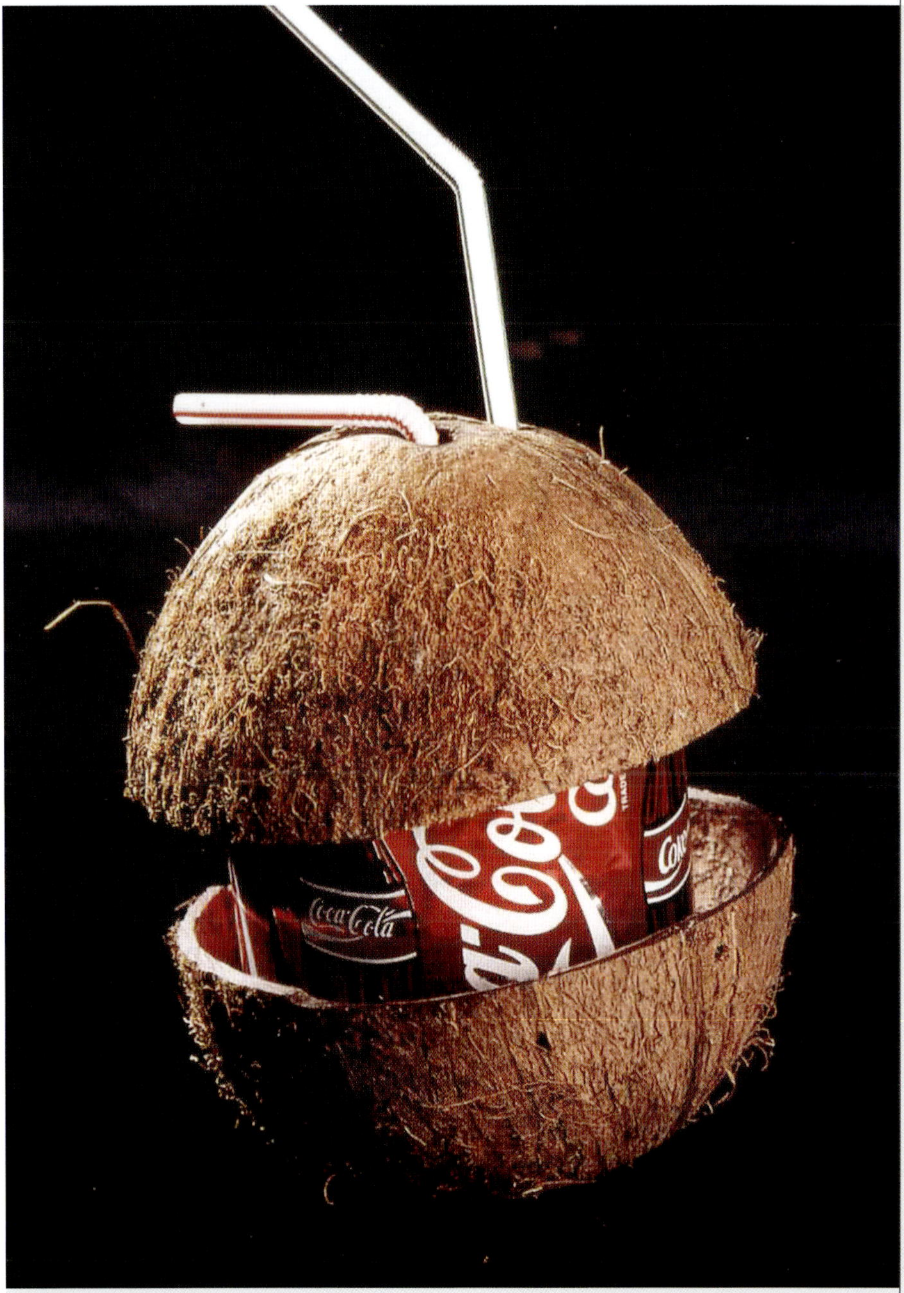

in New Zealand, as is the assertion of an identity, the loss of and consequent need to reinvent cultural traditions, and the acquisition of knowledge that enables the expression of these issues. These ideas are captured in Nanette Lela'ulu's *Little Man Sad Eyes* **[figure In.2]**. By positioning a young boy in front of ginkgo leaves (as a representation of New Zealand), his unease in his new environment becomes apparent. Migration, which is central to this artistic movement, has also enabled Auckland to position itself as the city with the largest Pacific Island population. This, coupled with the fact that most of these artists are New Zealand born, provides the synergies between the island and the urban.

The number of artists referencing a Pacific identity grew steadily between 1985 and 2000. The media that they worked with included the traditional (painting, sculpture) and the avant-garde (digital media, fashion), as well as literature, theatre and film. Given the Pacific notion of art as all-inclusive and as being an integral aspect of life (therefore perhaps throwing a wider net, as it were), the range of media used clearly reflects Pacific culture itself.

The majority of these artists have initially addressed issues of identity within the classroom—a venue of support for their artistic endeavours. Both secondary and tertiary programmes throughout New Zealand have seen a growth in Pacific Islanders asserting a creative identity. The result has been the development of both an art movement as well as a structure of support (as witnessed by the Pacific Art Award, the Tautai Contemporary Pacific Arts Trust and the Pacific Arts Committee of Creative New Zealand).

Financial and creative support have aided contemporary Pacific art and, at the same time, offered a market and venue for the flourishing of a Pacific idiom. Transferring secondary school accolades to either tertiary or art market success is not always easy. Many of those who plied their way through school subsequently shifted their focus, some entering other areas of the arts (design, advertising) or becoming art teachers themselves. The dream of being an artist is not always sustainable in one's daily reality. Artists such as Lyle Penisula, Pauline Hoeft-Cocker, Laugutu Poloai, Toegamau Sefo and William Furneaux, who showed great promise and were highly visible in the *Bottled Ocean* exhibition (1994–1995) and/or the book *Speaking in Colour* (1997), have shifted their focus. Others, including Riki Tangaroa, Loretta Young and Sale Jessop returned to their islands.[5] Young's *O le Ala O le Loto Alofa*

Figure In.2 › Nanette Lela'ulu, *Little Man Sad Eyes*, 2000. Photograph courtesy of the artist.

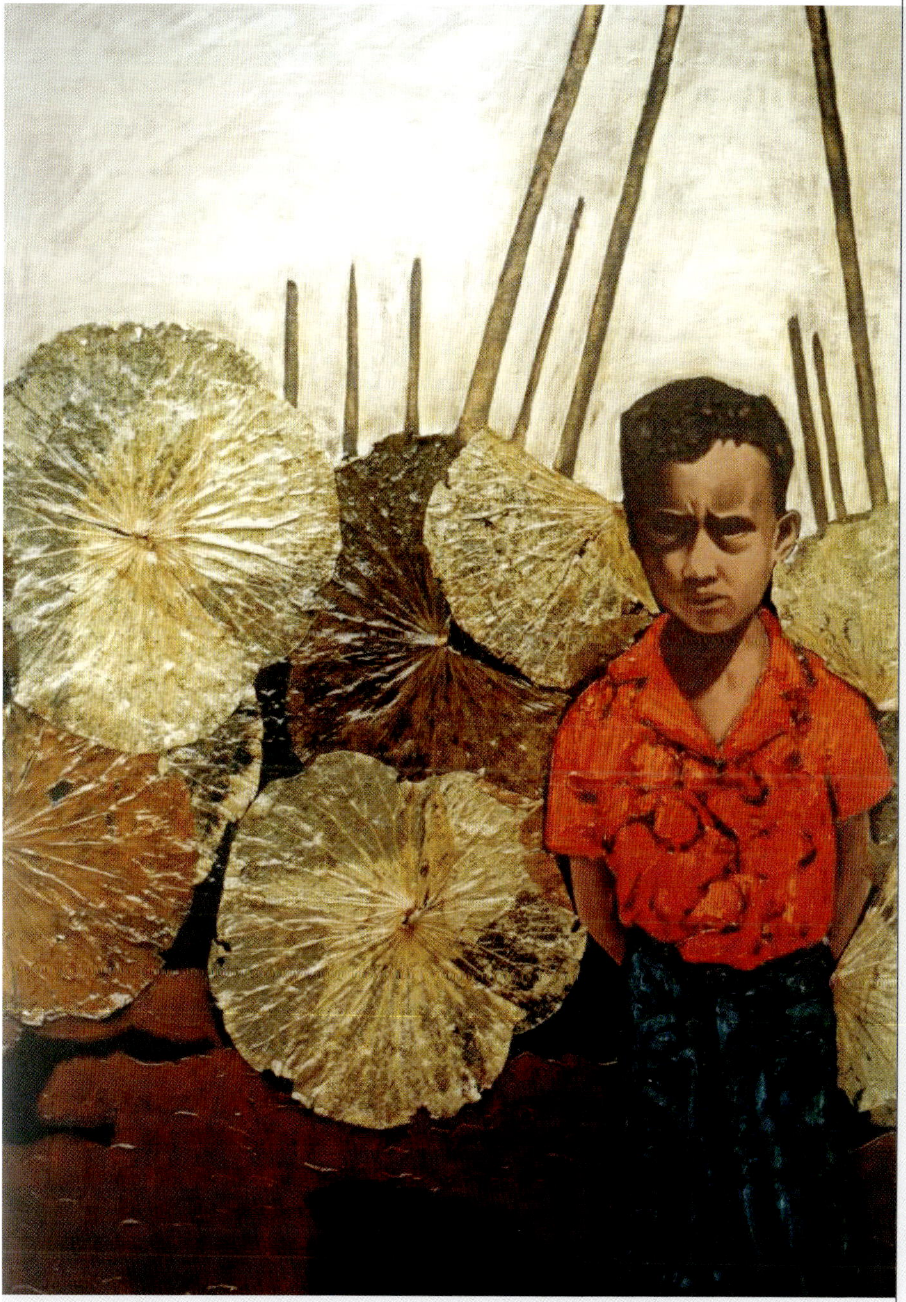

(The Road of Loving Hearts) **[figure In.3]** acknowledges that journey home. Others exhibit sporadically. However, a core of artists has remained steadfast throughout this period and has led the movement to national prominence and international acceptance.[6]

Having navigated institutional art education, having dealt with issues of identity and having acknowledged their position in New Zealand society, these artists are creating traditions that create a bridge between the world of their ancestors and their own global urban reality. Contemporary Pacific artists are as varied as any other group. They combine their ethnicity and their place within New Zealand to comment not only on their cultures but also on themselves as individuals. The label "Pacific" offers a cultural construct of understanding but it does not limit the variety of expression or the complexity of the issues that the artists draw upon. However negative this label appears, it has a function: it allows for a clear reference to Polynesian cultural traditions, it offers a platform and it distinguishes Pacific Islanders as the "other's other" (Mane-Wheoki 1995b: 16). It is this reality that reinforces the social and political agendas of their work. However, the socio-political aspects of contemporary Pacific art cannot be scrutinised in a bell jar. There are many strands that must be unravelled in order to understand contemporary Pacific art's inherent complexities.

In the 1960s and 1970s race relations and issues concerning human rights were at the forefront of indigenous concerns. The civil rights movement in the United States, apartheid in South Africa, a growing desire for independence from countries under colonial rule and, here in New Zealand, the "dawn raids"—all these events created a worldwide awareness of civil rights injustices.[7] Interestingly, these social problems heightened an interest in indigenous arts; yet, it took some time for those teaching the art of the Pacific to embrace these issues.[8] The arts of the Pacific (as taught by art historians in the United States and Europe) were explained via style areas and masterpieces. Gifted, pillaged or stolen, the art of the Pacific was no longer found in the Pacific, but housed in museums around the world.[9] For those concerned, traditional Pacific cultures no longer existed or, if they did, their art was not authentic because these cultures had been sullied by contact with the West.[10] To mark the bi-centennial of Cook's voyages, a number of exhibitions were organised (including *Artificial Curiosities* (1974) and *The Art of the Pacific Islands* (1979))

Figure In.3 › Loretta Young, *O le Ala O le Loto Alofa (The Road of Loving Hearts)*, screen print on patent vinyl, Astroturf and spray painted river rocks, 1996. Photograph courtesy of the artist.

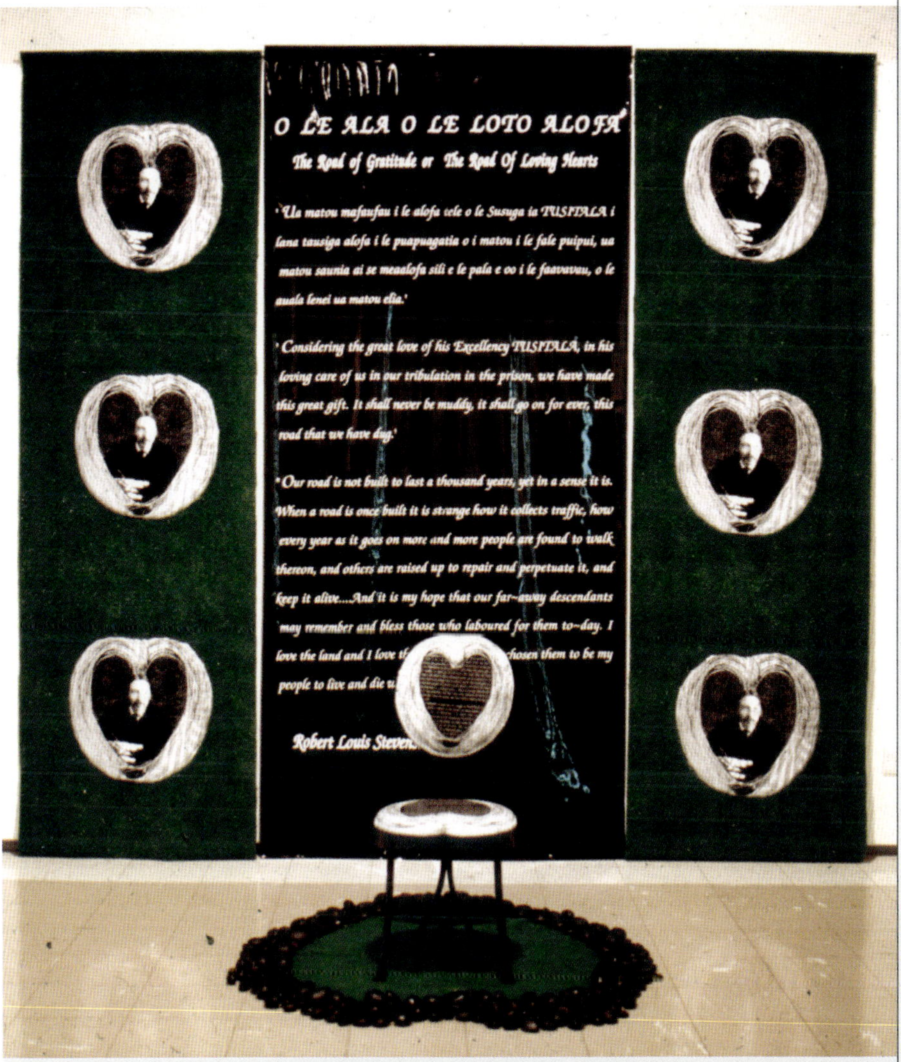

bringing together the taonga of Pacific cultures that had been collected in the 18th and 19th centuries. These exhibitions (along with *"Primitivism" in 20th Century Art: Affinity of the Tribal and the Modern* and *Te Maori*, both held in New York (1984)) opened up a vigorous discussion on a number of issues surrounding Pacific art, including ownership, value, evolution, tradition and authenticity.

As art exhibitions were the focus of debate in the United States, *Te Hokinga Mai* (*The Coming Home of Te Maori*) 1986—7 and *Whatu Aho Rua: A Weaving Together of Traditional and Contemporary Pieces of Taonga* (1989) not only ignited a discussion of art practice in New Zealand, but also demonstrated that 'contemporary Maori art making is contributing significantly to the reimaging of New Zealand's cultural identity and the reinvention of New Zealand's history' (Mane-Wheoki 1995b: 5).

This artistic debate was fuelled by memories of political and social confrontation. The dawn raids, the Springbok Tour, the creation of the Waitangi Tribunal, issues of sovereignty, indigenous protest and race relations—all remained a concern. This period of heightened political activity, coupled with a sense of betrayal, created a cultural divide not just between Pacific Islanders and New Zealanders, but also within Pacific communities themselves.[11] The shift from the island to the urban was complex. As New Zealand born Pacific Islanders embraced the notion of Pasifika (a self imposed label that fused their island heritage and their urban reality), they became more comfortable in their role as urban Polynesians.[12]

Drawing upon their traditions, creating new ones and asking that the viewer re-evaluate their perceptions of the Pacific, artists embraced the process of taking back or owning their representation. Language, both visual and literal, became an important tool in this process. Utilising and owning derogatory terms, such as the term "coconut", enabled the assertion of an identity at the same time as it questioned the stereotype. Jim Vivieaere, in his installation *E Manako to te Uto*, 1995 **[figure In.4]**, questioned stereotypes associated with Pacific Islanders. This piece—in black and white, there are no frangipani, no bright colours—was not only a visual statement of his reality, but also recognition of both the stereotypes and abilities of Pacific peoples. As such, the clichés, the icons, the traditions of and about the Pacific were both included and excluded. Pacific artists could, in this way, choose which stereotypes to promote or to denounce, and so this discourse reflected the reality of migration, the new social context of Pacific Islanders in New Zealand, the

Figure In.4 › Jim Vivieaere, *E Manako to te Uto*, window installation December 1995–January 1996, Auckland Museum. Auckland Art Gallery Toi o Tāmaki.

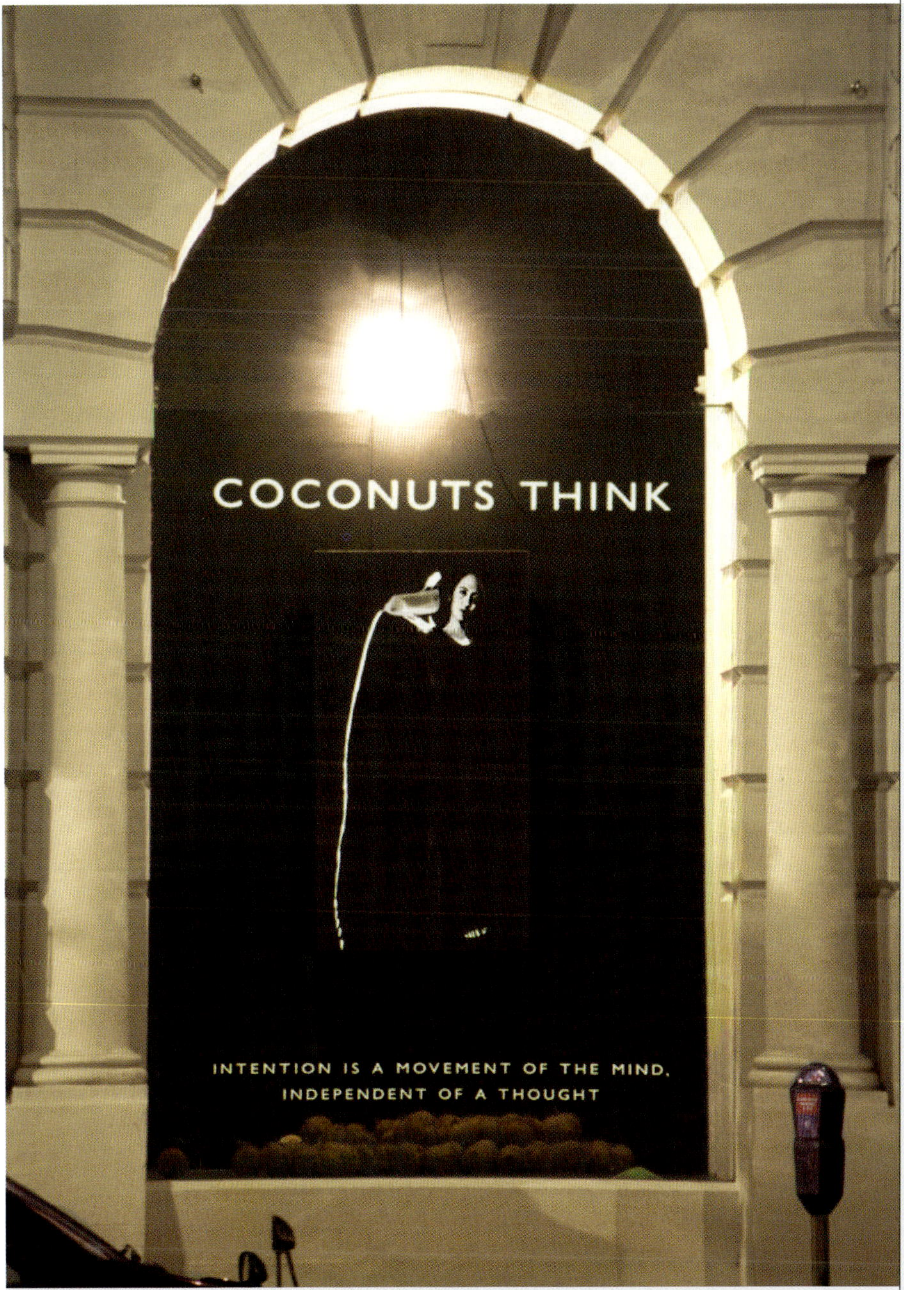

assertion of an identity, the loss of and the need to reinvent cultural traditions, and the acquisition of knowledge that enabled them to express these ideas.

Combining a number of voices and perspectives, many of which have changed over time, this body of work attempts to weave together ideas and histories without offering a priority to any one issue, voice or belief, or indeed any set of issues, voices or beliefs. It draws on the contributions of writers and critics of Pacific art—in particular Sean Mallon, Jonathan Mane-Wheoki, Pandora Fulimalo Pereira, Nicholas Thomas, Caroline Vercoe and Jim Vivieaere, all of whom have contributed greatly to our knowledge about contemporary Pacific art.[13] The work of Melanie Anae, Cluny Macpherson and Paul Spoonley is also very important in providing the social context of Pacific Islanders in New Zealand; and Phyllis Herda, Adrienne Kaeppler and Jehanne Teilhet-Fisk, amongst others, helped provide a theoretical and historical foundation for the contemporary.[14]

As noted, social and political changes were accompanied by changes in art production. We no longer speak of "Pacific art" as it was understood in the 1980s; for, as Susan Cochrane (1993: 175) noted, 'these art forms (contemporary Pacific art) are especially appropriate to the urban environment from which they emanate. A study of them reveals the type of social changes taking place in the artists' societies, and also demonstrates a range of opportunities has developed for artists to make and market art in the urban environment'.

This book, *The Frangipani is Dead,* attempts to provide not only a historical overview of the fifteen-year period from 1985 to 2000, it also analyses the issues that drove contemporary Pacific art. The most important factor was that of identity. This came into play in numerous ways, perhaps most commonly in the artists' desires to draw upon a cultural heritage, to comment on the politics of the post-colonial age and to position themselves within New Zealand. Pacific Islands artists felt an affinity with Māori as indigenous peoples, and as minorities within New Zealand; it is not surprising then, that indigenous politics underlay a desire to assert a cultural identity.

Offering a historical framework, Chapter 1 looks at the developments of contemporary Pacific art, primarily through the creation of travelling exhibitions (especially *Te Moemoea no Iotefa* and *Bottled Ocean*). These exhibitions not only opened doors for Pacific artists, more importantly, they placed Pacific art in New Zealand's art

Figure In.5 › Fatu Feu'u, *Miti Mitia*, oil on canvas, 2000. Photograph courtesy of Duncan Shaw Brown.

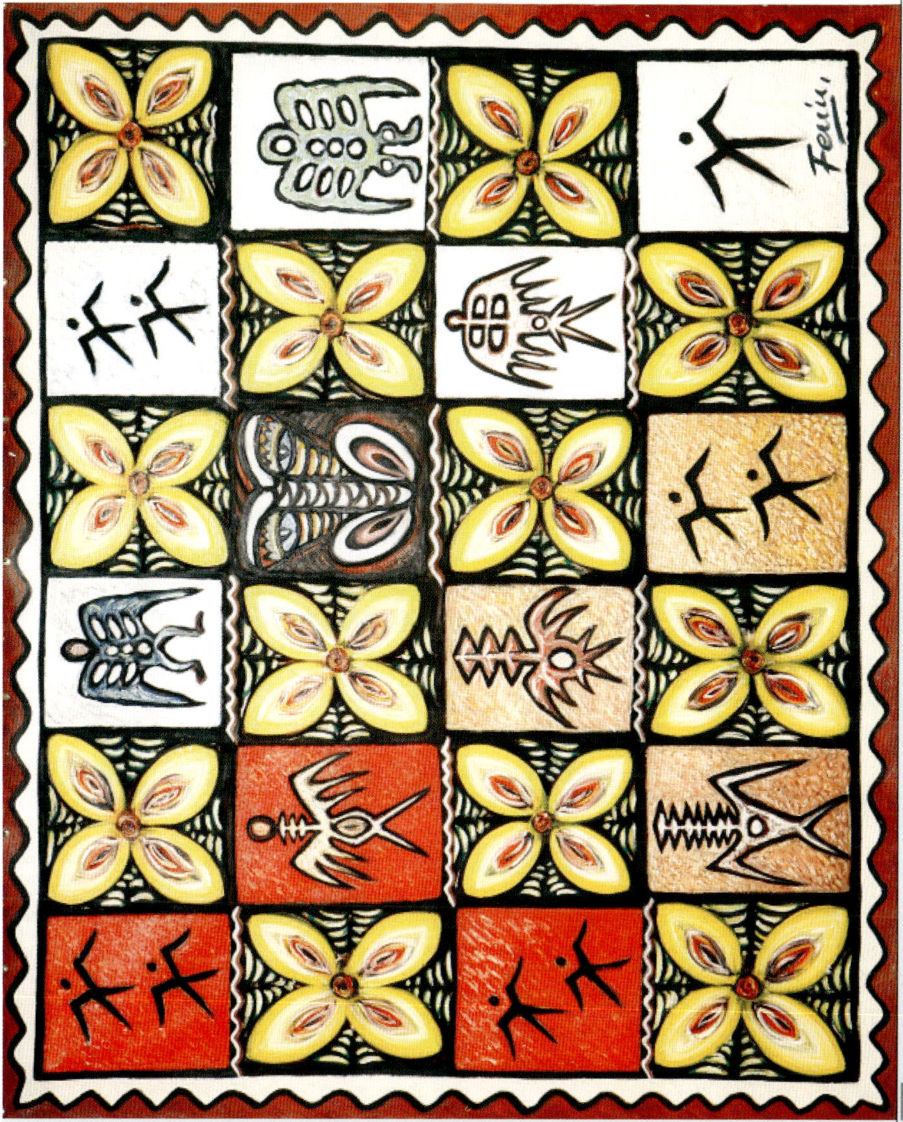

galleries and consequently brought Pacific art to the attention of New Zealand. *Te Moemoea no Iotefa* and *Bottled Ocean* were both landmark exhibitions, though for different reasons. *Te Moemoea no Iotefa* was the first exhibition of contemporary Pacific art to travel throughout New Zealand; it included ten artists whose work demonstrated a continuum from the traditional to the contemporary. *Bottled Ocean*, which also travelled throughout New Zealand, on the other hand, demonstrated a break from the past, positioning a group of young artists as the Pacific's future. In analysing these exhibitions as well as a move internationally (with New Zealand's participation in the Asia Pacific Triennial), this chapter provides the historical framework for the Pacific art movement.

Representation and identity were key elements, and the Pacific label was reinforced. However, this label also led to stereotyping. Chapter 2 looks at the importance of the label and the assertion of a Pacific identity by Pacific artists. Using the stereotype of tapa, tiki, and tatau[15] (all images easily recognised as Pacific), Pacific artists reinforced both their identity and their position within New Zealand. By utilising images and objects from a Pacific heritage, artists therefore reinforced the stereotype while positioning themselves as Pacific artists. The label opened doors, but identity is often a double-edged sword, and the conundrum of whether to own or to destroy the cliché is addressed in Chapter 2.

Just as identity is an underlying theme throughout this book, so is the negotiation and re-contextualisation of the stereotype. Chapters 3 and 4 address the ways in which Pacific arts attempt to balance the preconceived notions about the arts and cultures of the Pacific with their lived realities. In Chapter 3 the concept of abstraction is positioned as a traditional means of imaging a Pacific world. This is in distinct contrast to age-old beliefs in the primitive—beliefs that still linger and undermine both the acceptance and value of Pacific art. Offering the ability to work abstractly also reinforces contemporary Pacific art practice—not as hybrid but as a part of the continuum of a tradition. Such abstraction within Pacific arts practice—be it the utilisation of language and image, or the use of visual metaphor—results in the contemporary being supported by the past.

This is further developed in Chapter 4, which identifies how Pacific icons, such as textiles and lei, have been utilised to make assertions of a Pacific identity in an urban environment. This chapter looks again at stereotype and challenges the

Figure In.6 › Graham Fletcher, *Wallflowers*, enamel on aluminium, 2000. Photograph courtesy of the artist.

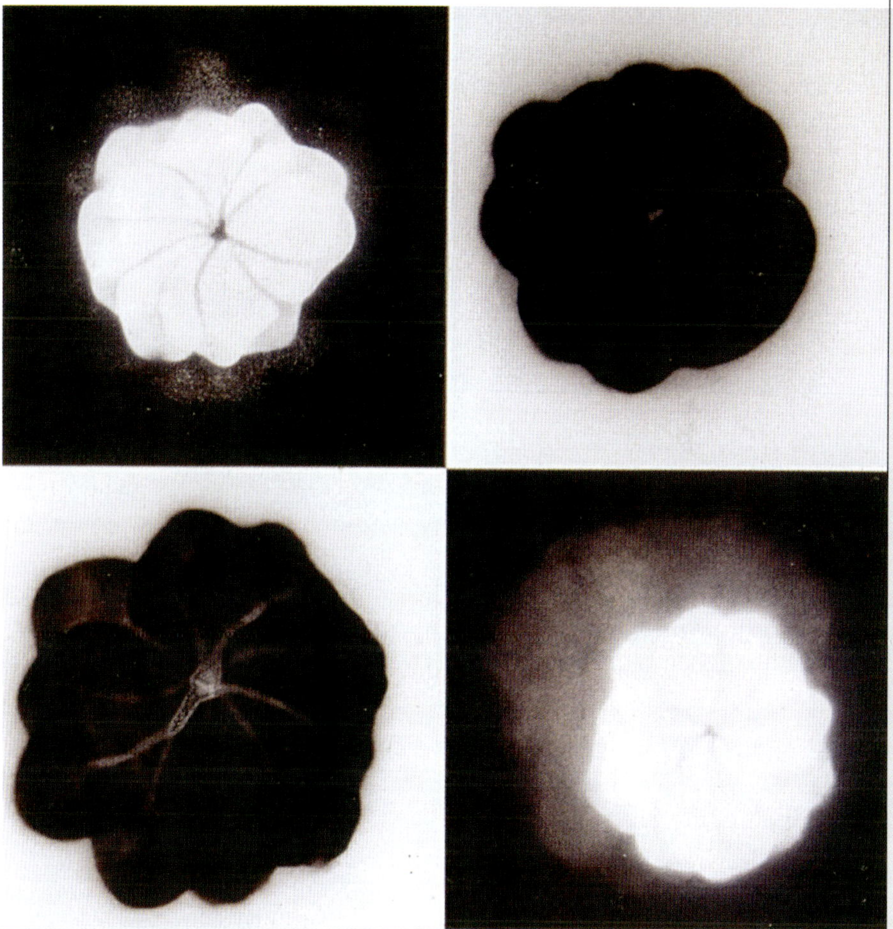

concept by providing cultural references for various icons. As objects of status and economic importance, such icons are more than clichés—they provide an essential foundation to an understanding of the art movement as well as to the identities associated with it. In moving beyond the stereotype, Pacific artists were and still are innovating the past, reinterpreting icons for a new generation.

Finally, Chapters 5 and 6 examine the need to self-represent—not only to move beyond the cliché, but to create new foundations on which to stand and speak. Again, identity plays a large role. As artists assert a Pacific identity—but one of their own making—the complexity of both owning and destroying the stereotype comes into play. In this process, the political in Pacific art takes centre stage as artists become their culture's critic. The images created address the social realities of urban Polynesian life—factory work, multiple jobs, abuse and suicide. Chapter 5 explores these issues, which combine with notions of cultural loss to create new directions for Pacific peoples. Chapter 6 looks at fashion, the music industry and the West's preoccupation with the hybrid. It highlights the creation of an urban language, of a reaction to global influences. In so doing, it outlines other possible responses which enable Pacific artists to both assert their identities and to position themselves on the world stage. How Polynesian artists embrace such genres as film, modern dance, opera, the theatre, fashion, hip hop music and dance is investigated. Hip hop artists refer back to the islands, acknowledging the need to reference one's cultural heritage. They are not suggesting a gloss—the stereotype of the frangipani—but the necessity of understanding one's history. With this knowledge there is strength in an assertion of an urban Pacific identity.

Changes in attitudes, in perceptions and in stereotypes are reflected in the title of this book—*The Frangipani is Dead*. The frangipani, a symbol of the Pacific, became a symbol of the Pacific art movement; its stylised form is a key motif that is used by many artists, especially Fatu Feu'u **[figure In.5]**. As a stereotype, its bright decorative appeal led critics to suggest that contemporary Pacific art was as fashionable and ephemeral as a frangipani itself. The book's title also places the movement of Pacific art into the broader category of New Zealand art—moving beyond the icon, beyond the cliché. Pacific icons such as barkcloth, tatau and tivaevae have become part of popular culture. For many artists this cliché has been a stumbling block, a constant that they had to work against. Ideologically it created not just a Pacification of

Figure In.7 › Andy Lelei, *You Make Me Nobody*, acrylic on canvas, 1999. Collection of the Macmillan Brown Centre for Pacific Studies.

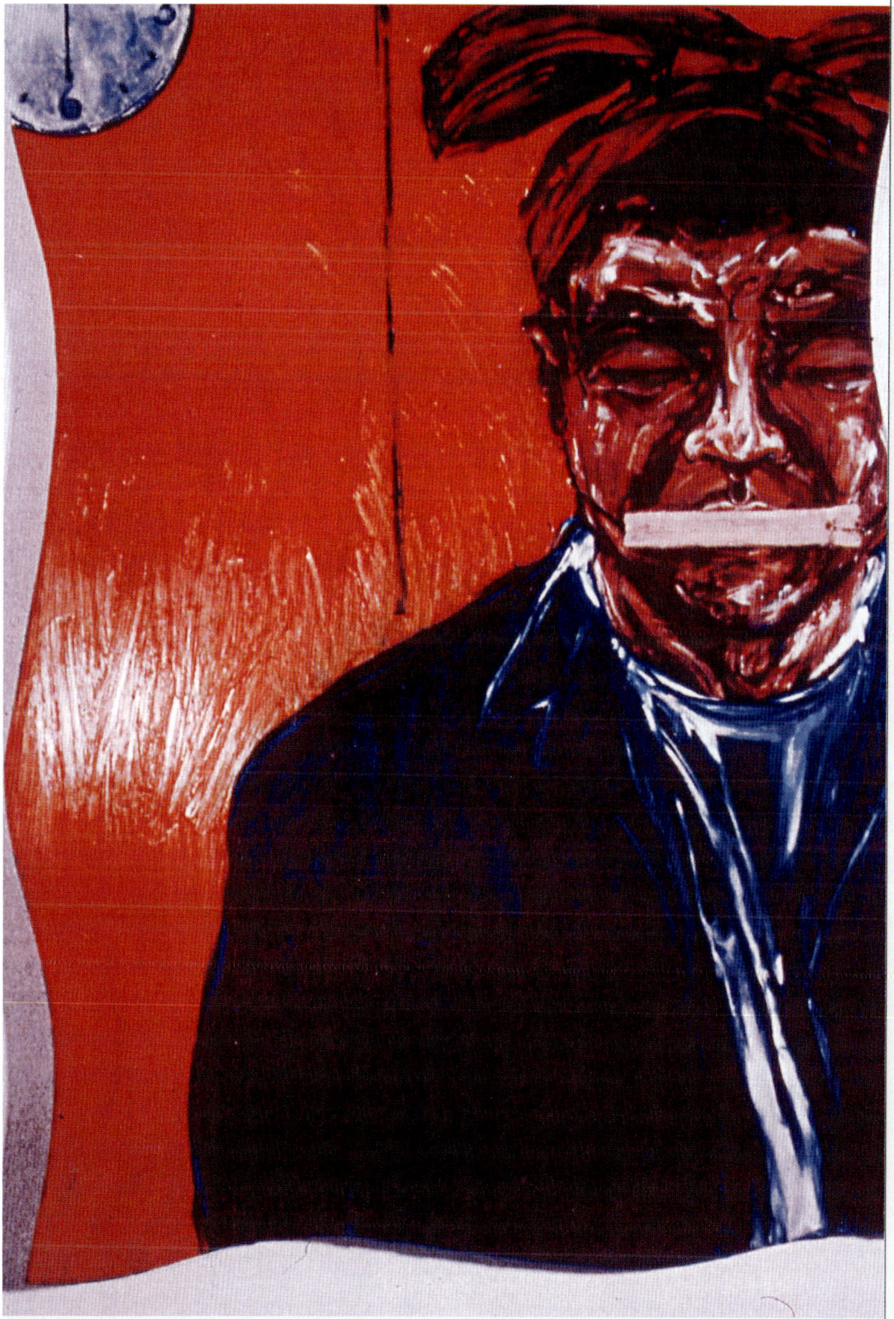

New Zealand, it further reinforced the stereotype. The frangipani, always bright, always colourful, represented the Pacific. In contrast, Graham Fletcher offers a different interpretation of the cliché in his black and white *Wallflowers* series **[figure In.6]**. Fletcher not only 'problematises the stereotype' (McAloon 2005: 5), he also focuses on the fragile nature of the frangipani and, implicitly, of culture. In this monochrome depiction, the realities of life for Pacific Islanders in New Zealand, a theme seen in Andy Lelei's[16] *You Make Me Nobody* **[figure In.7]**, are also addressed. It is this conflict, between the real and the imagined, that has played itself out in the artistic practice of contemporary Pacific artists. Perhaps more to the point, many artists believed that the image represented not who they were but an idealised/mythologised Pacific embedded in the minds of others. Therefore, the frangipani became a symbol of resentment. More than a stereotype or cliché, it symbolised a white attitude towards brown people, it created the box within which Pacific artists were so easily imprisoned. This book attempts to tease out the myriad ramifications of the meaning of the word frangipani and to show that many artists have indeed moved beyond the stereotype, leaving the frangipani, but not their cultural heritage, behind.

There is a constant ravelling and unravelling of the many strands that make up contemporary Pacific art. The stasis created in the cliché binds one to the past, but the movement and the artists themselves are looking to their future, and in so doing are constantly pushing the boundaries of their work. Employing the concepts of performance art, Michel Tuffery does just this **[figure In.8]**. Creating performances that include his sculptures, traditional dance 'crews', music and food, he blends the island and the urban. It is this give and take—the synergy between place and time—that is the foundation of contemporary Pacific art.

This book traces the development of the Pacific art movement between 1985 and 2000, exploring the movement's beginnings, the artists involved and the key issues that underlay their practices as they evolved throughout the fifteen-year period. It is hoped that readers will examine, and perhaps re-evaluate, their perceptions of the Pacific and recognise the lived Pacific reality that is New Zealand.

Figure In.8 › Michel Tuffery, *Junior dancing on Laumei* at the Sydney Olympic Arts Festival, 2000. Photograph courtesy of the artist.

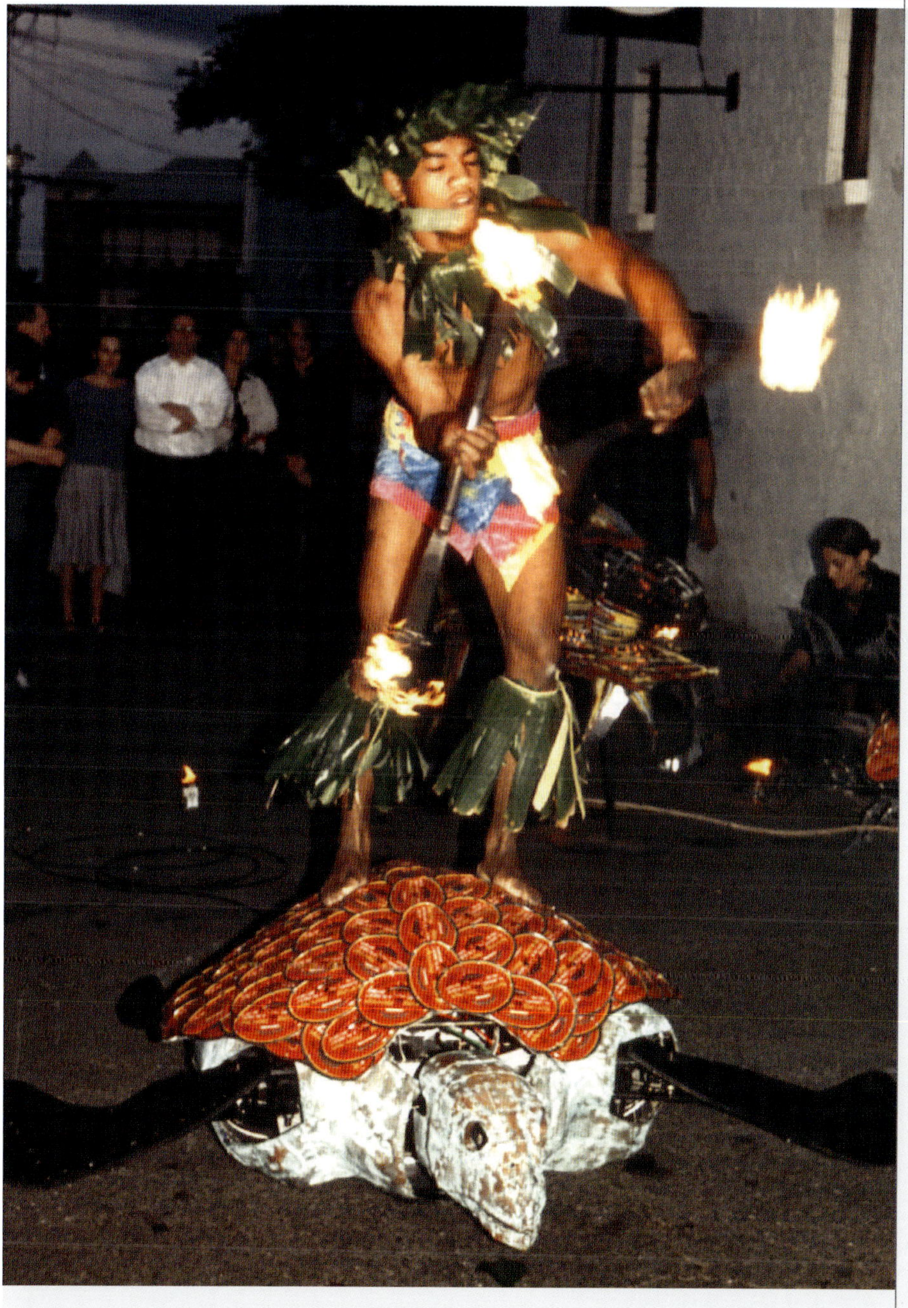

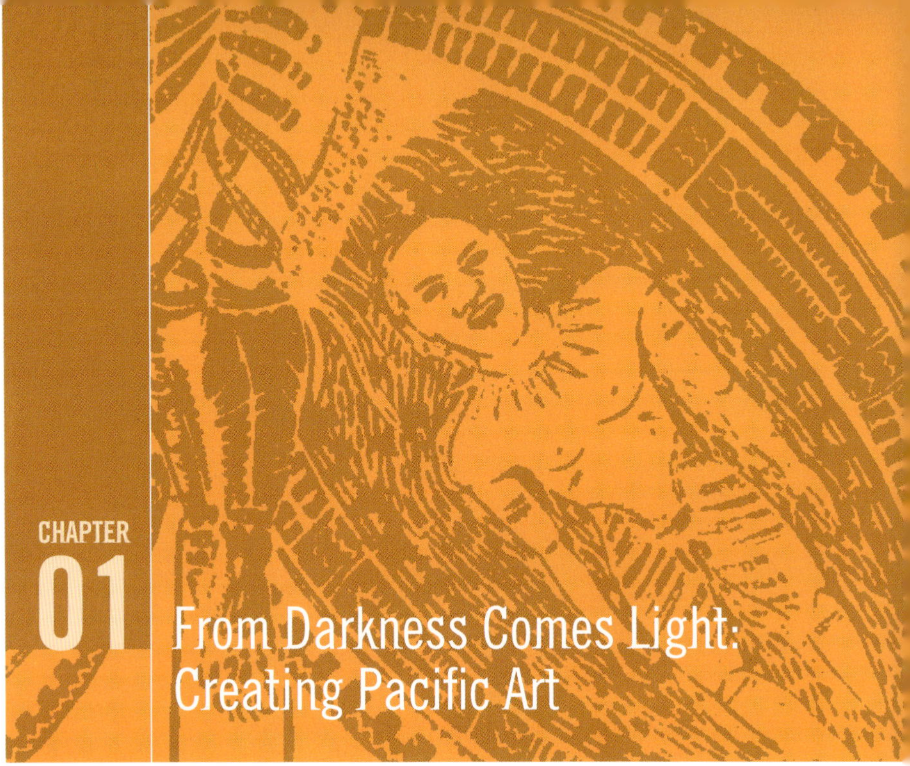

CHAPTER 01

From Darkness Comes Light: Creating Pacific Art

For many, the *Te Maori* exhibition, which opened in New York in 1984, was the seed that enabled both the growth and recognition of Māori art throughout New Zealand. It provided the opportunity to re-situate Māori art production within the New Zealand cultural landscape. *Te Maori* and its triumphant return (*Te Hokinga Mai*) in 1986 heightened the awareness and vitality of Māori art and culture many had left for dead.[1] While Māori began to accept new cultural production as part of their system of taonga, Pacific Islanders in New Zealand began to look to their cultural foundations as well. An acceptance of the fact that Pacific cultures are alive and producing art has now moved previous discussions from the museum to the islands, and from the islands to the art galleries. Ephemeral arts, women's art, utilitarian objects, dance, theatre and music, once not a part of the discussion, are foci today. The ways that Pacific Island artists integrate their urban lifestyles with the cultural icons that have surrounded their childhood have created these vibrant art forms. The result is a patchwork that binds together stereotypes and myths, the authentic and traditional, the eclectic and eccentric, the island and the urban.

The combination of a new sensibility towards indigenous arts in New Zealand, with a touristic and political interest in the region has seen the Pacific become a key player in New Zealand's popular culture (Stevenson 1999). The position of Pacific as fashionable is reinforced by the following comments from Stacy Gregg of *More* magazine:

> There's a new feeling abroad in this land. It's fresh. It's vibrant. And it's ours. Nobody else's. It's that Pacific sort of feeling . . . . for so long we had no discernable culture of our own—not one that we could share anyway. We were just watered down British for so long. Sure we had Maori culture, but while it was one that New Zealanders of European ancestry could certainly enjoy, it didn't always feel theirs, somehow. There wasn't a mood, a soul, a spirit, that *everyone* could grasp and enjoy.
>
> Well, it's coming . . . . A Pacific sort of feeling is starting to bubble through art, music, leisure, sport, lifestyle . . . . It takes time for a nation to develop its personality . . . . We're pulling together all the influences that make us a modern Pacific nation and creating something anew. Pacifica is a little bit Maori. A little bit European. Add a spice of Asia. A vibrant splash of Polynesia. An injection of California . . . . It's not born of one culture. It's an expression of many. Therefore, it threatens no one. It's a mood, a style, a feeling. This is Pacifica.[2]

The development of the Pacific label was significant, as it afforded the practice of a number of artists to enter the mainstream New Zealand arts environment. The conundrum of the Pacific label—a label only a few artists have been able to escape—remains problematic. As noted above, it was the label that New Zealand embraced. This, in turn, has fuelled the development and dynamism of contemporary Pacific art in New Zealand. Both artists and exhibitions can be seen as equivalent phenomena—each asserting difference, addressing issues and pushing the confines the label creates.

Pacific artists, in attempting to move beyond the cliché, created anew, asking that their viewers re-evaluate their perceptions of the Pacific. In this process of taking back or owning their representation, artists were picking and choosing which aspects of their traditional past to offer for public scrutiny. Key to this discourse is the relationship between the island and the urban, histories of migration and immigration, the loss of cultural traditions and knowledge, and the desire to redress this loss. This new social and cultural reality combines a traditional past with the present.

In what one may call the beginnings of contemporary Pacific art in New Zealand, a group of artists (Fatu Feu'u, Johnny Penisula, John Pule, Filipe Tohi and Jim Vivieaere) began to reposition their art production as Pacific **[figure 1.1]**. They, coupled with a group of younger artists just completing art school (Ioane Ioane, Lily Laita, Lyle Penisula and Michel Tuffery), began showing together. These artists were working in different media, using different imagery, and yet were associated by means of a Pacific heritage. Taking advantage of a newly accepted contemporary indigenous art practice, these Pacific artists were able to create their own niche—a niche based on both their cultural heritage and the phenomenon of contemporary indigenous art movements seen around the world.[3] As New Zealand was positioning itself as a Pacific island, artists with a Pacific heritage were able to exploit the familiar in order to open doors.

Samoa House in Auckland (also known as Maota Gallery and Tautai Gallery) was a key site in the mid to late 1980s; a gallery-run artists' co-op, it provided exhibition space and a venue for the nourishing of this fledgling artistic community. More than just a gallery, Tautai hosted workshops and was 'a meeting place for anyone concerned with Pacific identity in the arts' (Stacey 1988: 87–89). Gwen Stacey (87–89) noted that 'the gallery is a welcome addition . . . [it] brings together a group of artists who share a commitment to producing work that reflects a Pacific perspective', and concluded her commentary by saying, 'the concept of a Pacific identity is especially pertinent in New Zealand . . . It is to be hoped that the Tautai gallery may act as a navigator guiding us on a journey towards a post-colonial identity in the visual arts.'

With the growing recognition of Pacific art, dealer galleries and community centres became interested in hosting Pacific exhibitions.[4] Group Pacific shows became regular occurrences in Auckland and Wellington, as did solo exhibitions at dealer galleries. The politicisation of culture was a key item on the agenda. Māori protests, Pacific overstayers and independence for Pacific nations had led to an acknowledgement of a Pacific presence in New Zealand, which was also recognised in the arts. Contemporary Māori artists were leading the way while the elders debated how to position the contemporary.[5] This process of debate extended to Pacific artists whose work was seen as similar to, yet different from, that of Māori artists. The differences—the realities of their situation, their life experiences—became the cornerstone of this Pacific art movement.

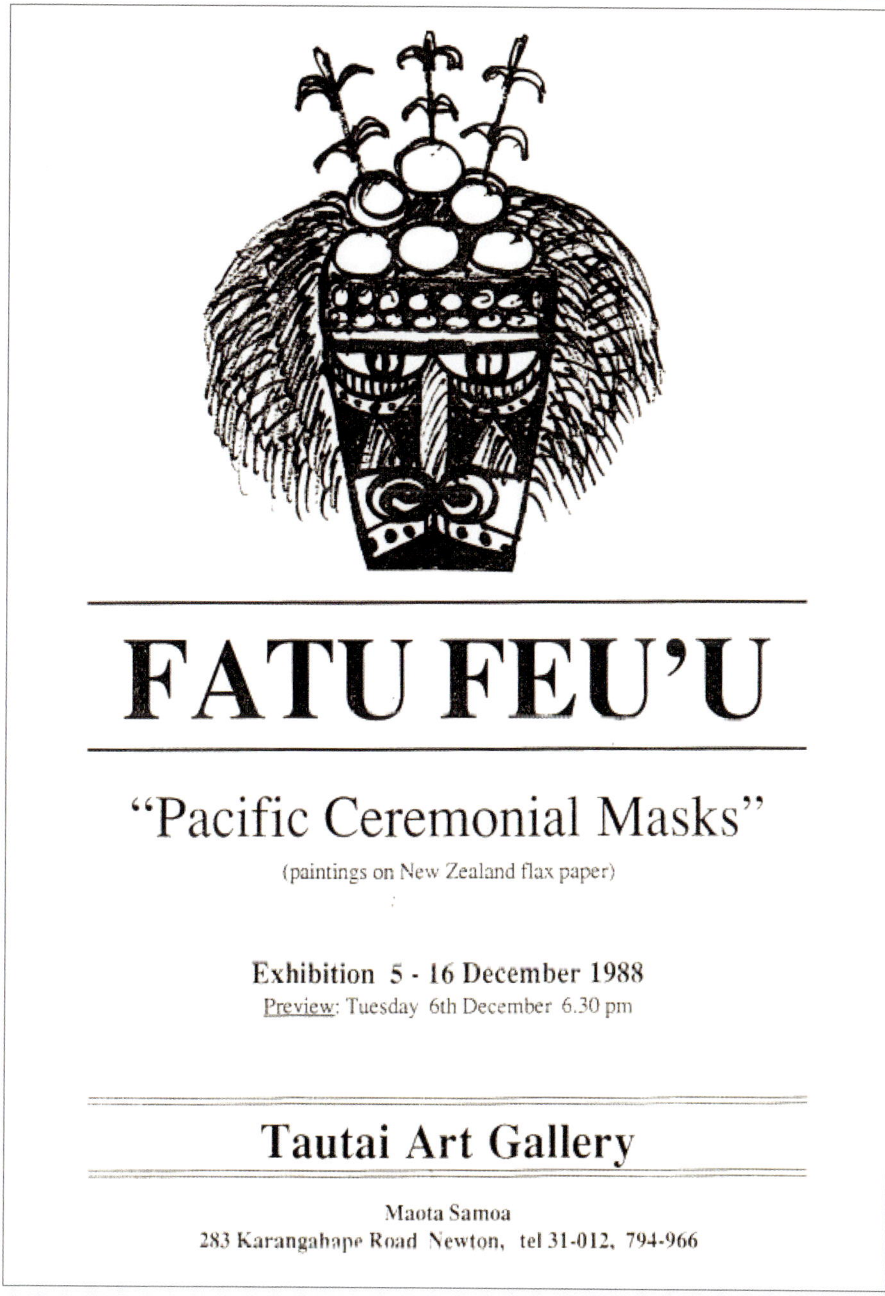

Figure 1.1 › This poster for an exhibition of work by Fatu Feu'u (1988) asserts the Pacific nature of the work. Illustrated with a 'mask' image whose headdress includes influences from various Pacific cultures.

In 1990 when the groundbreaking exhibition *Te Moemoea no Iotefa (The Dream of Joseph)* opened, Rangihiroa Panoho (the curator) had a group of known Pacific artists to draw from and include in the exhibition. Fatu Feu'u, Ioane Ioane, Lily Laita, Johnny Penisula, John Pule, Filipe Tohi and Michel Tuffery had already been exhibiting and would soon move from the margins to the centre, from small exhibitions to inclusion in national exhibitions. The Pacific became part of a New Zealand reality as *Te Moemoea no Iotefa* introduced contemporary Pacific art into New Zealand discourse.

A travelling exhibition hosted by the Sarjeant Gallery, *Te Moemoea no Iotefa* illustrated the dynamism and the vitality of change in Pacific arts. Leaving behind discussions of the traditional and the authentic, Panoho wove together the various aspects of Pacific culture as it persisted in New Zealand [**figure 1.2**]. In the accompanying catalogue, Panoho reinforced the lived reality of Pacific Island suburbs—of stunning and vibrant cultures—when he stated:

> One remembers growing up with Tongan neighbours. Neatly planted rows of taro down one side of the house. The root. The smell of pale pink/purple taro boiling in the big metal pot with coconut cream. Plastic lei around Catholic pictures in the living room and sometimes huge woven mats on the floor . . . Samoan fine mats wrapped around waists and jandals on hot church Sundays . . . . The umbilical cord with the islands has not been severed. The traditions are still there—the visual vocab has simply been extended. (Panoho 1990: 4)

The exhibition brought together material culture from the Pacific—items usually found in museums and libraries, including mats, tivaevae (the current production of traditional objects) and a Samoan fale, work from New Zealanders referencing the Pacific and contemporary Pacific art.[6] In this construction, Panoho was both moving beyond and including the stereotype, giving voice to the past and the future. In so doing, the myriad realities of Pacific art were brought together and seen as a whole. The catalogue also included interviews between Panoho and the ten contemporary artists involved. Their statements reflect the stage of Pacific art practice at that time and their desire to move beyond the boundaries of race. The need to incorporate the Pacific community into the gallery system for both their own support and for understanding of their work was important to these artists and to the visibility of their

Figure 1.2 › Rangihiroa Panoho (far right) interacts with artists from one of the weaving workshops associated with the *Te Moemoea no Iotefa* exhibition. Note the inclusion of both contemporary and traditional art works. Photograph by John McIvor and courtesy of Rangihiroa Panoho.

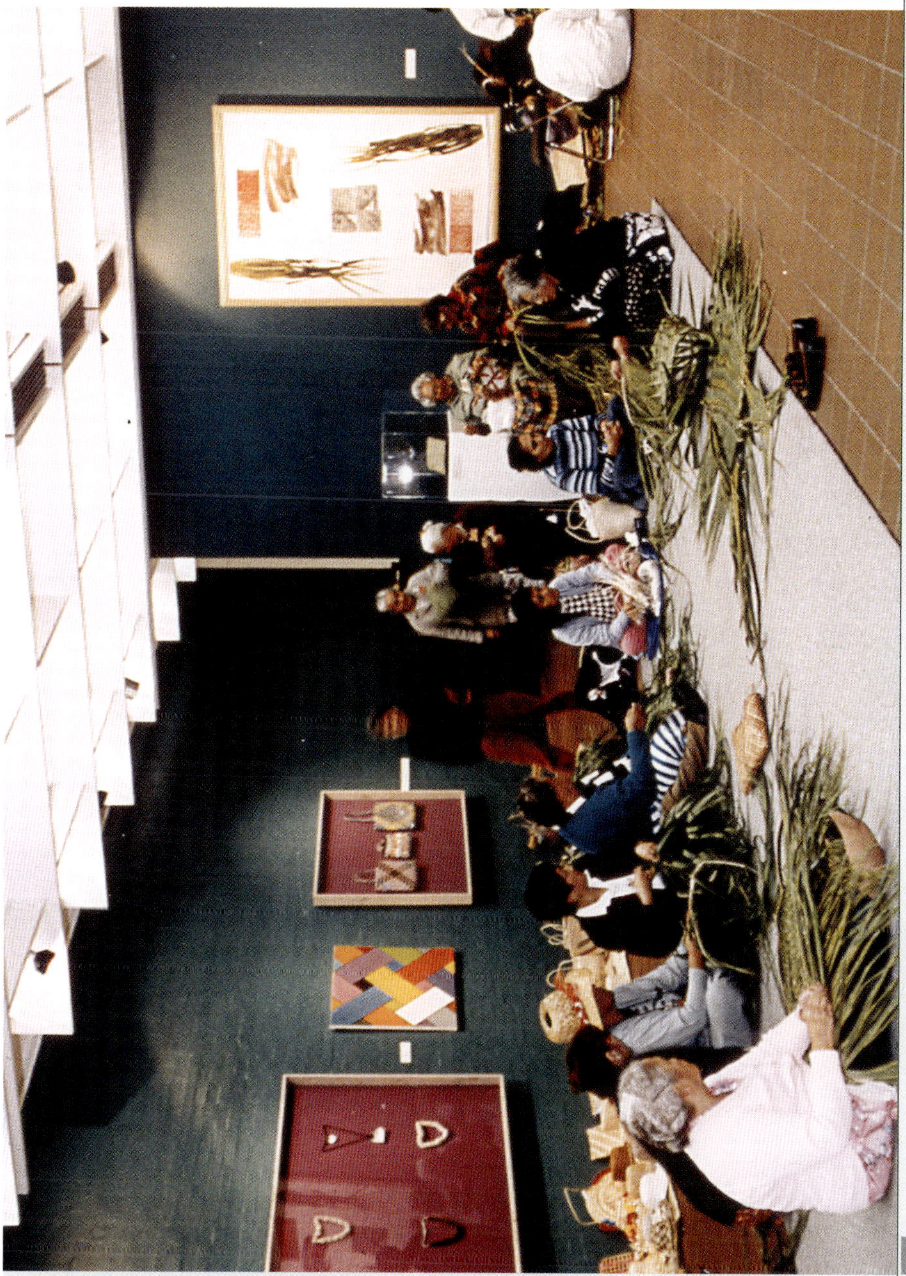

communities. The alliance between artist and community has remained an integral aspect of the contemporary Pacific art movement, affording it an affinity to Māori art practice and distancing it from the individual in Western art practice.

Yet, at the same time, the market audience for this work was not the Pacific Islander. Taonga—barkcloth, mats, tivaevae and lei—are easily incorporated into the urban lives of Pacific peoples. Art, however, is a different entity. Although the acknowledgement of Pacific artists by their communities was important, it was essential that Pacific artists interact with the New Zealand art market as well. *Te Moemoea no Iotefa* began this important dialogue by demonstrating that contemporary art was an extension of the cultural heritage and traditions of Pacific peoples. Michel Tuffery suggested that many of these art forms were indeed familiar to the New Zealand public. It was a matter of repositioning and acknowledging this presence (Panoho 1990: 31).

With the success of *Te Moemoea no Iotefa*, Pacific artists found exhibition space more readily available to them, and the growing recognition of their art meant that dealer galleries and community centres became interested in hosting Pacific exhibitions. In 1993, Michel Tuffery was one of two New Zealand representatives at the *First Asia-Pacific Triennial (APT) of Contemporary Art* in Brisbane. Interestingly, the other artist from New Zealand was Robin White, a printmaker who Tuffery has credited as an inspiration in his own practice. This pairing reflected the curatorial brief of *Te Moemoea no Iotefa*—of balancing the use of Pacific imagery by the insider and the outsider.[7] As Panoho successfully demonstrated, the imaging of the Pacific is not simplistic. Moreover, its complexity reflects the lived realities of New Zealand: New Zealand as a colonial power, New Zealand as a Pacific island and New Zealand as the home of the largest Pacific population. Demonstrating the diversity of Pacific imagery enabled both *Te Moemoea no Iotefa* and the New Zealand participation in the *APT* to position the arts of the Pacific as vibrant and vital parts of an eclectic whole.[8]

With a growing interest in Pacific art, Exhibitour asked Jim Vivieaere if he would curate a travelling group exhibition. Vivieaere soon found himself the spokesperson and authority of Pacific art. This new role was one that sat uneasily with Vivieaere, and in the process of organising the exhibition he spent much time and effort undermining and subverting institutional desire. The result was *Bottled Ocean: Contemporary*

Figure 1.3 › Jim Vivieaere with Leon Van den Eijkel, exhibition flyer, *Bottled Ocean*. Photograph courtesy of the Wellington City Art Gallery.

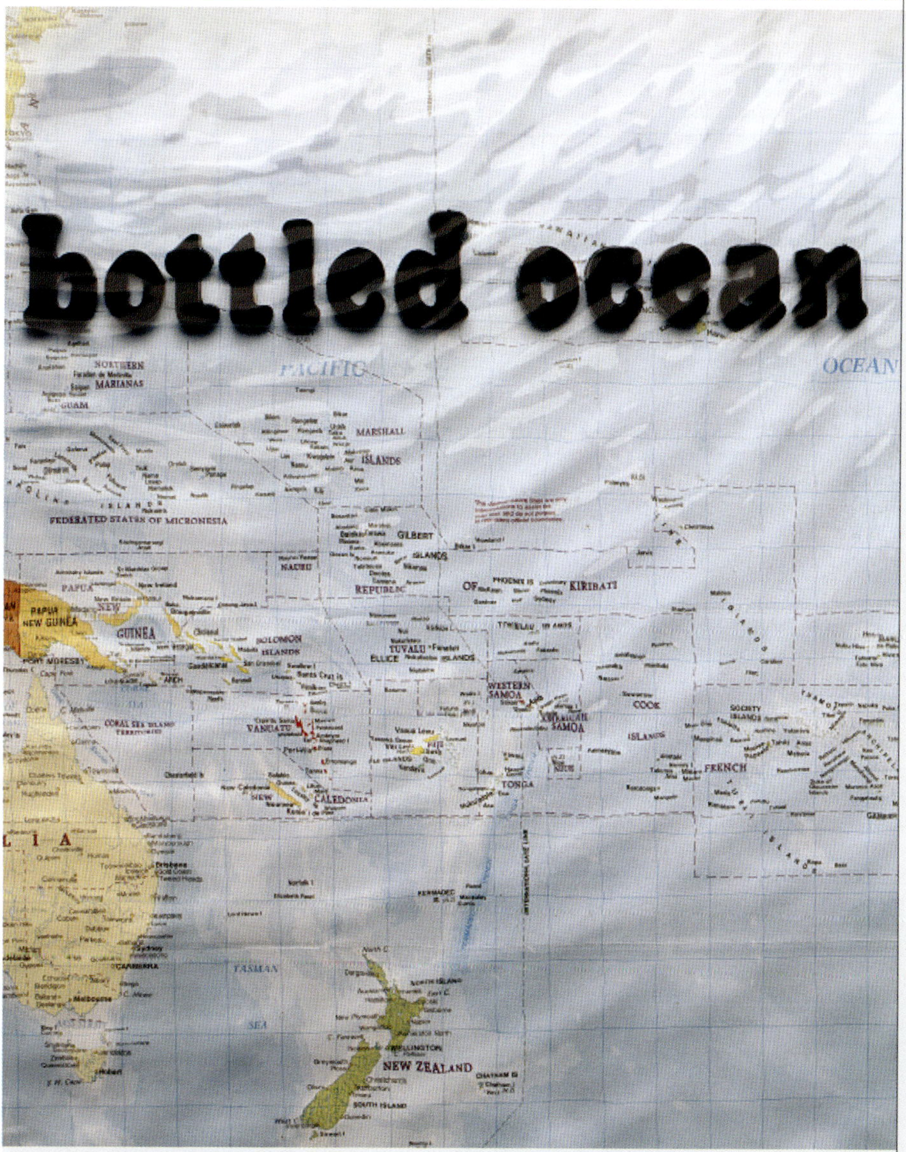

Polynesian Artists **[figure 1.3]**, which toured New Zealand in 1994–1995.[9] Every venue offered a different configuration, both in exhibition design as well as the artists included. There was a core of twenty-three artists, with others added along the way.[10] Aside from the basic fact that each gallery space was different, Vivieaere's artistic input was therefore the creation of each exhibition—the constant rethinking and reformulating of the idea **[figure 1.4]**. He did not want to afford the opportunity of cliché. He wanted the vibrancy of the work to speak for itself. Yet the process created as many limitations as it created opportunities. In his Auckland curatorial statement, Vivieaere (quoted in Thomas 1996b: 343) commented 'Bottled Ocean the concept carries the limitations of a pigeonhole, the categorisation of Brown Pacific Peoples into a single island of consciousness . . . . Creativity is informed by who we are and where we are at and for most Pacific Island artists much of this process is unfinished and still finding voice'.

His concerns about labelling, tokenism and ghettoising Pacific arts were valid. Vivieaere, who had employed the culture card in establishing Pacific art, was now fearful of the cliché. He did not want an exhibition of brown artists to be seen as such. He did not want to pigeonhole or label these artists who were just finding their feet. The key that opened the door could close it. The academic dialogue concerning centre and margins, hybridity, creolisation and indigeneity did not aid this unease. The exotic continued to prevail. Justin Paton (1996: 125) noted 'the centre, such as it is, has made the margins its business—mainstreamers are out, outsiders in'. Being fashionable added to this conflict.

Wendy Vaigro reviewed the exhibition at its Palmerston North venue and noted this ambivalence:

> The deep organising principle of the show is the circulating current of the Pacific Ocean, which both separates and connects its islands. As the ostensible organising principle of 'Bottled Ocean', 'Pacific Islandness' is utilised as a term that references, ironically, attempts to homogenise Polynesian artists working in New Zealand . . . . In challenging the closure of aesthetic and political categories and conventional curatorial practices, Jim Vivieaere creates 'Bottled Ocean' as a meta-exhibition. The result is a subtle and thoughtful show that eludes ideological control and 'authoritative discourse' at every turn. Vaigro (1995: 44–45)

Figure 1.4 › Here Michel Tuffery's *Pisupo Lua Afe* 'enjoys' the exhibition. Note also Laugutu Poloai's *Economical Resources* (left) and Ani O'Neill's *Kua Marino te Tai* (right). Photograph courtesy of Jim Vivieaere.

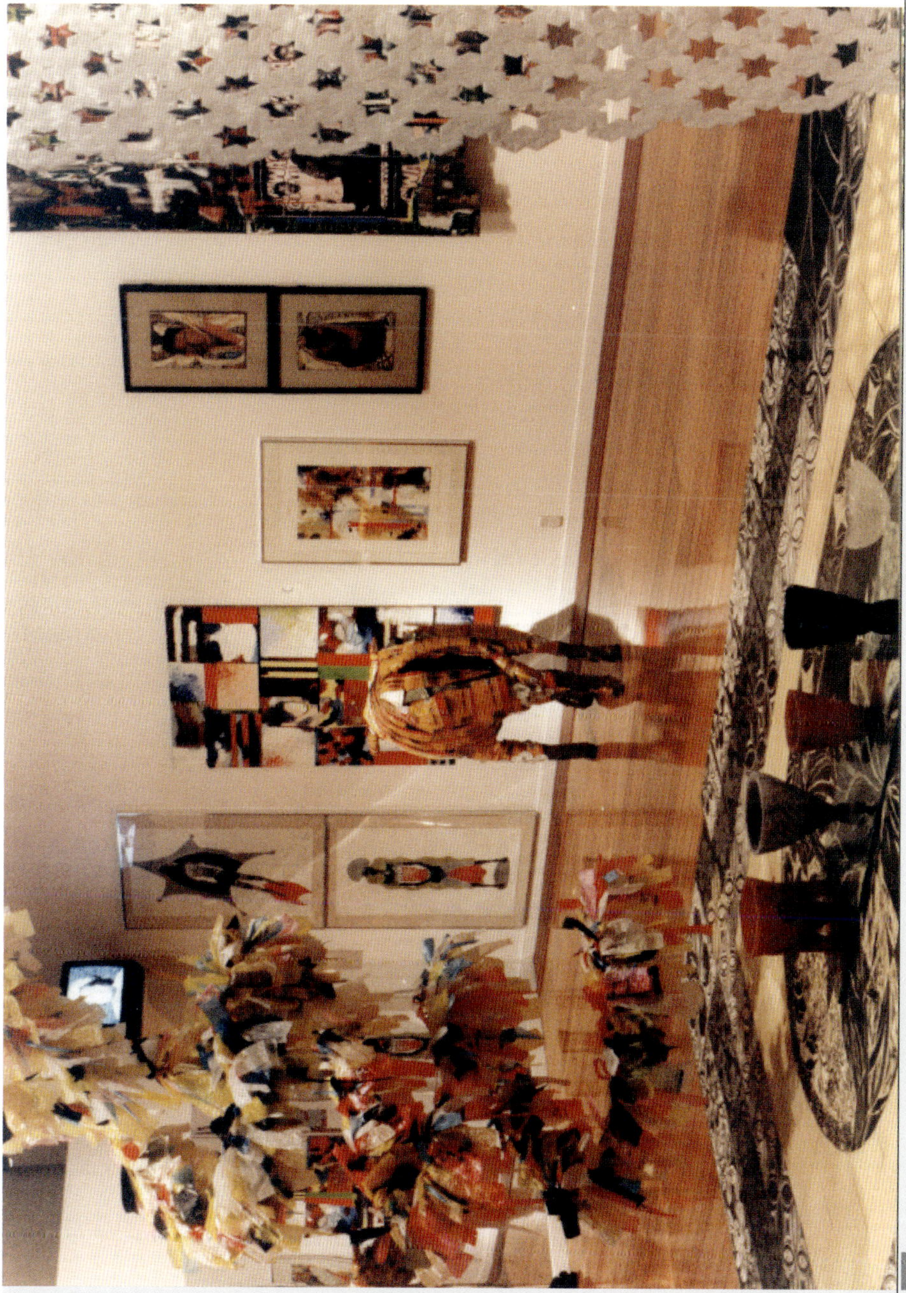

Vivieaere wanted to exhibit more than an exotic stereotype. Yet, by suggesting that the Pacific works communally, not individualistically like the West, other stereotypes were reinforced. Balancing prejudice and ignorance with the desire to entice and promote, *Bottled Ocean* became infused with the paradox of identity. In the exhibition catalogue, Vivieaere (1994) stated 'with exhibitions of this sort one wonders how Pacific cultural origins and traditions can be made a source of creative possibilities rather than constraints. Some works refer to the past, or express themes of transition and current entrapments. The artists are exploring their uneasiness with their blurred identity. Conflict exists between their assumed heritage and their urban experience'.

With a curatorial agenda focused on balance, the issues of identity that were being addressed by Pacific artists also suggested a balance. Michel Tuffery juggled his Samoan, Cook Island, Tahitian and European heritages and in so doing, he created works such as *Tiangi*[11], a Christ figure with a pe'a **[figure 1.5]**. Lyle Penisula demonstrated his hybrid realities in his work as well. *Father and Son* **[figure 1.6]** makes clear reference to Penisula's mixed heritage—an urban Polynesian proudly wears his marker of identity, a taulima. In both of these images there was an attempt to scrutinise the hybrid nature of genetics as well as the play between the traditional and the contemporary. Each artist played upon his unique circumstance, while at the same time welcoming the Pacific nature of his identity.

Both *Te Moemoea no Iotefa* and *Bottled Ocean* positioned contemporary Pacific art as integral to the New Zealand art environment. It is interesting to note that in the four years between these exhibitions the Pacific label moved from a sign of cultural pride to a stereotype to be challenged. The balance between positioning oneself as an indigenous person and being labelled—of asserting an identity or being placed in a box—was precarious. As a result, those who were engaging with a Pacific heritage were soon to loathe the label they had created. A new art movement had quickly transformed into a cliché.

Nicholas Thomas (1995a: 204) commented that Fatu Feu'u 'has given consumer culture in New Zealand a distinctive Pacific accent' **[figure In.5]**. Feu'u was adept at marketing his vibrant images, which were easily transposed to different media. Recognised as the "father" of Pacific art, Feu'u has deliberately and successfully invented a contemporary pan-Polynesian art, a shared tradition rather than one

Figure 1.5 › Michel Tuffery, *Tiangi*, woodcut on flax paper, 1989. Photograph courtesy of the artist.

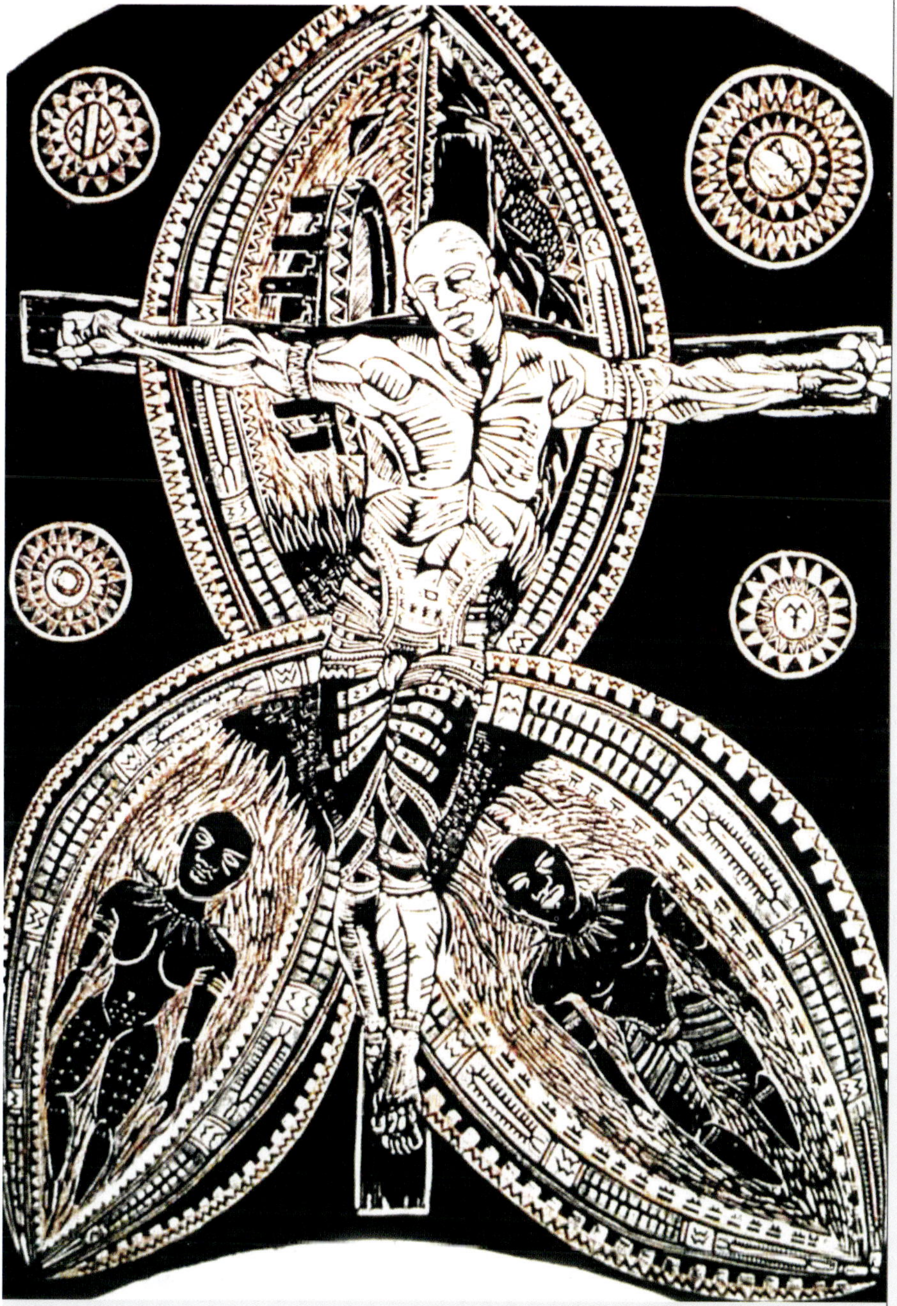

specific to himself (Thomas 1999: 262). As John Pule commented on pan-identities, 'the one common thing that will keep us together is the fact that we are all Islanders' (Pule quoted in Mallon and Pereira 1997: 99). It is in this way that Feu'u responds to his reality of living in Auckland. Here, he finds the interactions between Pacific Islanders merge to establish a vibrant culture. It is not the culture of his homeland; it is a blend of creative endeavours, a mix that enables a dynamic expression in the arts. This is the heart and soul of New Zealand; this is the pulse of contemporary Pacific art.

Fatu Feu'u's use of frangipani motifs offered a Pacific flavour; barkcloth was now wallpapering the set of Shortland Street; and Pacific art became a souvenir of a sun-drenched holiday. Feu'u's motifs, particularly his frangipani, became associated with the art practice of many aspiring Pacific artists, as well as with his own work. Pacific artists referencing traditional practices (with barkcloth, tatau, carving and plaiting) created easily recognisable work without the political overtones embedded in much contemporary Māori art. This signature motif quickly became cliché and the hallmark for assessment of other Pacific artists.

Feu'u's practice, however, is not simply a refashioning of barkcloth imagery or an appropriation of a tradition. Pacific imagery, especially barkcloth patterning, references a traditional balance between men and women. The motifs reinforce the balance of social obligation, authority and power that are inherent in barkcloth production and exchange. These ideals became essential to Feu'u's practice, and their incorporation into his work through the use of the motifs highlights the non-representational nature of Polynesian art—veiled meaning and metaphor prevail as objects and motifs become representative not only of a person or a position, but of the ideologies and obligations they hold.

These ideals were reiterated in the conceptualisation of *Te Moemoea no Iotefa*, which positioned Feu'u firmly in New Zealand's art world. The balance between the past and present referenced fa'aSamoa, while simultaneously announcing a shift from the islands to the urban. Finding success, yet loathing the stereotype, led both artists and curators to move beyond issues of identity. Distance enabled an urban critique of the island. Artists looked to the islands and addressed what they perceived to be contradictions and problems. They were choosing which parts of the stereotype they would embrace.

Figure 1.6 › Lyle Penisula, *Father and Son*, acrylic on hardboard, 1993. Photograph courtesy of the artist.

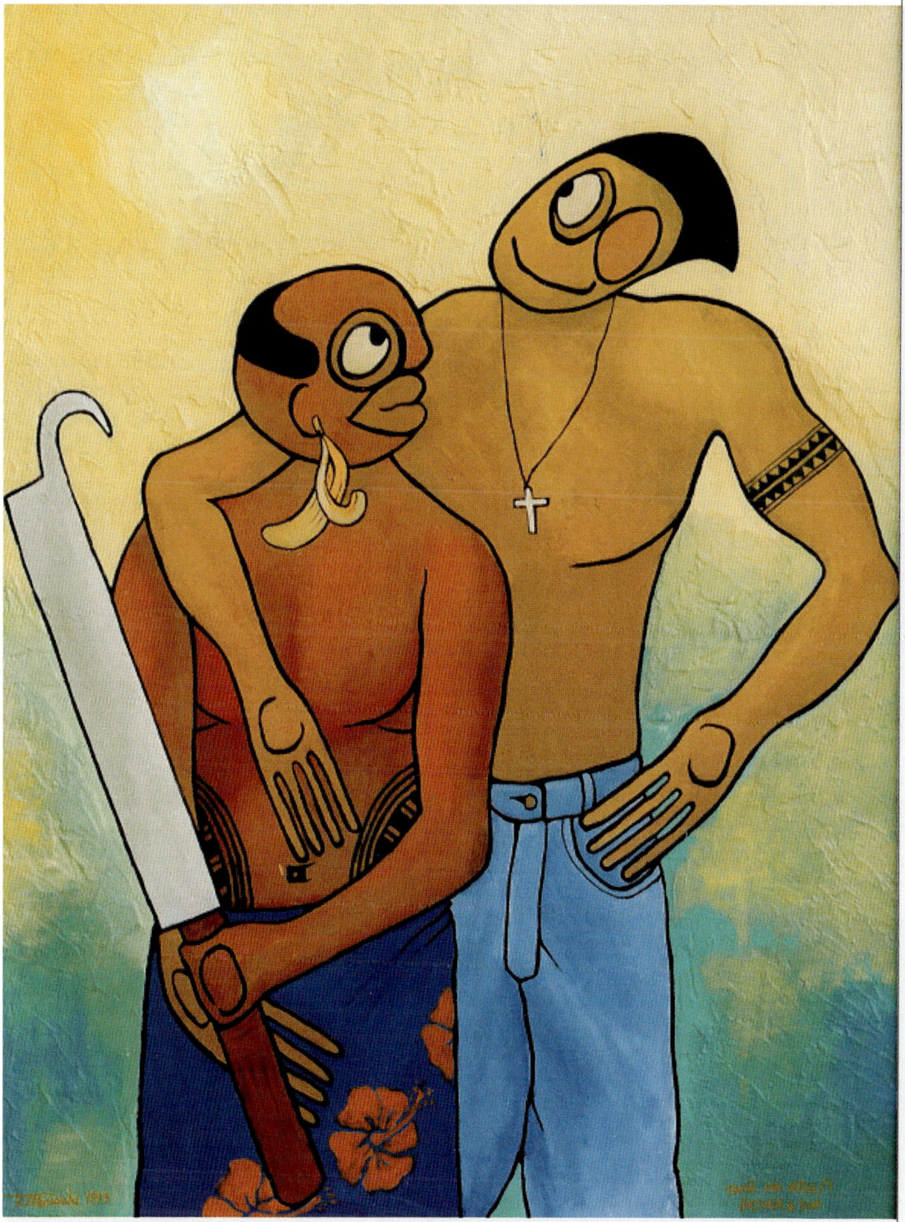

The Pacific cliché has become the artist's muse. The icons of the Pacific are invested with humour to address issues of tourism, representation and colonialism. Ani O'Neill, with *Tangaroa* **[figure 1.7]**, confronts the audacity of an emasculated god being reinvented as a virile tourist icon. The god of the seas and, for many, of creation, Tangaroa was the concern of men, not women. The missionaries emasculated this important god in their attempts to destroy him and the beliefs imbued in his image. O'Neill is not attempting to reinstate the prowess of this fertile being, but is actually creating a virile stuffed toy in his image. Placing him in the domain of women, O'Neill recognises their position as the purveyors of culture within the Pacific diaspora. In this way, the image offers both a critique on missionisation and on tourism, and at the same time readdresses a cultural icon and its importance today. *Tangaroa* is not the only icon that O'Neill has regenerated. Double entendre is her muse and tourist icons are ripe fodder for O'Neill's critique. She has opened the gallery door to an often marginalised artistic tradition with her mat of plaited ribbon *Kua Marino te Tai* **[figure 1.4]**, which offers an urban take on an island ideology (Stevenson 2001b).

Another side to Polynesia humour is the way that it often conceals biting criticism. Works such as Michel Tuffery's *Pisupo Lua Afe* **[figure 1.4]** offered a humorous take on a major staple for Pacific peoples—tinned beef. A bull of tins, a tinned beef—the simple pun almost denies the complexity of a sculpture imbued with the task of integrating social commentary with environmental critique. An introduced species which dominates and destroys the fragile island ecosystem is an obvious metaphor for missionisation, colonisation and the continued exploitation of Pacific resources.

Asserting their voice—a Pacific voice—also created problems. Thomas (1996b: 319) commented 'the works of artists who announced an interest in their own otherness enhanced the audiences' interests in exoticism and difference'. The Pacific net that they had eagerly embraced now seemed a strangling device. The experience led Vivieaere (quoted in Thomas 1996b: 345) to state that 'the only reason we are here is that we are Polynesian—not on our merits but because we're the 'other' . . . we don't need Polynesian shows. I would like to see it [Bottled Ocean] as the last'.

The conviction gained from the *Bottled Ocean* experience—that exhibitions can move beyond the issues of race and pigeonholing—supported a conceptual framework for the Second *APT* in 1996 that 'avoided the sterility of political correctness' (Neale 1996: 56). The curatorial team (Jonathan Mane-Wheoki, Margo Neale and Jim

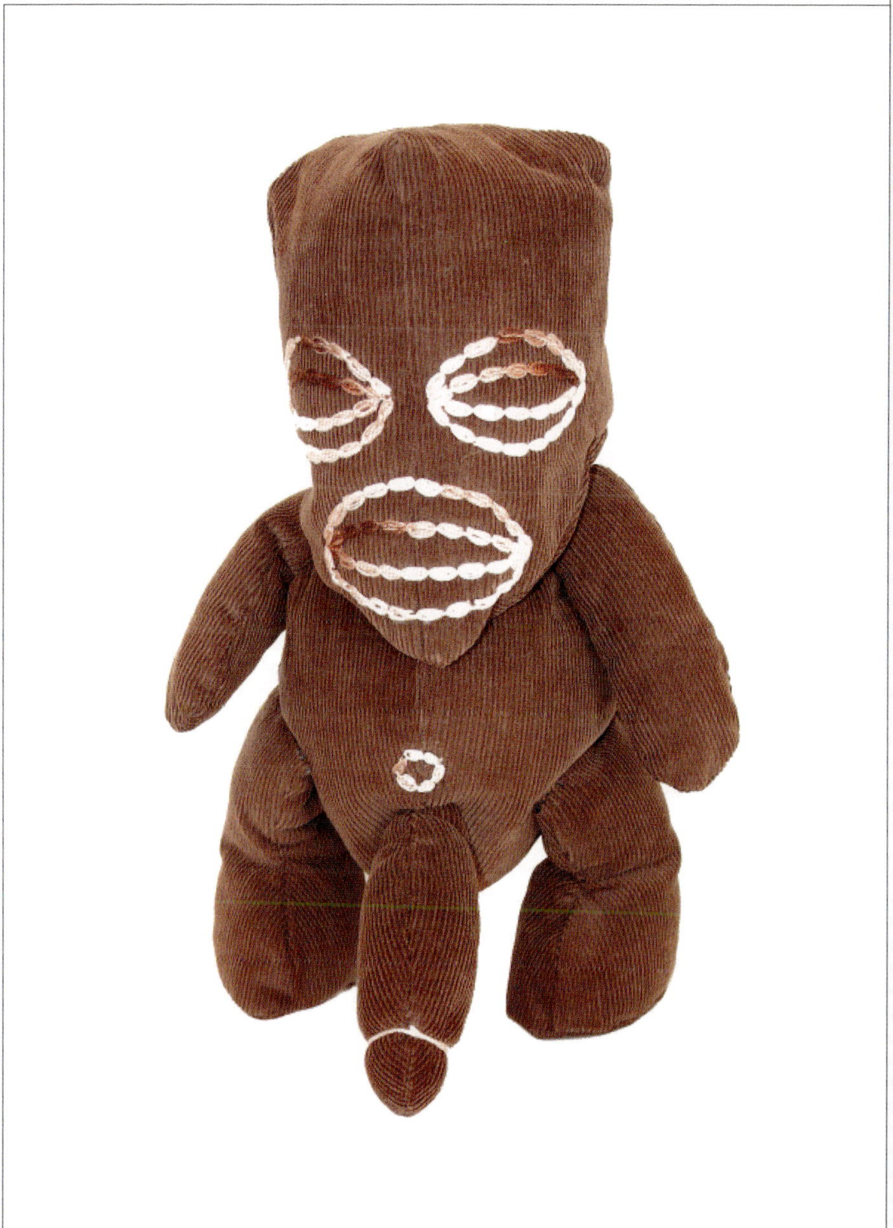

Figure 1.7 › Ani O'Neill, *Tangaroa*, corduroy and embroidery, 1992. Photograph courtesy of the artist.

Vivieaere) brought together artists with Māori, Pacific, Chinese and Pākehā heritage as a collective representation from New Zealand. Again drawing upon collective notions of identity, as well as a sea-faring metaphor of travel—the waka—they asserted the 'ambiguities of blurred boundaries, blurred cultural identity and the assertion of independence' (Neale 1996: 57).

The conceptual basis of New Zealand's participation in the *APT* was founded on Vivieaere's subversion of the expected. The double waka metaphor both undermined the institution's numbers game of allocating space for only two New Zealand representatives, and at the same time promoted a Polynesian presumption of collective individuality. That collective identity, however, was a New Zealand identity. This inclusiveness was fuelled by Vivieaere's abhorrence of the pigeonholing of Pacific artists. Drawn more from the reflection of New Zealand's myriad realities evident in *Te Moemoea no Iotefa*, the waka construct enabled a broader and truer vision of the role and position of Pacific art in New Zealand. A Pacific umbrella allowed for the inclusion of more Pacific artists, acknowledging their participation in the New Zealand arts community. The conundrum of identity and label remains, yet the ideological focus has shifted. Issues-based exhibitions have superseded exhibitions with issues.

Giles Peterson has been at the forefront of this change. In 1995 with *Emerging into the Light*, his curatorial attention focused on issues surrounding women's art practice in New Zealand and so he avoided the pigeonhole entrapment of a "Pacific" exhibition. Notions of nationality did, however, underlie his next exhibition—*Pacific Dragons: Art of Protest and Promise from Fifteen Nations of the Rim*. Although the net was thrown wide and far, the focus was the relationship between Māori and Pacific—between New Zealand's indigenes and those of other Pacific Rim nations. Using a concept not based on race has enabled the promotion of Pacific artists without the pigeonholing effect feared by Vivieaere.

Weaving its way through these efforts is another strand—the re-centering of New Zealand's world, and the role that the Pacific plays in its lives and art. The promotion of New Zealand as a bicultural nation has provided a vehicle for artistic production and patronage. It is here that Peterson finds his niche. Working diligently to promote Māori and Pacific artists, he has curated a number of exhibitions, including *Island Crossings* **[figure 1.8]**, which travelled to Australia.[12] These exhibitions along with

Figure 1.8 › View of *Island Crossings* at Global Arts Link, Ipswich, Australia. Photograph courtesy of Giles Petersen.

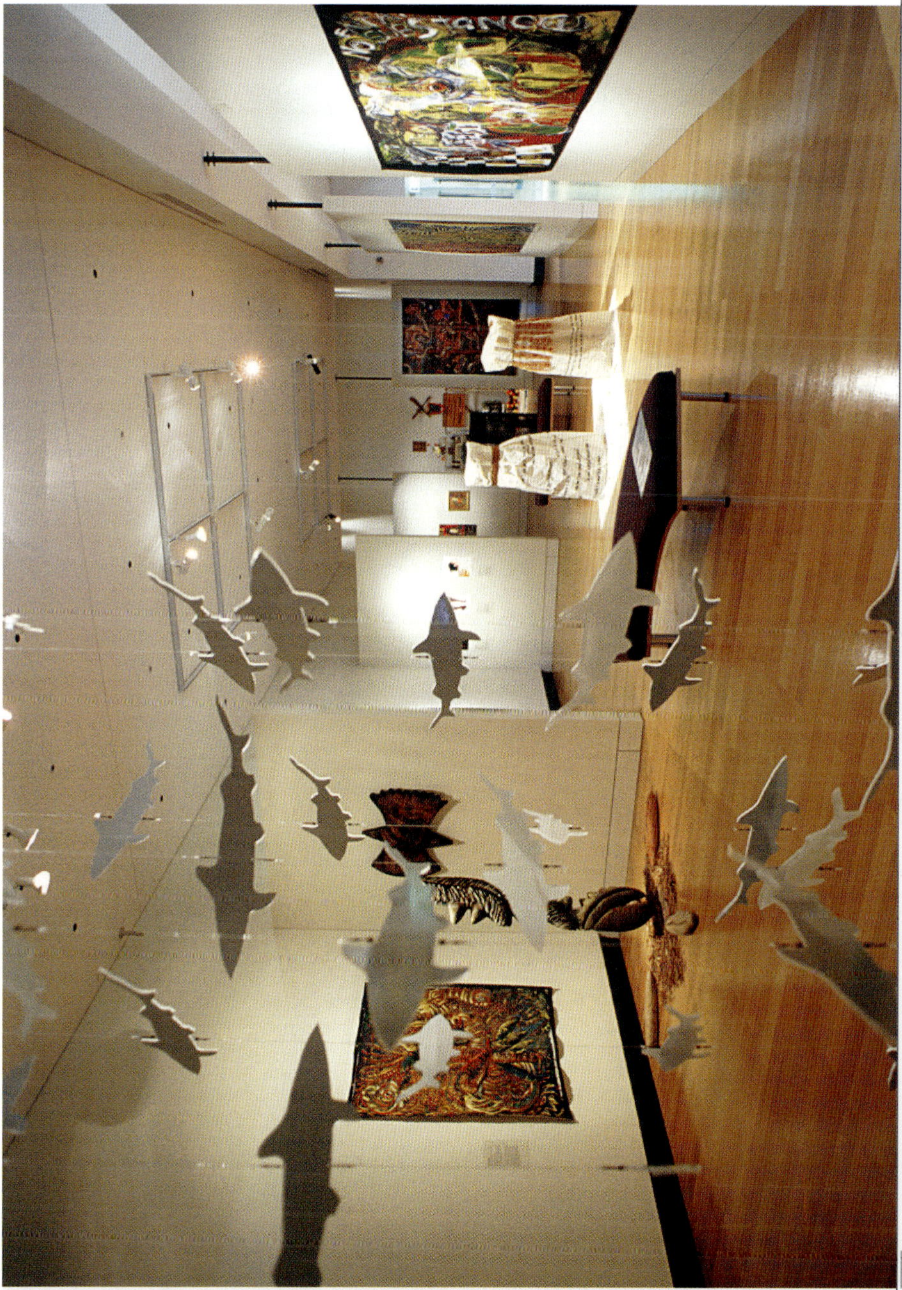

others in Australia, New Caledonia, Samoa and Germany have heightened an international awareness of Pacific art. The *APT* has been a cornerstone for promoting the Pacific, but others like the Sydney and Noumea biennials have also enabled New Zealand's Pacific artists to position themselves as players in an international artistic context. They are no longer just Pacific artists, or the "other's other".

The move offshore, seeking wider audiences and international recognition is something that the Tautai Contemporary Arts Trust has committed itself to. In 1995 Tautai was reorganised into an official trust whose primary goal was and is to promote Pacific Island artists in New Zealand and overseas. Since 1996, the Tautai Contemporary Arts Trust has organised exhibitions of Pacific artists in Samoa, New Caledonia, Australia and Germany. In that role it has been an advocate for both recognised and emerging Pacific artists. Tautai has also held annual exhibitions in Auckland and is involved in the organisation of workshops, symposia and networks that have afforded it the ability to reach beyond its membership to the wider Pacific community. The trust has collaborated in many ways with the Pacific Arts Committee and Te Waka Toi (the Pacific and Māori funding bodies of Creative New Zealand), whose primary roles are to support the arts.

In the early 1990s, New Zealand also saw the development of Pacific theatre, writing and music (discussed further in Chapters 5 and 6). Pacific Underground, based in Christchurch, produced a number of plays that addressed key issues within the Pacific community: immigration, racism, economic realities and cultural obligation.[13] Theatre groups in both Auckland and Wellington provided the platform for other writers as well. *The Semisis* exposed a New Zealand television audience to Pacific humour.[14] Opera, hip hop and mainstream radio were also introduced to a Pacific vibe. Pacific artists quickly became key practitioners in each of these artistic areas, providing New Zealand with another voice, another set of stories.

The Tautai Contemporary Pacific Arts Trust, once the sole support of Pacific artists, was joined by numerous other trusts in the late 1990s; these trusts were created to provide opportunities to emerging and established artists, as well as to provide community support and a platform from which to speak.[15] This network of support enabled Pacific arts to flourish, providing endless possibilities for Pacific artists. Jim Vivieaere (1999: 226) noted the 're-appropriating of Polynesian ideas and values by Polynesians' and coined the term "polynisation". Many efforts, however, have been

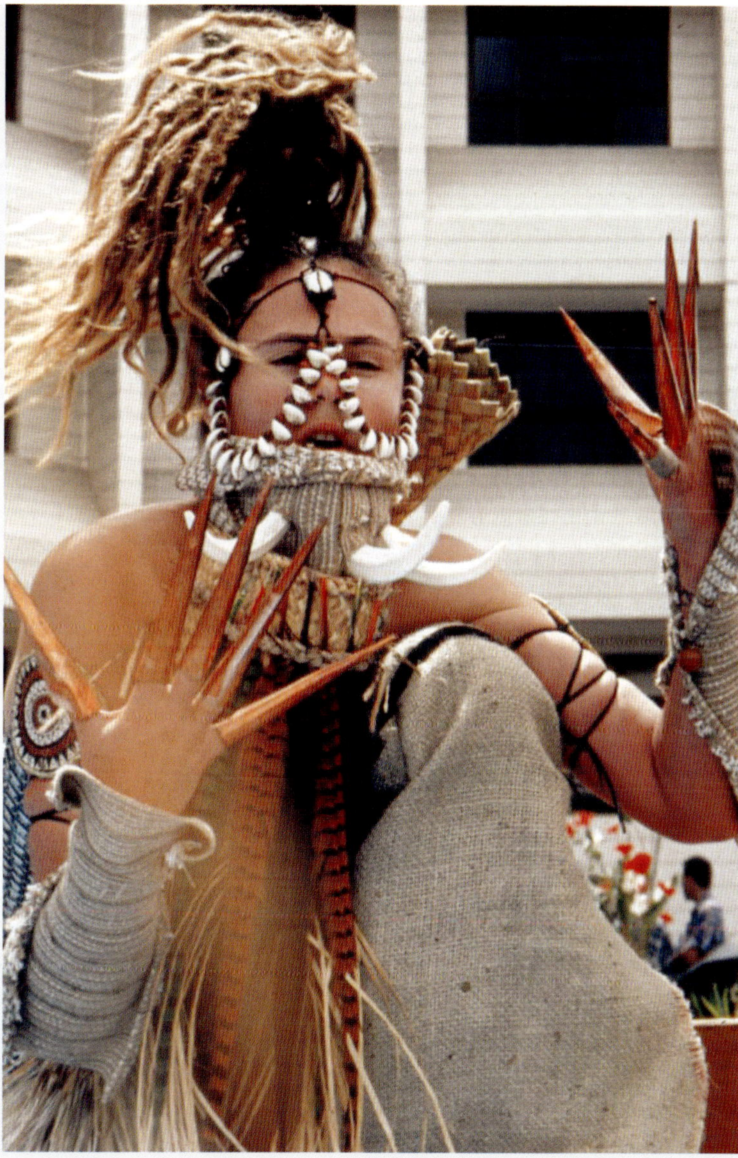

Figure 1.9 › Pacific Sisters performing at the Seventh Festival of Pacific Arts, Apia, Samoa, 1996. Photograph courtesy of Karen Stevenson.

more a containment than a building of a Pacific identity. “Pasifika”, a term utilised by New Zealand born Pacific Islanders, reflects a lived urban reality—it is rap music, hip hop, and urban Pacific fashion and design.[16] Its focus is the sophistication and savvy of New Zealand's street culture. *Pasifika* addresses the urban reality of islanders and their attempts to balance notions of identity and loss, migration and place, youth and age, tradition and change. This is clearly exemplified in the phenomenon that is The Pacific Sisters **[figure 1.9]**. Challenging the established art canon, The Pacific Sisters combined costume, tradition, dance and the catwalk with the energetic rhythms of hip hop. They and other artists connected the past and the future, producing new voices of self-representation that challenged the comfort and serenity of the stereotype.

Current directions move issues of race beyond the post-colonial and the post-modern, integrating new technologies, attitudes and ideas. The continual reappraisal and redefining of Pacific art has enabled the steady growth in the number of artists referencing a Pacific identity. Bolstered by the support of the trust network, government granting bodies, residency programs, and commissions associated with regional and local exhibitions, Pacific art has developed into a distinct movement.

A conceptual shift is clearly recognisable. In the beginnings of Pacific art practice in New Zealand, artists defined themselves through cultural markers. The icons of Polynesia—barkcloth, tatau, the lei, as well as bright colours and flowers—allowed the creation of the stereotype. *Te Moemoea no Iotefa* channelled this energy, drawing comparisons between the island and the urban, between the past and the future. Today a polynisation has occurred whereby reinterpretations of Pacific traditions are created for a contemporary audience. Artists draw upon a cultural knowledge of ideas and materials to (re-)present the myth, the cliché. In so doing they offer a cultural critique that underlies this growing artistic movement. Ambiguity, an underlying theme for *Bottled Ocean*, allowed both the artists and the creative endeavour to challenge, to experiment and to renegotiate their place within New Zealand. Urban Polynesians who have navigated institutional art education, who have dealt with issues of identity, and who have acknowledged their position in New Zealand society, created Pasifika. These artists have referenced traditions that create a bridge between the world of their ancestors and their own global urban reality. It is this reality that reinforces the social and political agendas of their work.

Speaking again of the waka, Justin Paton (1996: 125) noted 'while some of these makers have their sights set on the future, others are guided by the rudder of the past, and while some seek the safe harbour of older certainties, others aim to map and re-map new identities'.

We find a balance in a space that nourishes the complexities of cultural change. Acknowledging the social consequences of migration and integration, contemporary Pacific art practice negotiates with the past, creating a vibrant new movement. How artists represented not only themselves but also the cultures they wished to emulate became key. As Pacific art moved from stereotype to metaphor, the materials and ideas that they presented reflected at once the ambiguity and the complexity within the lives and realities of contemporary Pacific artists in New Zealand.

CHAPTER 02

Tapa, Tiki and Tatau: Conceiving Identities

The creation and assertion of identities is something that Pacific peoples have done for millennia. It was, therefore, not a European presence that inspired these creations, but the inherent travelling of Pacific peoples and the consequent interaction between them. Many Pacific Islanders live in New Zealand, as do New Zealanders with a Pacific Islands heritage. This heritage has become the basis for a vigorous new expression of contemporary art. The body of knowledge from which this art form comes is, for the most part, culturally Polynesian. By drawing upon their cultural heritage, contemporary Pacific artists have created new contexts for traditional imagery. In so doing, they have constructed a vibrant artistic movement on which personal and cultural identities may stand.

The creation of identity is both a fashion statement and a political tool. Identities are constructed and manipulated; their inconsistencies and contradictions mirror our multifaceted contemporary society. As individuals or as groups, we place ourselves vis-à-vis others. Identity, in this sense, is not static. The assertion of identity creates distinctions—between races, culture, gender and place—and is often an impetus for creative expression and artistic practice. The use of symbols to create identities, both national and personal, is significant. As the island countries of the Pacific placed themselves within an international arena, symbols based upon cultural heritage were used to signify a national identity.[1] The importance of identity at the national level is essential to the creation of a nation state trying to survive its colonial legacy.[2] Symbols of cultural identity can also be seen as signifiers of difference and resistance (Hereniko 1994: 420), an attitude clearly seen in the politicisation of art in the Pacific.[3]

Government officials across the Pacific have chosen national symbols—icons of identity—as a means of promoting their island nations. A venue for the promotion of Pacific identities is the Pacific Arts Festival. In a photograph from the 1996 Festival in Samoa [**figure 2.1**] a young delegate from Tonga dances in a costume made of plaited pandanus; she is supported by a gentleman dancing in barkcloth. These costumes suggest both the importance of these textile traditions, as well as their role in asserting a contemporary identity. Images such as this, together with European colonial representations of the primitive (tourist fantasies of a South Seas paradise and expressions of post-colonial indigeneity) fight for prominence as assertions of identity are revealed. In the process, tourism and how the Pacific is perceived by the West are integrally tied to culture and identity in the Pacific. The use of both the beauty of the islands and their associated misconstruction results in culture and tradition becoming a means to economic independence and growth. In reference to the Cook Islands, Jeff Sissons (1995: 161–162) suggested that they have created a 'nationalism of seduction, consumption and commodified indigeneity'.

Just as island nations strive to promote a particular identity, so do individuals. However, personal identity stems from a deeper source—from a history upon which one can draw.[4] The label "Pacific" has both a racial and cultural distinction, as well as a geographic one. Artists utilising the label draw upon both a cultural heritage and their physical presence in the Pacific. The fact that this artistic movement—contemporary Pacific art—occurred in New Zealand reinforces this Pacific presence. Yet, even though New Zealand has positioned itself as a Pacific island, for the most part it is not the island referenced by contemporary Pacific artists. When New Zealand has been the focus of artistic endeavor, it is a Pacific Islander's relationship and/or struggle with it. New Zealand is not the idealised paradise of the Pacific. As such, the context of contemporary Pacific art punctuates a cultural heritage, giving credence to the old, creating anew. As Ioane Ioane said, 'my cultural background reveals itself'[5]; for Ani O'Neill, one's heritage cannot be ignored—'it's in the blood' (O'Neill quoted in Naigulevu, 1995). For others, it is part of a personal history that was probably lost in migration. It is the ground upon which they stand.

The assertion of identity as a cornerstone of the contemporary Pacific art movement was important because it enabled artists to position themselves as individuals in a larger arts community. The recognition of Māori art as both taonga and an artistic endeavor in its own right opened doors for Pacific artists. Nevertheless, Māori and Pacific artistic practices are distinct, displaying differences that have their basis in the politics of art, culture and identity as these are played out in New Zealand. Māori are tangata whenua, Pacific Islanders are not.[6] This had led Jonathan Mane-Wheoki to label Pacific artists, "the other's other" (Mane-Wheoki 1995b: 16). An assertion of a Pacific identity, based on the icons of the Pacific, created an arts practice that immediately symbolised Pacific, not Māori. Embracing these icons, reinterpreting the stereotype to reinstate the convention to a meaningful position, Pacific artists have asserted an identity. The arts offer visual and verbal interpretations of social, cultural and political practices. They are not simply decorative, but are interwoven into the political, forging a Pacific identity.

Simultaneously, the Pacific itself has an identity. For over 200 years it has held a place in the Western imagination. Coupled with notions of paradise, the artistic and cultural traditions of the Pacific have been seen through a skewed lens. These misconceptions continue to be promoted, and have become a part of political and economic policy as they foster economic growth (Stevenson 1990 and 1992). At the same time, these fictive beliefs are perpetuated for their internal value as symbols of enduring cultural unity, as well as for their significance to foreigners, particularly tourists (Sissons 1995: 153). How does the day-to-day reality of island life blend with the fantasy, the myth? Duro Ra'apoto commented:

> They call me Tahitian, but I refuse this. I am not Tahitian. This denomination has an essentially demagogic, touristic, snobbish and rubbish vocation. "Tahitian" is the *pareu* shirt whose material is printed in Lyon or in Japan; it's the Marquesan *tiki* called Tahitian as well as the *tapa* of Tonga, Uvea, or Samoa sold in Papeete under the Tahitian label . . . Tahiti is an exotic product made by the Western World for the consumption of their fellow-countrymen. Ra'apoto (1988: 3)

In the 1980s identity, tradition and authenticity were at the centre of a heated academic debate.[7] Most problematic was the fact that Western academics were dismissing the cultural politics being played out in the Pacific, thereby scoffing

Figure 2.1 › Tongan dancers at the Pacific Arts Festival, Samoa, 1996. She is wearing a costume created from plaited pandanus and the gentleman in the rear has donned barkcloth; both important textile traditions in Tonga. Photograph courtesy of Karen Stevenson.

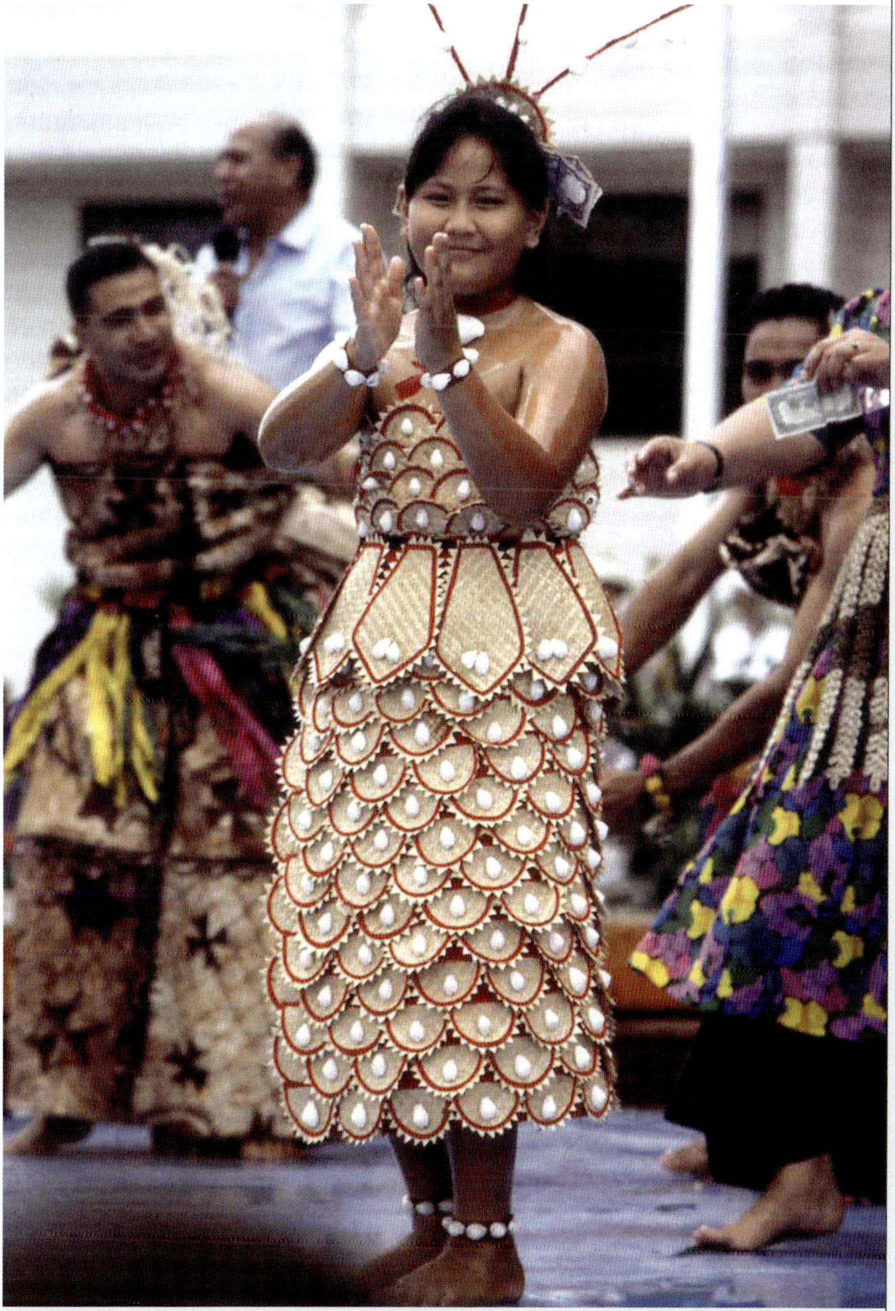

at the authenticity of cultural practices that upheld assertions of sovereignty and national identity. This led Roger Keesing and others to query the touristic nature of the arts, to explore how cultural practices were reinvented for the tourist market (Keesing 1989: 19–42). Albert Wendt was one of the first to question these Western academic attitudes. In reference to the many art publications that illustrate the art of the Pacific, Albert Wendt wrote:

> My objection to this literature is that it gives the impression that our ancestors' art is still the Oceanic Art of today; or, that if it isn't, it ought to be; or that we have not produced any worthwhile art since the papalagi came: or that if we are producing some art it is not 'authentic' Oceanic Art and therefore not worthy of serious discussion. Wendt (1983: 198)

A result of these debates was the assertion of an indigenous voice. No longer willing to allow the West to create and/or evaluate the parameters of cultural practice, Pacific peoples demonstrated the important links between the past and the present. Cultural icons became symbols of sovereignty. However, an acknowledgement of contemporary arts, as opposed to tourist art, was slow in coming. Jane Moulin (1996: 129) stated that 'arts contribute to forming cultures—they are capable of leading the way to change, rather than passively telling what has already transpired'. Bernard Narokobi (1990: 17) affirmed the importance of contemporary art production when he observed that 'whilst there is a total transformation, a revolution, a break with the past, it is clear that the break is not a rejection of the past. Rather, it is an expression of the past in a new, exciting and creative way . . . The past is depicted in the present . . .'.

Thus, tapa, tiki and tatau are utilised to both reference and critique—to own and to re-present the Pacific. Pacific artists, therefore, attempt to balance the stereotype with their lived reality. They draw upon cultural and artistic traditions that make up many preconceptions about the Pacific. In so doing, tapa, tiki and tatau have been re-contextualised to assert a cultural, artistic and personal identity. As a result, the Pacific's cultural heritage is integrally linked with the contemporary; the past and the present combine through the use of cultural icons. Duro Ra'apoto (1988: 6) asserted that 'if the imagination can be defined as the faculty to create something new from something old, then it is our duty to understand, to become impregnated

To

George

My first grandson

Please look after this gift.

It is very special to me.

Love

Grandma

xxxx

On your Christening

Figure 2.2 › This example of Samoan siapo incorporates the vane swastika motif. One can trace this motif to the Lapita culture. It remains a prominent motif in contemporary art. Auckland War Memorial Museum Tamaki Paenga Hira, AM9602.

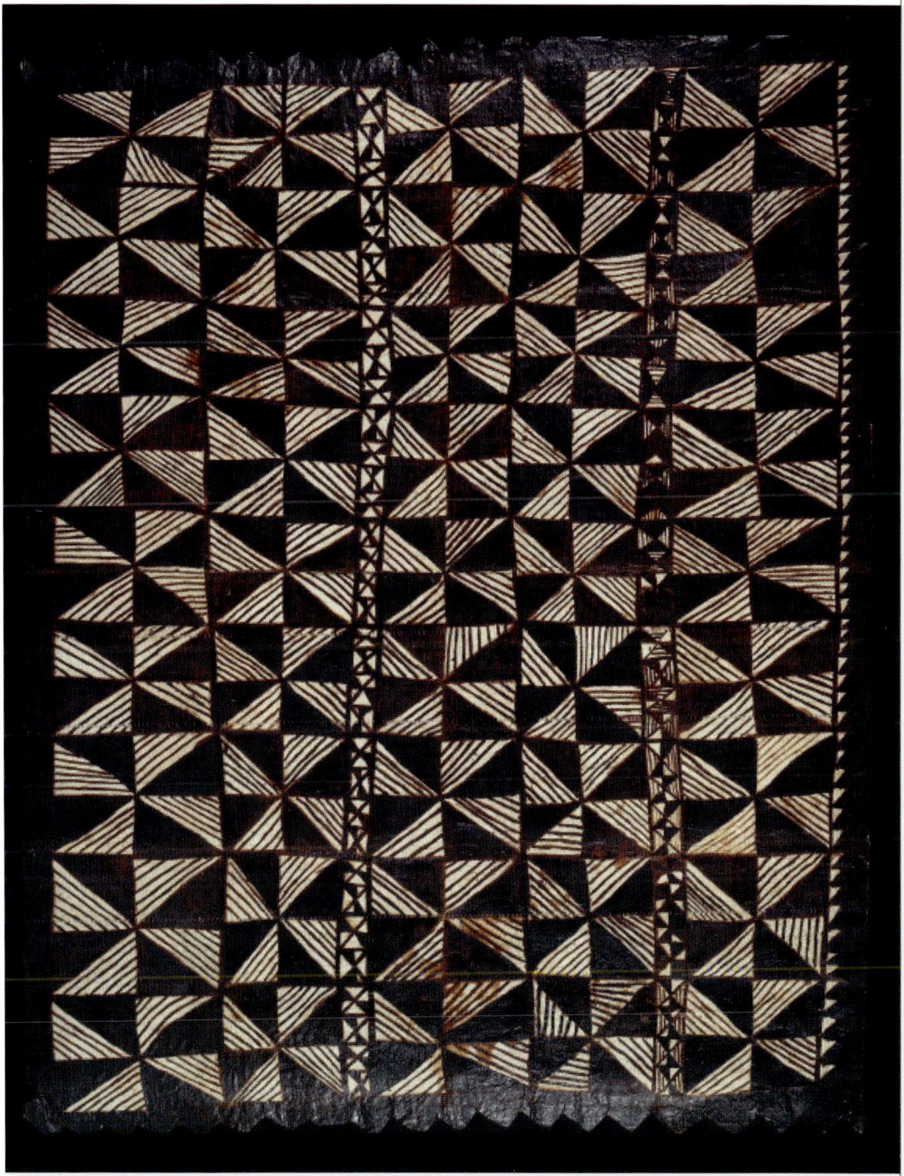

with our past, our culture, our language, to create a new world in our image and in our dimension'.

Many contemporary artists from around the Pacific have taken up this challenge. They have looked to the past and drawn their imagery from it. Many of the images they use are conceived as metaphor: the lizard, the shark and the patterns of tatau. Many are images that we have come to recognise as Polynesian: the dusky maiden, the palm and even the frangipani. Both as metaphors and reality, these images are used to illustrate the cultural heritage and history of the Pacific.

Tapa, tiki and tatau are three art forms integrally woven into the cultural foundations of Pacific arts [figure 2.2]. They are ubiquitous and are as much a part of the Pacific as the swaying palm. These art forms were the visual manifestation of the social, economic, religious and political systems in Polynesia. As such, their use as national symbols, as signifiers of cultural and political identities, is astute and allows artists to become 'impregnated with our past' (Ra'apoto 1998: 6). Decisions on which icon or cultural practice to position as a signifier of identity also enabled Pacific peoples to re-present their arts and, in so doing, to assert their value. This allowed for the stereotypical interpretations of Pacific art to be balanced by an indigenous perspective.

Tapa, tiki and tatau have become clichés to many people. This chapter explores the ways in which artists have embraced these icons and how they have recontextualised them. A brief overview of their traditional value clearly demonstrates that Pacific artists are not paying homage to the masterpieces of past civilisations, but are recreating the motif to re-establish its prowess today. An affirmation of ethnicity and cultural pride results at the same time as homage is paid to a cultural heritage. Artists draw from both a past and a present; they appropriate imagery and ideas that enable the creation and expression of a Pacific practice.

The first visitors to the Pacific collected tapa, tiki and tatau. In particular, Cook—perceived to be a visiting chief—was gifted large quantities of barkcloth; however, he and his men had no concept of what this cloth meant within the social, economic and political systems of the Pacific. They recognised its role as clothing, and clearly as being a gift within the trading relationships that developed, but its underlying importance—the necessity to give cloth in all transactions—eluded the visitors. The

Figure 2.3 › Detail of a club, u'u, from the Marquesas. The head of this janus-figured club comprises numerous tiki images, which would both protect the warrior and imbue the club with a spiritual essence/power. E150. 1114, Oldman Collection, Canterbury Museum.

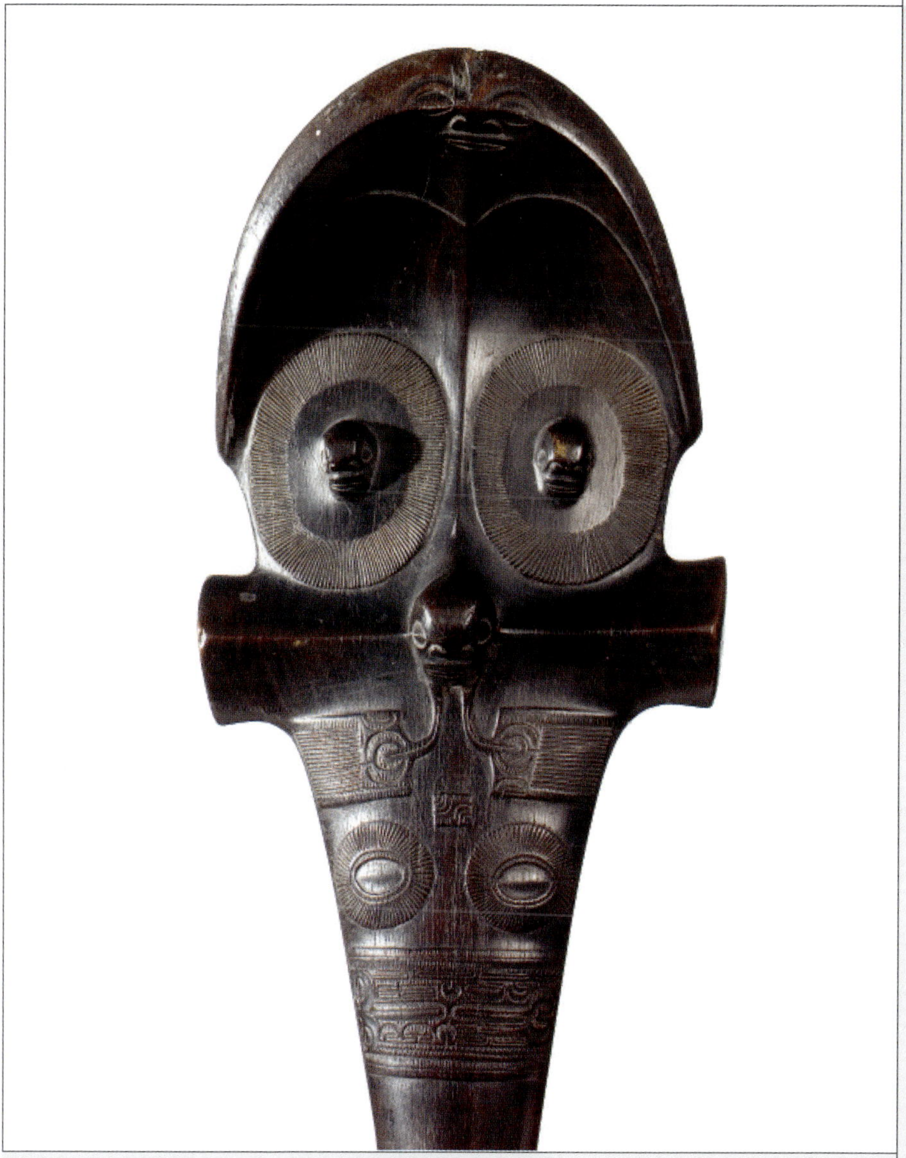

same can be said for tiki and tatau. Tiki were seen as grotesque idols and tatau as a new fashion to introduce to Europe. This superficial attitude has remained and the essence of these art forms continues to be misunderstood.

The importance of textile arts and their integrated relationship within Pacific communities has been overlooked. Often dismissed as merely clothes by the West, recognition is growing that their use was much more than protecting the body, that textiles protected the community: they created and maintained relationships, demonstrated wealth and status, and enabled an artistic ability to be recognised. Being labour intensive, textiles were highly valued and necessary in any economic or chiefly exchange. The domain of women and a cornerstone of traditional economic practices, barkcloth reinforced social relationships. Men, however, also played a role in its creation: they aided in the cultivation and harvesting of the paper mulberry, they created the pounders and also carved upeti boards.

Carving was the realm of men and, as such, tiki were their domain. Whilst cloth visually portrayed social relationships and obligations amongst people, the carving of god images, or more precisely containers of their spiritual essence, enabled the relationship between men and the spirit world **[figure 2.3]**. Tiki and their role in Pacific societies were also misunderstood by the West. Seen to be primitive renditions of the human form or idols of worship, the West could not comprehend the abstract nature of these physical manifestations. Created with an emphasis on the head (the seat of one's mana), these became symbols of the primitive and, therefore, of the exotic nature of the Pacific. As such, they quickly became images associated with tourism—images symbolic not only of a culture, but of a fantasy.

With the introduction of Western cloth and of a new belief system, the importance of tapa, tiki, and tatau waned within Pacific communities. However, the use of barkcloth remained integral to Tongan society as did tatau in Samoa. Both of these art forms were visual markers of status within highly stratified social systems. Both art forms signal relationships and not only provide a link to the past but also remain a marker of identity today. Tatau, on the other hand, continues to be linked to its genealogical past, its motifs referring to histories and traditions. In a series of photographs **[figure 2.4]**, Greg Semu not only documents the acquisition of tatau in Auckland, but also commented on its social and cultural complexities. His images do not focus on the exotic, but on the process; not on a changing tradition, but on

Figure 2.4 › Greg Semu, *First Tatau Session, Velvet Crescent*, 1994. Auckland Art Gallery, Toi o Tāmaki.

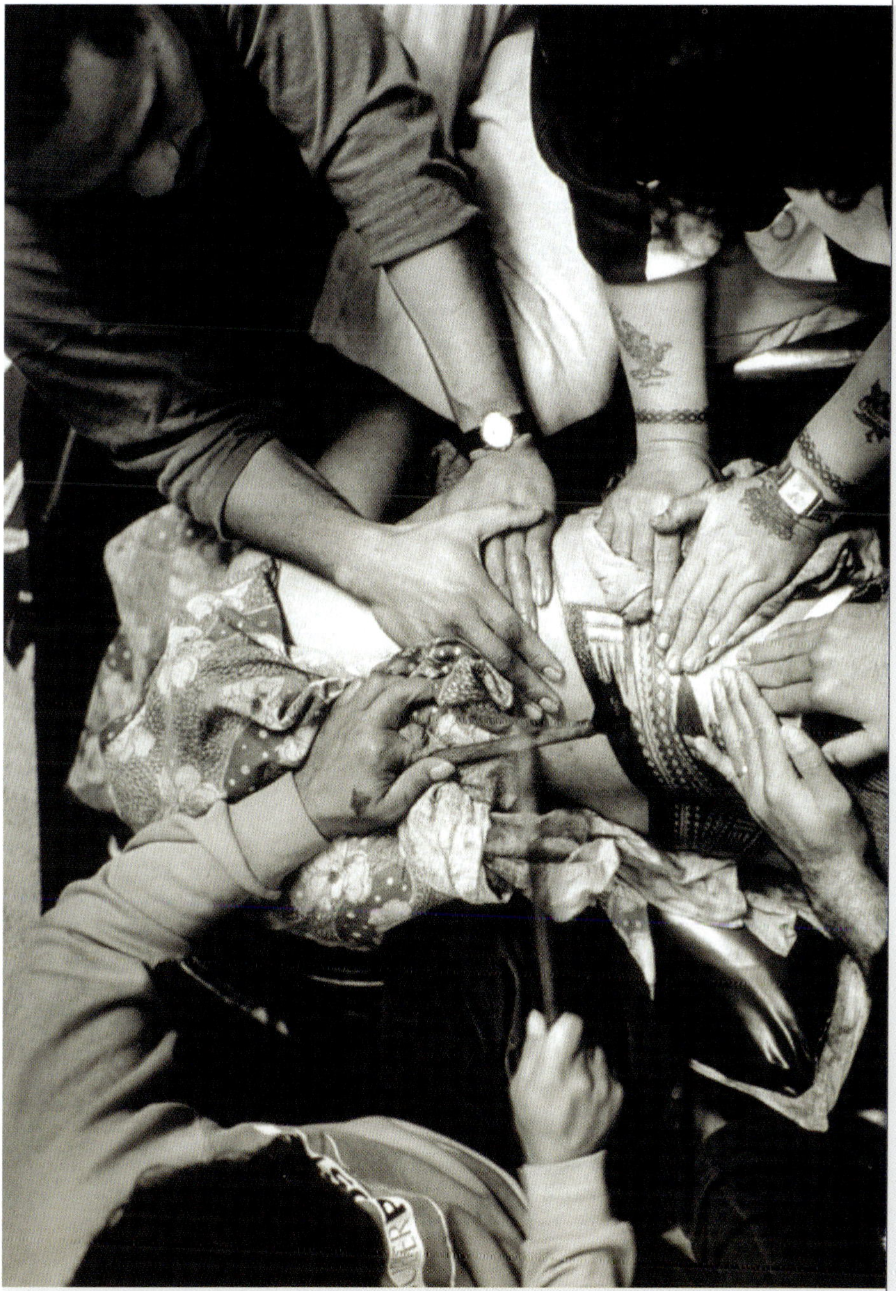

the cultural identity asserted. Tatau both adheres to the past and innovates, with the creation of new patterns from its historical inventory of motifs. The past and the present work in tandem to enable an assertion of a Pacific identity, an identity seen in Lyle Penisula's *Samoan* **[figure 2.5]**. His subject, lying on a piece of barkcloth and wearing a lavalava not only displays a pe'a, but also a taulima and ankle tatau. Contemporary Pacific artists have drawn on these art forms in particular: arts that both understand and reinforce the balance found within Pacific societies. The result is the reconfiguring of icons—drawing from, but not copying—and thereby providing a new generation with a new understanding of their traditional past.

Pacific women were quick to incorporate new dyes, patterns and motifs into their barkcloth, and this has become a symbol of innovation, easily reinterpreted in new media for a new audience, so that these new art forms are examples of both a steadfast adhesion to the past as well as an example of innovation. Fatu Feu'u has created a practice drawn from tradition—from, in fact, the only painterly art form in Samoa: siapo. Working, most often, on a large scale with a grid, Feu'u emulates the basic design foundation of siapo; but this is where the relationship ends. His practice actually draws on the three essential art forms in Samoan culture: siapo, tatau and oratory; the male and female presence is a constant, both traditionally and today. This imagery has been reinterpreted through the eyes of Feu'u—through his personal history of migration and of creating an identity for himself in a new home.

Conserve for Tomorrow **[figure 2.6]** combines three painted canvasses and four carved staffs. The staffs (composite images of chiefly staffs, warriors clubs and an orator's whisk) balance the three painted canvasses (which incorporate frangipani, masks, spirit birds and the vane swastika). There is a balance of male and female in relation to the motifs used, as well as the art forms that are referenced.

Some critics have questioned Feu'u's use of siapo motifs, commenting that it is a woman's art. Siapo is more than that, however: it creates and balances relationships within the community. Feu'u's use of the grid, of the symbols, of the patterns—on canvas, not barkcloth—is not a contradiction or cliché, since he reinterprets the essential function of siapo as a cultural icon. Women, through symbols, remain present in his art and provide the necessary foundation of balance—between men and women, life and death, the past and the present. His works are visual markers of new relationships and the social interactions these embrace.

Figure 2.5 › Lyle Penisula, *Samoan*, acrylic on canvas, 1993. Photograph courtesy of the artist.

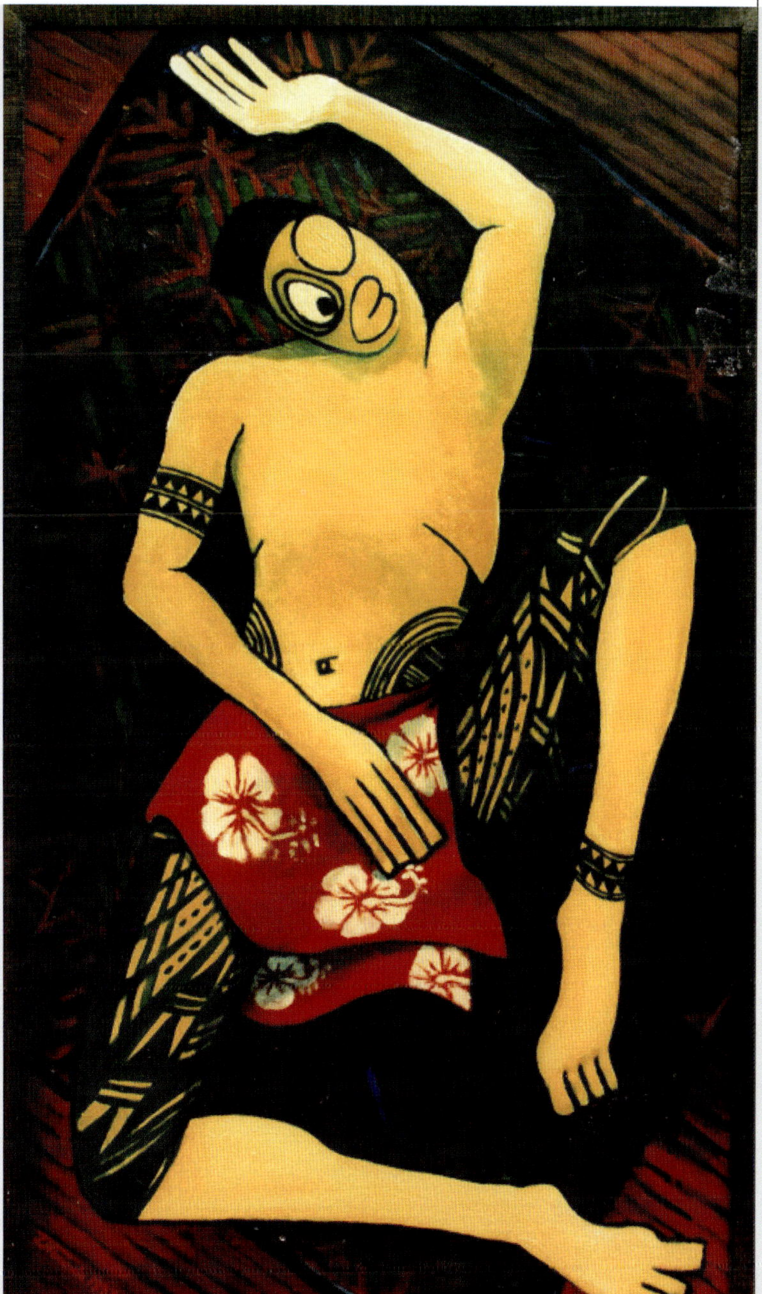

The patterns associated with tatau can also be seen in this light. Feu'u uses these motifs as a means of inclusion, of bringing together the old and the new, of allowing a forum for their presence in today's world. *Roads to New York* **[figure 2.7]** combines these ideas. They mark more than status or manhood—they are protective of the person; they are an identity clearly associated with Samoa.

This notion of protection is key to Feu'u's work, which often incorporates masks and spirit and/or bird images. These relate to the spiritual world, not only of the ancestors, but also of the present. They represent more than legends and convey an important idea that ancestors and beliefs protect us. He speaks of spirituality, of pride in his culture, of empowering these traditions—of reinterpreting them in a modern context. Feu'u (1995: 67) wrote '[our] strength . . . lies in our identity as Samoans, with our culture as the backbone that can be recreated and shaped to the demands of our society'.

Feu'u has had to interpret his works for his public—the New Zealand public—so as to make the meaning behind the symbols clear. This, too, is part of the tradition—of using art to convey, to explain, to interpret one's world. As a result, he has made his work accessible, which has brought success. Unfortunately success is often criticised as commercialism, and so Feu'u has played both the role of mentor and scapegoat amongst Pacific artists.

In contrast to this, John Pule has created works that seem to mock the viewer—to purposely veil the meaning. *Liku* **[figure 2.8]**, a word painting in Niuean, is deliberately esoteric and confronts his New Zealand audience (Cross 1993: 43). By not translating his text, Pule forces the mainstream (his viewer) to become the other. In the mid 1990s, however, Pule shifted direction, creating a practice that combined a loose interpretation of Niuean hiapo **[figure 2.9]** and his own visual vocabulary. As with Samoan siapo, hiapo was a significant art form that embraced the social system. Traditional motifs were abstracted fauna, which were frequently depicted in a circular pattern. Abstraction is maintained in Pule's work and the circle remains integral in his overall patterning. *Perturbed Visitor* **[figure 2.10]** demonstrates the potency of these images, which create an interesting synergy as the viewer travels from motif to motif. Looking closer, one recognises the metaphors, the references to Christianity (often accompanied by sorrow), the gods (strong and fierce), land (heritage, genealogy), migration, sexuality and language.

Figure 2.6 › Fatu Feu'u, *Conserve for Tomorrow*, oil on canvas, wood and barkcloth, 1992. Photograph courtesy of Giles Petersen.

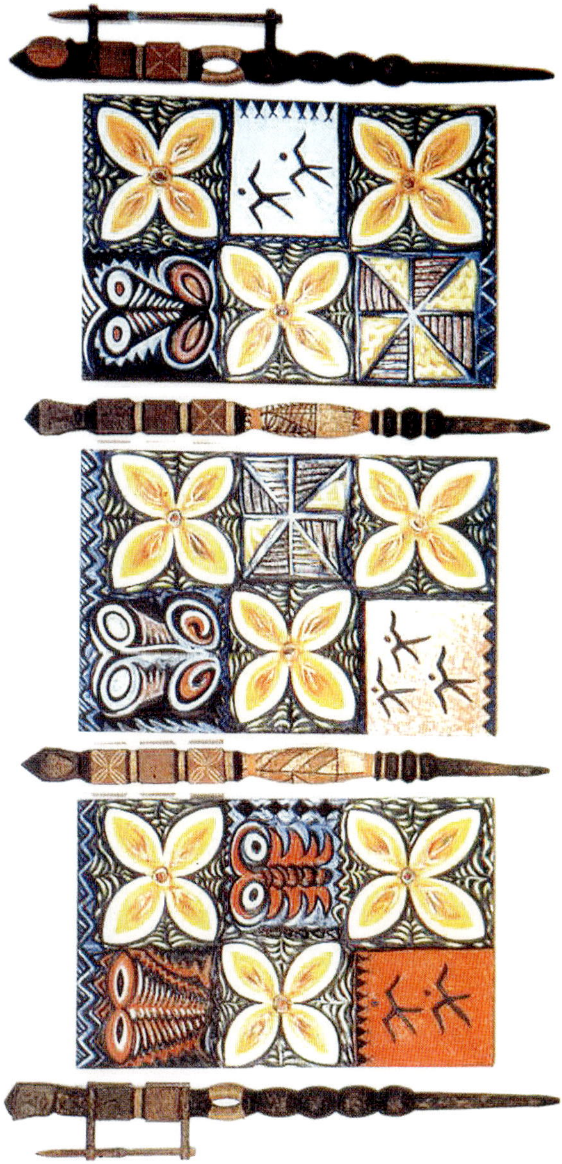

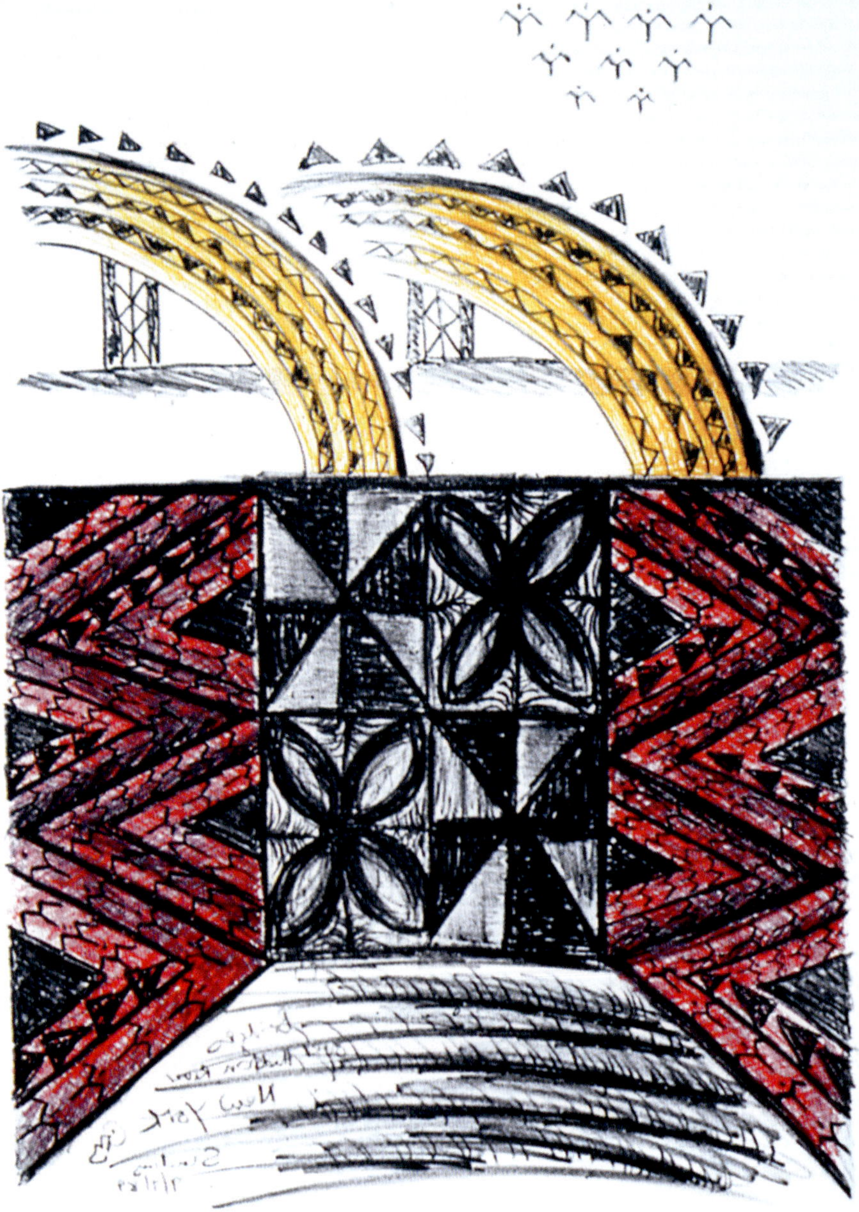

Figure 2.7 › Fatu Feu'u, *Roads to New York*, lithograph, 1990. Photograph courtesy of the artist.

Figure 2.8 › John Pule, *Liku*, 1990, acrylic on canvas. Photograph courtesy of the Sarjeant Gallery Te Whare O Rehua Wanganui.

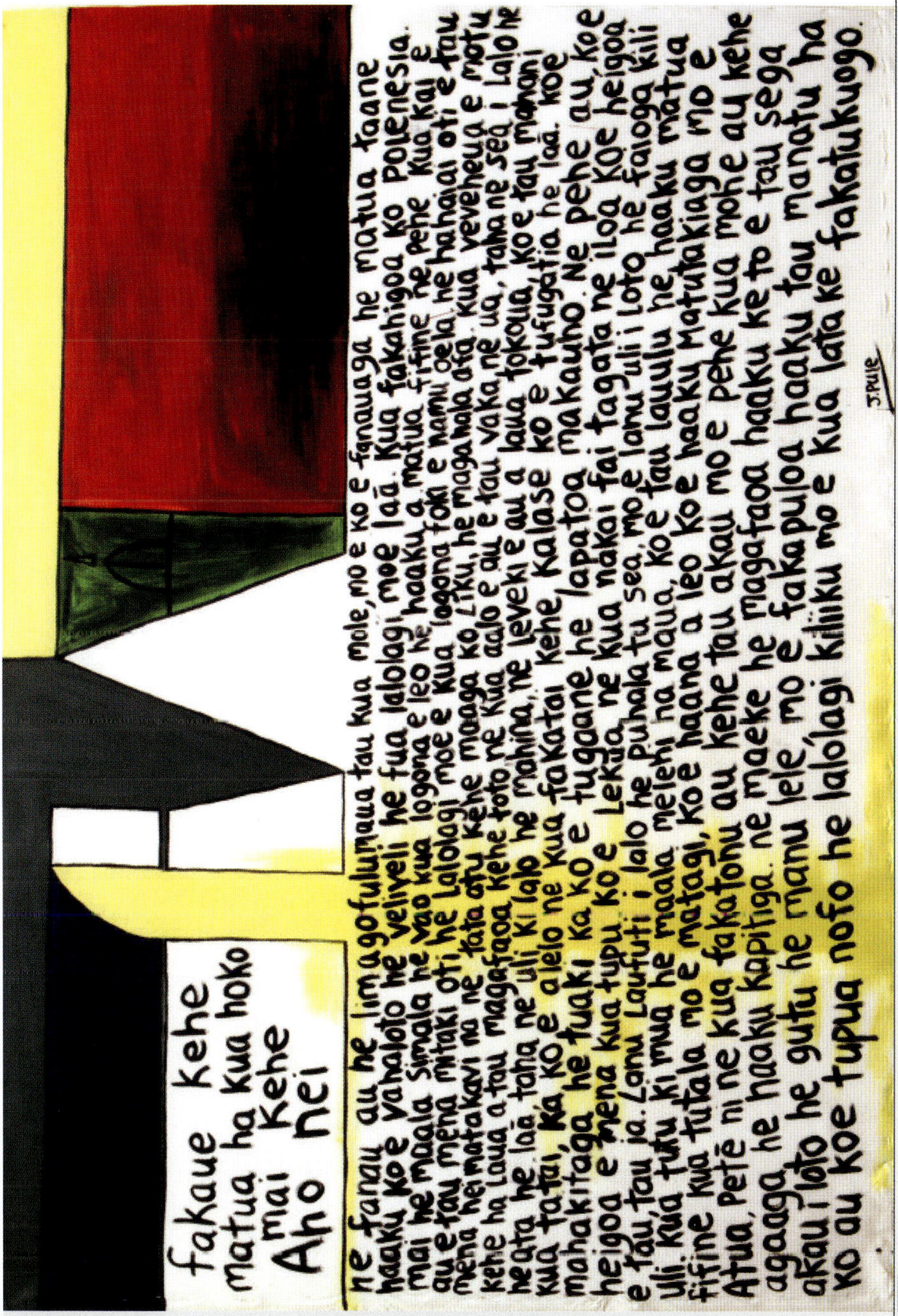

Both Feu'u and Pule have been the focus of much discussion vis-à-vis their use of the barkcloth tradition, but this dialogue reiterates much of the misinformation surrounding Pacific arts. They are neither appropriating this art form, nor are they emulating its traditions. What is important is the pattern and its reinterpretations, which offer meaning to a new generation of artists. As Nicholas Thomas (1994: 100) stated, 'Pule typifies the position of a younger generation of Polynesians who, without turning their backs on tradition or identity, do not uncritically support the form of tradition that their elders sustain'.

Veronica Vaevae also drew upon barkcloth and tatau patterns in her digital work *Mix that Scratch* **[figure 2.11]**. Critics could not see the obvious relationship between it and barkcloth. The repetition of motifs drawn from barkcloth and tatau created patterns of interaction. More importantly, Vaevae utilised a Western system and infused it with Pacific patterns, thereby asserting a Pacific identity within the Western framework.

Yet Vaevae's and Pule's work, like Feu'u's, is more than a series of motifs that the viewer can associate with the Pacific. In the past, the patterns and motifs created by Pacific women were invested with metaphor; so too are contemporary renditions. The more innovative these art practices become, the more traditional they are. For example, the shark is a recurring metaphor in Pule's work. In Western traditions the shark is often viewed as a fierce predator and an object of fear. In many Polynesian legends the shark is an aumakua—a protector—but the shark has many guises. It can be deceitful and cunning, luring victims in its direction. It is sexually charged, strong and potent. It is a life force. Traditionally a symbol of strength, today it becomes a metaphor of identity.

Hence we see a relationship between the past and the present, between motifs and metaphors, between social and spiritual relationships. Feu'u incorporates masks and spirit birds; Pule's fantastical beings pay homage to the gods and provide an alternative to the imposed Western religion of Christianity. Incorporating spirit images, using their names, giving them faces, allows contemporary Pacific Islanders a glimpse into the past, where knowledge was received through social interactions—interactions referenced by tapa, tiki and tatau. Stories of the gods and their relationships with people have turned into legends. Pacific Sisters, in 1998, gave new life and meaning to the legend of Tuna and Sina, their contemporary take providing not only a new

Figure 2.9 › This example of Niuean hiapo exemplifies Niue's move away from the grid in their barkcloth design. It also demonstrates the diversity of barkcloth pattern found in Polynesia [see figures 2.1 and 2.2]. Auckland War Memorial Museum Tamaki Paenga Hira, AM30088.

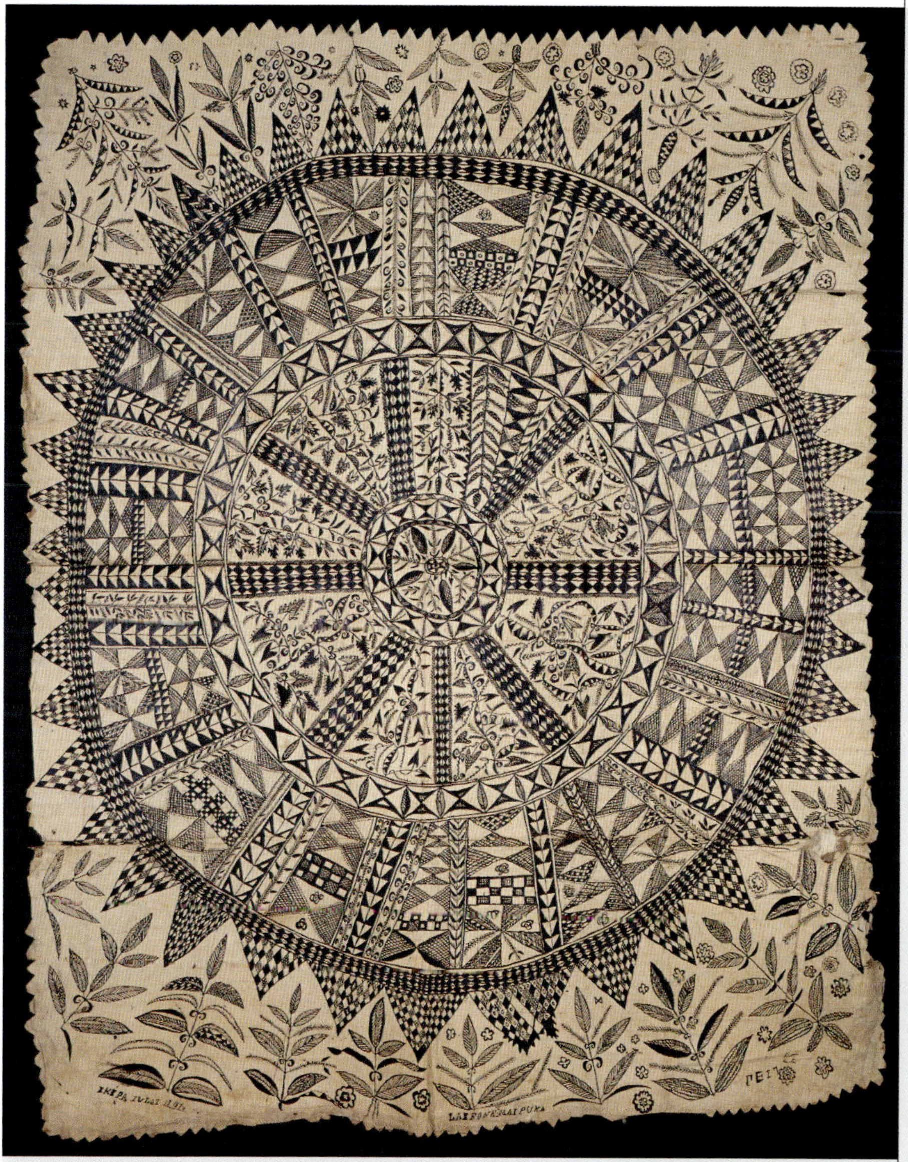

context and new audience, but also a body of knowledge for a new generation.[8] Using video, sound, dance and pantomime, Pacific Sisters offered a contemporary look at a traditional legend. O'Neill believes that the stories bring Polynesian cultural history to life. Many are pan-Polynesian and O'Neill finds that the variety of outside influences offers insight into each island's colonial past. This reinterpretation of a Polynesian legend transmits both knowledge and comfort through a shared (experienced) cultural heritage. 'The legends are our history. They cannot be denied and they are important to know.'[9]

Attempting to maintain some relevance between the past and the present, O'Neill positions herself firmly in New Zealand as an urban Polynesian. Her practice draws from the past—a past it questions as she reinvests cultural icons with new meaning. In *Tangaroa* **[figure 1.7]** she challenges the use of a god as a tourist image and questions how one can create images—images that were once invested with mana—'just to make a buck'.[10] Her benign stuffed toy becomes invested with a myriad of cultural and political issues.

Asserting a Cook Islands identity, yet positioning herself firmly in New Zealand, O'Neill creates a position from which she can question, critique and embrace Cook Islands icons. She noted 'my art to me, is really looking at my situation as a Rarotongan. I have always felt privileged to have had that background'.[11] The ability to question Western constructions of the Pacific as well as the willingness of Pacific peoples to embrace and/or own them leaves contemporary Pacific artists in a cultural no-man's-land. Underlying Pacific stereotypes are social, cultural and political issues, and these are addressed by the artists. Identity and/or the creation of an identity become an integral aspect of their arts practice. Positioning oneself as Pacific—taking on and embracing that mantle—provides a voice and a responsibility. Frequently this responsibility is placed on them by their culture—they become its representative and as such they develop a relationship with the community. This, however, is often fraught, since their artistic practice often positions them as their own culture's critic.

The politics of identity is, therefore, a key factor in contemporary Pacific art. For some artists like O'Neill, it is just who they are. For others, asserting a specific identity associated with a cultural heritage becomes important, particularly if a loss of cultural knowledge transpired through migration. There is also the issue

Figure 2.10 › John Pule, *Perturbed Visitor*, woodcut and lithograph, 1994. Photograph courtesy of PaperGraphica.

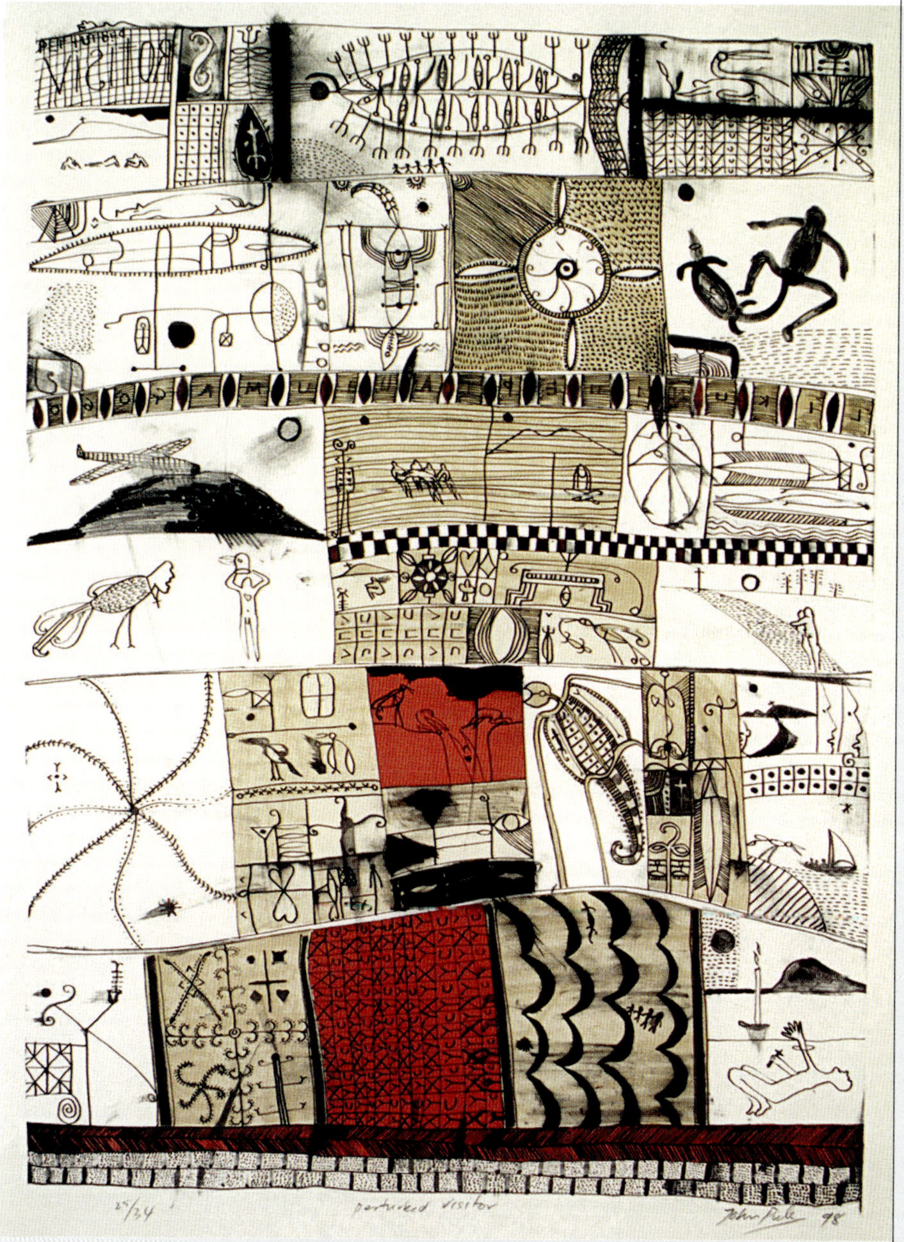

Figure 2.11 › Veronica Vaevae, *Mix that Scratch*, video still, 1994. Photograph courtesy of the artist.

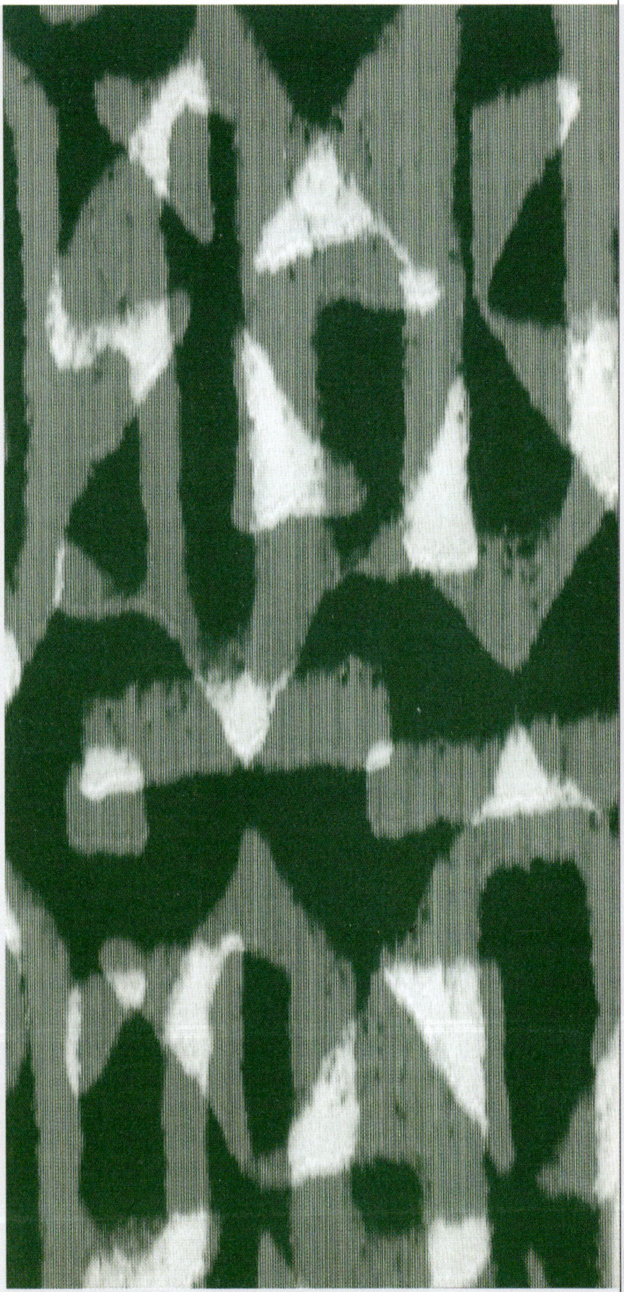

Figure 2.12 › Dagmar Dyck, *ngatu 60 ae 62*, acrylic and oil stick on canvas and tapa, 2000. Photograph courtesy of the artist.

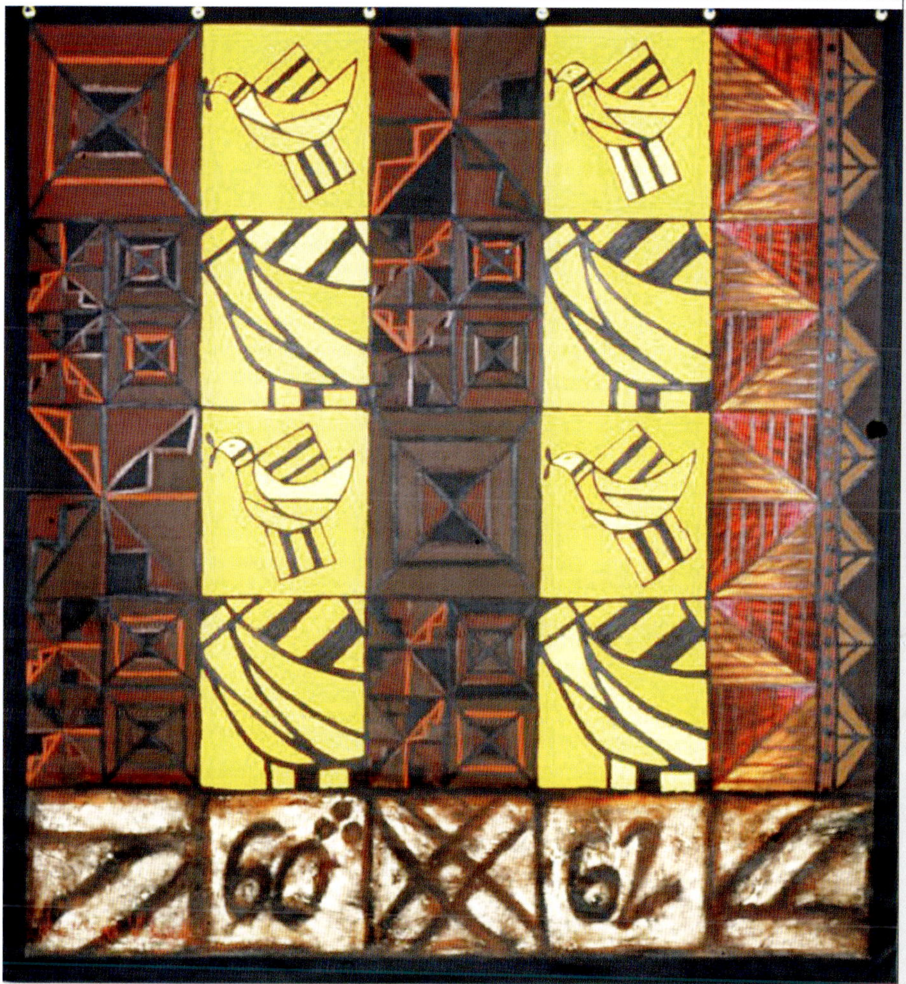

of negotiating the multiple identities often found in modern New Zealand, of negotiating a place in a new land (even though you were born here), of being the other's other. As many Pacific artists can draw upon multiple Pacific heritages, on multiple identities, they must learn to negotiate their place in New Zealand society. Michel Tuffery is of Samoan, Tahitian and Cook Islands descent. Acknowledging a Samoan background, he was amazed at the negativity associated with that label. Positioning himself as Tahitian, on the other hand, was a complete contrast—Tahiti is exotic and imbued with romantic stereotype. He positions himself in New Zealand. Lily Laita, of Māori and Samoan heritage, commented that 'labels place people in a box. I don't fit in a box'.[12] A Pacific identity creates labels—labels Pacific artists detest; labels they refute.

Therefore, positioning oneself as Pacific results in a predicament. Living in New Zealand, artists often do not belong to the islands they reference. As Michel Tuffery has said, 'if you're born here, you've got no identity'.[13] So, Pacific artists draw upon the stereotype—on tapa, tiki, and tatau—to create both a relationship to the islands as well as a home. Owning and critiquing the myth establishes them as urban Polynesians. The desire to identify with the islands when they do not belong creates inconsistencies and contradictions that translate into metaphors in their arts practice.

One example is in Dagmar Dyck's work. In the mid 1990s she incorporated Tongan objects into her work. At that time the objects chosen intrigued her and the relationship asserted was that of being Tongan. By 2000, however, Dyck focused her attention on textiles, and on the patterns and objects associated with women. This shift provided a depth to her work, an opportunity to assert not only an identity, but also knowledge. Her painted ngatu (*ngatu 60 ae 62)* became metaphors of identity **[figure 2.12]**. This process of negotiation can also be seen in the work of Michel Tuffery and Lily Laita. Tuffery clearly represents himself as a member of two cultures. He often uses the lizard (Pili) as a metaphor for himself—the outsider looking in, listening, observing, learning and acquiring knowledge to be used someday. In *Lua Pili Siva*, Pili wears a pe'a, thereby asserting a Samoan identity **[figure 2.13]**. Tatau reveals his Polynesian ancestry. Laita, on the other hand, is more ambiguous. Her images do not trumpet Pacific and often have multiple references—Māori, Pacific and New Zealand references, which bridge her identities. *Pari'aka* is a good example of this as it makes reference to her cultural heritages. It was created after a visit to

Figure 2.13 › Michel Tuffery, *Lua Pili Siva*, lithograph, 1992. Photograph courtesy of the artist.

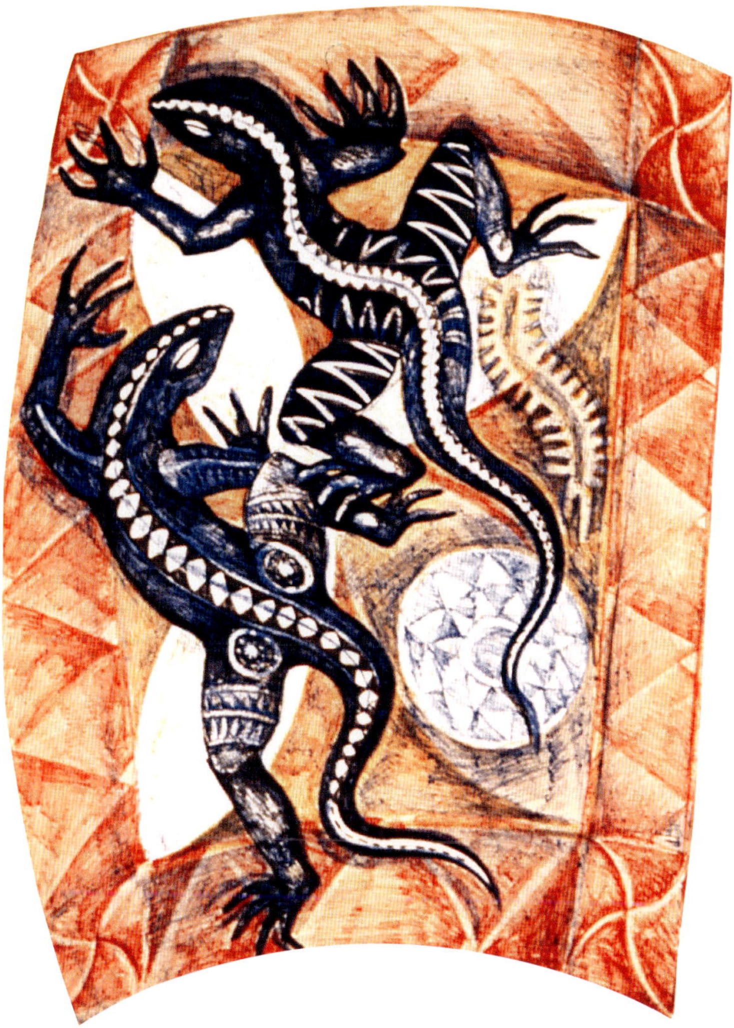

Pari'aka, and Laita (quoted in Griffin 1992: 87) stated 'it was the first time I'd ever been in one place at one time where two of my cultures were present at once'. In contrast, *Taeao Lalata* **[figure 2.14]** focuses on Laita's Samoan identity, and on the space/place of women—their roles in society.

Laita's work, like Tuffery and Pule's, is a construction of images, experiences and words. However, these words, which are not to be taken at face value, become metaphors of identity. Laita finds people's attempts at understanding—of grabbing at the words, at her identities—inappropriate. She has said that 'sometimes if Pacific Islanders see something in my work they go "oh" because they have the (Samoan) words to go by even if they don't understand the painting. It's like a clue but often it's a distraction because it's more often than not only a small part of the painting.'[14] (Laita quoted in Panoho 1990: 26)

Playing with words, combining English, Samoan and Māori, Laita exclaims in the title of the exhibition *Sum Niu Mahi* (1998) that she has done 'some new work'. The integration of words in Laita's work does not have the political resonance associated with Pule's. However, Laita does not shy away from controversy and is quite outspoken in regards to art, labels, racism and the Pacific bandwagon. Her celebrity status as a woman, a Samoan, a Māori means little. 'It's like, wow! Three for the price of one!' (Laita quoted in Findlay 1992: 47). She is keenly aware of her position, yet refuses to wear the label.

By embracing and re-contextualising the stereotype, Pacific artists are creating a position for themselves and their arts practice in New Zealand. Clearly this is complicated by cultural and identity politics—by the need to negotiate a position that enables their voice. The Pacific voice and the cultural heritage on which it stands not only empower those speaking, but also provide a platform for the Pacific community. This heritage, woven together with cultural icons—tapa, tiki, and tatau—serves the artists discussed here as a means of representing the Pacific and themselves. The genesis of a Pacific art is cemented in both a personal and public quest for balance. Bold or even subtle statements of identity punctuate difference. Pacific artists are doing more than reinterpreting a past. They are utilising new materials and technologies that bridge the space between the island and the urban, providing a foundation for cultural growth. References to tapa, tiki and tatau place this work within the Pacific. Yet, more than a rehash or play with the exotic, Pacific artists are creating a new visual language: the imagery of identity.

Figure 2.14 › Lily Laita, *Taeao Lalata*, acrylic on canvas, 2000. Photograph courtesy of Deborah White, Whitespace Gallery Auckland.

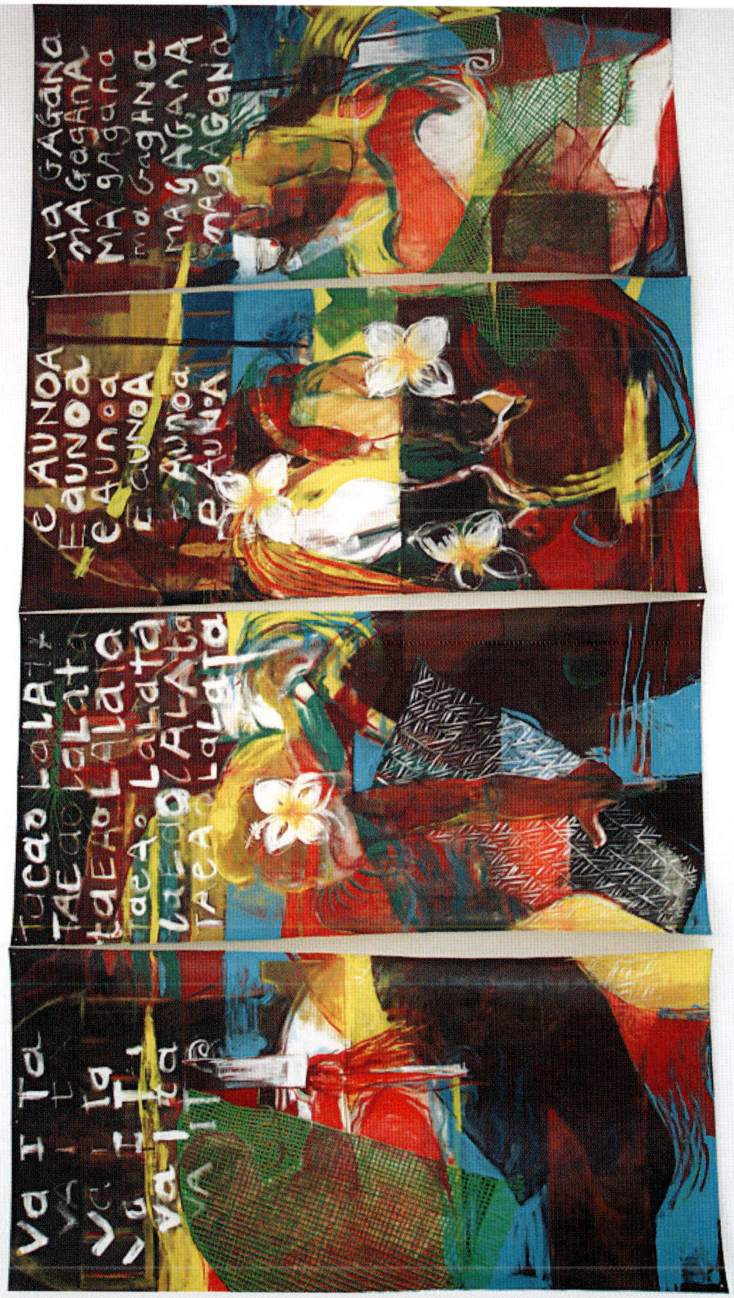

CHAPTER 03

Indigenous Abstraction: Reaffirming the Past

A Pacific Island cultural aesthetic has developed over the past millennia, changing as new materials and methods became available. As the Polynesians navigated their oceans, lashing technologies and the plaiting of sails were essential to their well-being. In each phase of migration artists quickly learned to manipulate new technologies in such a way that their function remained clear, enabling cultural knowledge to be passed from one generation to another. The patterns created in lashings are also seen in tatau, barkcloth, plaiting and on Lapita ware. This suggests that these designs are more than a pleasing aesthetic: they are integrally entwined into Pacific lives and have been part of this cultural whole for millennia. Referencing astronomical, navigational and environmental knowledge, these abstract concepts became mnemonic devices that allowed for the dissemination of cultural knowledge.

These facts contrast significantly with the stereotype of Pacific. The Pacific and its traditions have been seen as primitive, heathen, exotic and, more recently, as a tourist destination or a souvenir. These stereotypes, reinforcing ethnocentric beliefs, left the Pacific in the wake of the West. Images, oratory, and both the ability and necessity to think abstractly have been misunderstood. The West has claimed abstraction as its own; however, abstraction (as defined by the West)[1] has been the foundation of Pacific art production. Adrienne Kaeppler, whose work focuses on Tonga, yet embraces the entire Pacific, has suggested that the underlying purpose of art production in the Pacific was and is to make the invisible visible (Kaeppler, 1985: 120). This, combined with the facility to speak and move metaphorically, has reinforced the principles of abstraction within Pacific art.[2]

The stereotype, in equating Pacific tradition with notions of the primitive, did not allow that Pacific peoples have the ability to think and act abstractly. Yet the Pacific's sculptural images are abstract **[figure 2.3]**. In attempts to account for this, it was suggested that their creators did not have the ability to depict a realistic human form. The fact that they do not depict humans had escaped those promoting the concept of the primitive. As a result, ethnocentricity has perpetuated a lack of understanding, as well as the inability to value Pacific art traditions.

Within the rhetoric of the contemporary, Pacific tradition plays an important role in cultural politics. By 1985 tradition was a word burdened with more than a decade of academic debate amongst anthropologists, art historians and theoreticians.[3] Linnekin (1990: 151) noted its position in public debate when it was utilised by academics as well as cultural politicians to make assertions about the validity and character of changing cultural practices. It became a vague term rooted in an idealised past, yet manipulated in the present. It was jargon. For many Pacific artists, however, tradition was and is associated with both an older generation *and* the islands, with practices not always a part of their urban lives. Tradition became a composite of cultural practices that included language, music, dance, oratory, textiles, body adornment, and the importance of genealogy, protocol and the church. These were not practices to belittle or discard, but practices to learn from and utilise as a foundation for innovative contemporary art practice.

These traditions have integrally linked Pacific peoples and places to stereotypes of the exotic—the islands, bright colours and flowered clothing. Pacific Island art production is seen as communal[4] and/or linked to indigenous spiritual ideologies.[5] These stereotypes place Pacific cultural traditions into a bell jar that refutes the notion of innovation. Pacific Islanders, however, believe that tradition embodies knowledge, the interpretation of which was and is constantly changing, as it is passed down or discovered, and modified for contemporary social, economic, political and cultural means. As such, the interplay between abstraction and tradition becomes complex in the current environment as artists choose which traditions to draw upon.

Historically, a gender division of labour and artistic endeavour created a balance where women worked with soft, pliable materials and men with hard materials (Teilhet 1983). Navigation, oratory and spirituality were in the realm of men, while women produced and nurtured status relationships. As balance was the key, this framework also allowed for change and innovation. Technical knowledge was shared, yet often used differently. For example, the same plaiting techniques were used to plait sails, mats, and baskets; the patterns found therein were also seen on barkcloth, in tatau and village gardens. These patterns, associated with particular practices, became mnemonic devices to protect and pass on cultural knowledge. Gender roles and/or notions of gender divisions of labour, however, have not survived the move from island to urban. This creates an arena where artists combine their interests with an acquired knowledge that frequently was not handed down but was developed through research. The balance necessary in the past has become reinterpreted by artists today. As a result, cultural knowledge is transmitted via new cultural traditions.

These traditional art forms, though constantly changing, have consistently reinforced the cultural traditions of Polynesia, creating a valued artistic system.[6] This chapter looks at the artistic practices of artists who balance the notion of tradition and abstraction. This underlying principle is essential to the understanding of contemporary Pacific art, as it enables artists to draw from a wide range of practices and patterns, so permitting their artwork to sit easily within the traditions of Western art.

Pacific peoples use their art production as a means of cultural preservation. Men created the means to interact with the spirit world so as to provide for and protect their families. Carving, building and tatau enabled these social and spiritual interactions. In contrast, women created wealth, symbolised relationships, and demonstrated both a personal and cultural aesthetic—all through textile production. These various art forms were central to their lives, so much so that their identity was entwined in their production. Their works move beyond the utilitarian, beyond the decorative: they embody all that is valued within the culture itself. These traditions provide a foundation for innovation in contemporary Pacific art.

There are two distinct strands of contemporary Pacific art as currently practised in New Zealand. These reflect a social and geographical reality: an older generation

Figure 3.1 › This stall at the Pasifika Festival in Auckland, 2007, is selling a variety of contemporary textile products; some utilising traditional (pandanus) others using modern (plastic) materials. Photograph courtesy of Hilary Scothorn.

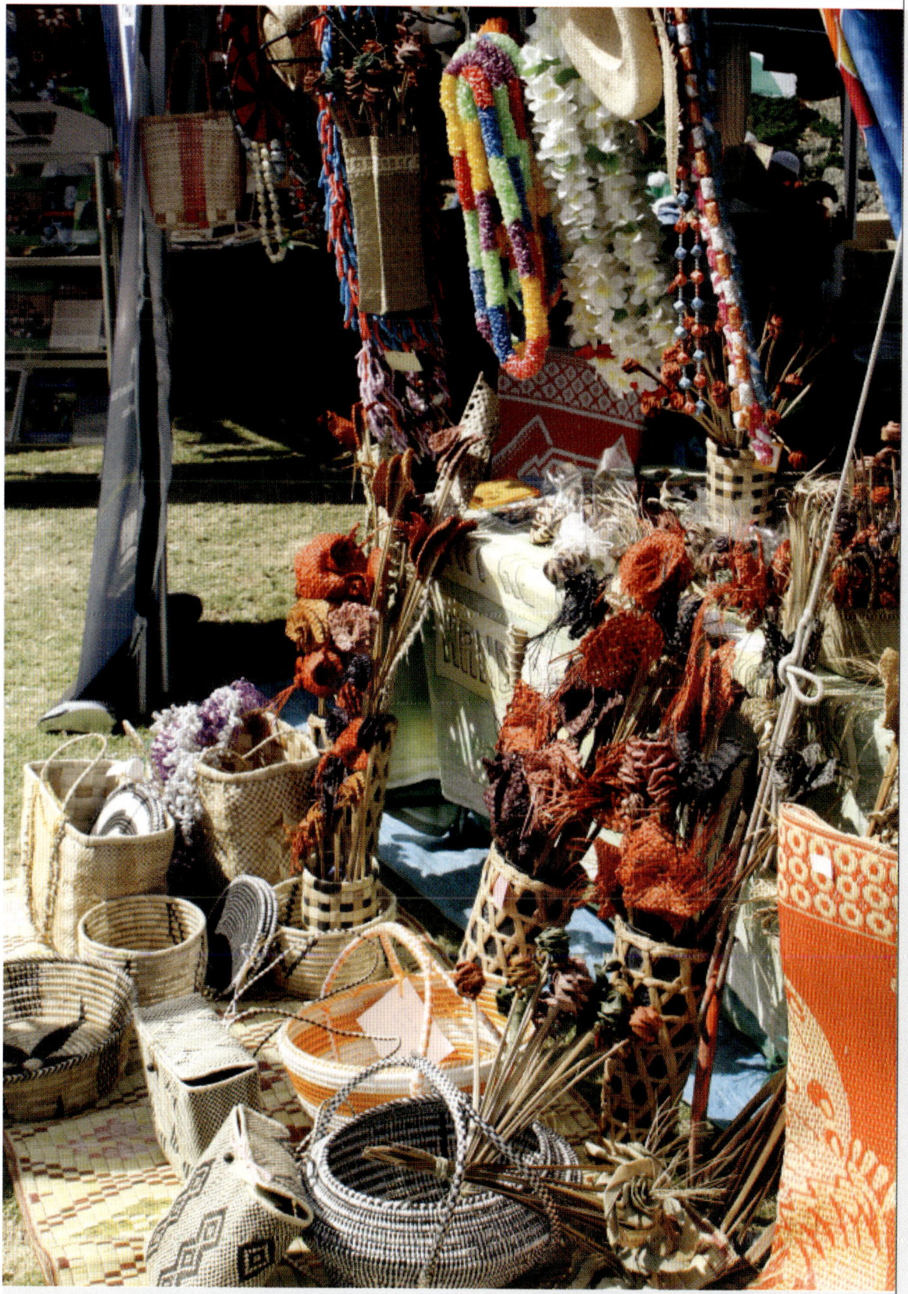

tied to the islands, and a younger generation exploring the vitality of their urban environment. The result is the continued practice of valued traditions, as well as the reinterpretation of these traditions in a contemporary manner. Textile koloa, in its varied forms, enacts for Tongan women aspects of Tonga's past and what it means to be Tongan in the present (Herda 1999: 166). Similarly, for Cook Islands mamas textiles offer 'stability to a society in a state of change' (Sheffield 1996), while 'it is within the [Niue, Tokelau and Tuvalu] communities in particular that we have witnessed the greatest innovation, experimentation and adaptation of the old (weaving techniques) with the new (forms and materials)' (Pereira 2002: 80).

Bound together by a cultural aesthetic, innovation provides the link between contemporary and traditional values in Polynesia **[figure 3.1]**. These art forms are essential to the creation and perpetuation of a strong Pacific identity. As Rangihiroa Panoho (1990: 6) noted, 'down at Freemans Bay, Niuean women are busy cutting and assembling large amounts of different coloured plastics. Fertiliser, lunch bag wrappers, drinking straws, polybubble lei. Industrial wrapping plastic band is woven skilfully into mats, kete, and hats. The umbilical cord with the islands has not been severed. The traditions are still there—the visual vocab has simply been extended'.

Ani O'Neill and Filipe Tohi are both the recipients of knowledge associated with the genre of textiles—tivaevae, plaiting and lashings. Tivaevae are associated with women, lashings with men; and both women and men used plaiting in their artistic and also their everyday lives. Tivaevae utilise appliqué techniques that were introduced to Pacific women by missionary wives. As an art form, Tivaevae replaced barkcloth production in Tahiti and the Cook Islands by the late 19th century: the function and nature of barkcloth production was transferred to tivaevae. Tivaevae ta'orei referenced plaiting motifs, because the pieces of material (cut into small squares) created similar patterns to those utilised in mat production. Tivaevae generally evolved to embody floral patterns, and in the Cook Islands these also included elaborate embroidery **[figure 3.2]**. The traditions, patterns and technologies continue today both in the Cook Islands and New Zealand. They have been passed to Ani O'Neill by her grandmother.

Women's art has always been greatly valued in the Pacific. They were not only the makers of wealth, their products were essential in gifting, exchange and status

Figure 3.2 › Detail of a Cook Island tivaevae showing its embroidery. Photograph courtesy of Hilary Scothorn.

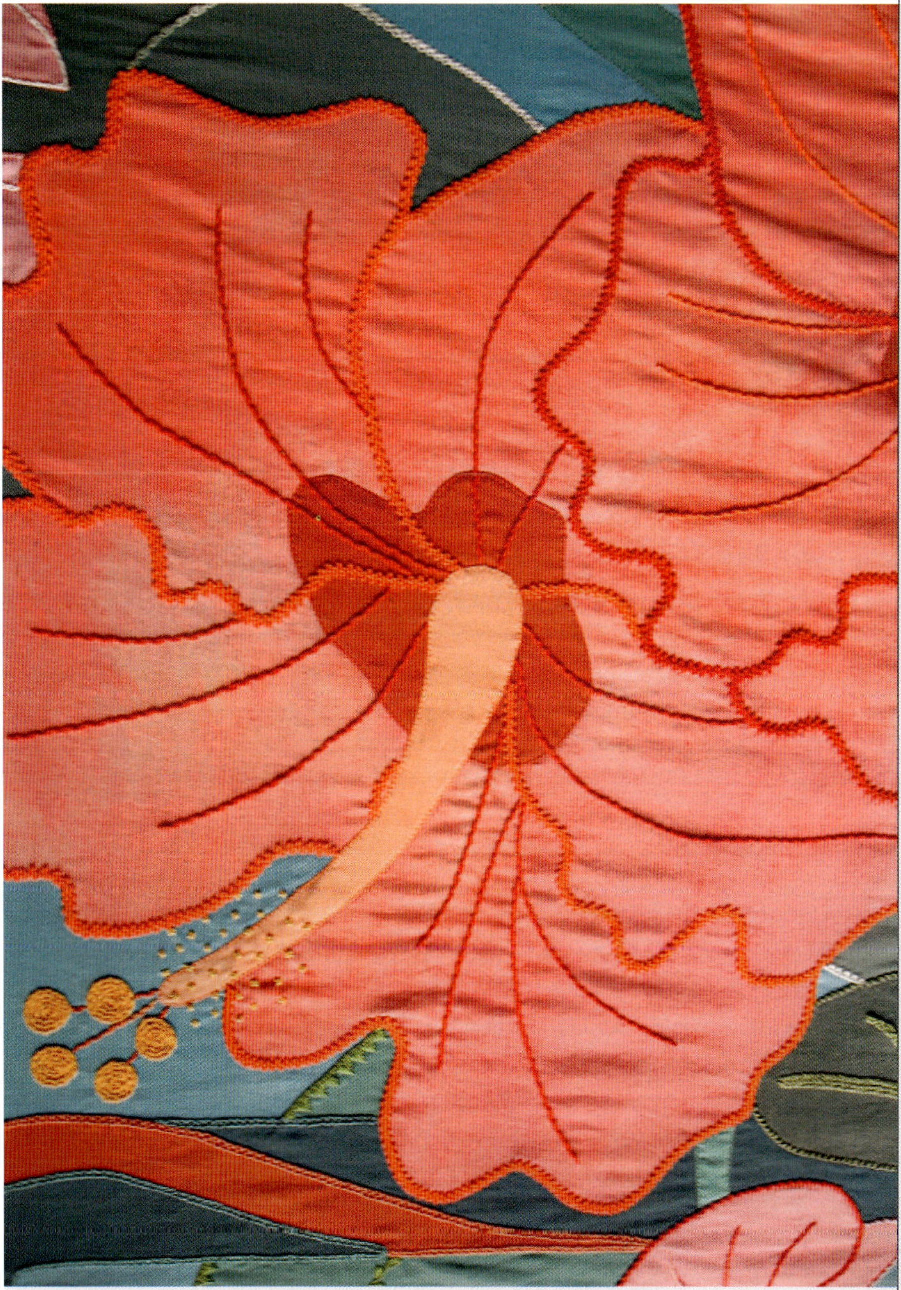

relationships. These art forms represent the importance of the domestic, of women as the purveyors of culture. O'Neill believes that the cultural and traditional value of needlework (the "labour of love" often sidelined by our hi-tech society) should be recognised.[7] Tradition, transmitted between women, is seen as reinforcing the very soul of Polynesian art. O'Neill offers a new context to traditional art: a context where the pliable and repetitive arts traditionally associated with women can be reinterpreted for an urban audience. She embraces the art forms associated with Cook Islands women and effortlessly intertwines these with the notion of art taught within the institution. Using her culture as a springboard, she catapults herself into the contemporary art world, reinvesting her practice with tradition.

Based in urban Auckland, O'Neill has bridged her divergent realities in her art practice. In such work as *Rainbow Country* **[figure 3.3]** her medium is crocheted wool. Her "paintings" offer abstract expressions that reference both the islands and their traditions. In these, O'Neill focuses on the issues of value vis-à-vis women's work. By referencing these objects as paintings, their placement within the gallery setting affords them a legitimate art status, while challenging the attitudes that dismiss women's work as craft. O'Neill's ability to place these neo-traditional works within the gallery setting also reinforces the position of the traditional arts in New Zealand. Her acknowledgement of the mamas provides a platform for their work as well. Drawing upon the communal work ethic of Pacific women, O'Neill often incorporates a market within her exhibitions, whereby tivaevae, mats, baskets and hats are also brought into the gallery context. Clearly one tradition has not replaced the other. They work in tandem to create a balanced whole.

O'Neill has also drawn upon plaiting and braiding technologies to create works derivative of mats—for example, *Star by Night* **[figure 3.4]** and *Kua Marino te Tai* **[figure 1.4]**—and lei (*ei line, Sweet Rap)*. These draw upon the genres of art traditionally created by women, referencing their role and value within the cultural traditions of the Pacific. Both *Star by Night* and *Kua Marino te Tai*, composed of plaited ribbon, recreate mats with modern materials. The pattern created, a star, offers a relationship to the Pacific skies, to navigation and to the foundation of Pacific cultures.

The use of pattern is also at the heart of Filipe Tohi's investigation into lalava or lashings. Tohi's drawing of a cross pattern, *Fakalava* **[figure 3.5]**, is clearly related to the positive and negative space seen in O'Neill's *Star by Night*. Tohi's work

Figure 3.3 › Ani O'Neill, *Rainbow Country*, steel and wool, 2000. Photograph courtesy of the artist.

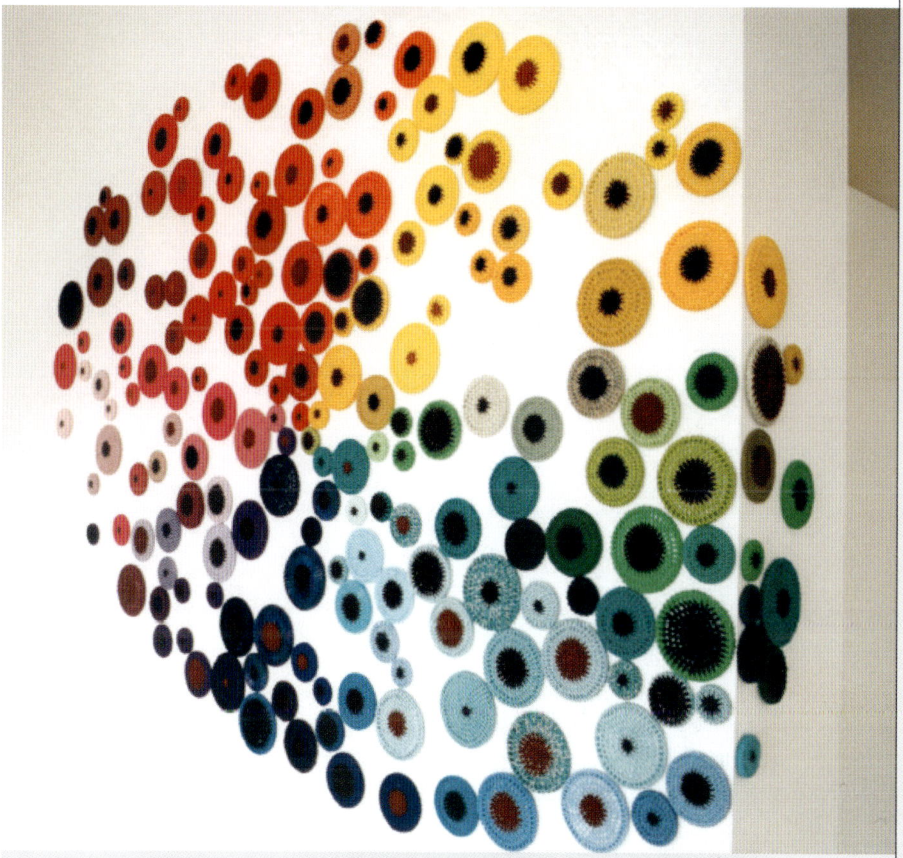

Figure 3.4 › Ani O'Neill, *Star by Night*, florist ribbon, 1993. Photograph courtesy of Ani O'Neill/Museum of New Zealand Te Papa Tongarewa (1997-0037-1).

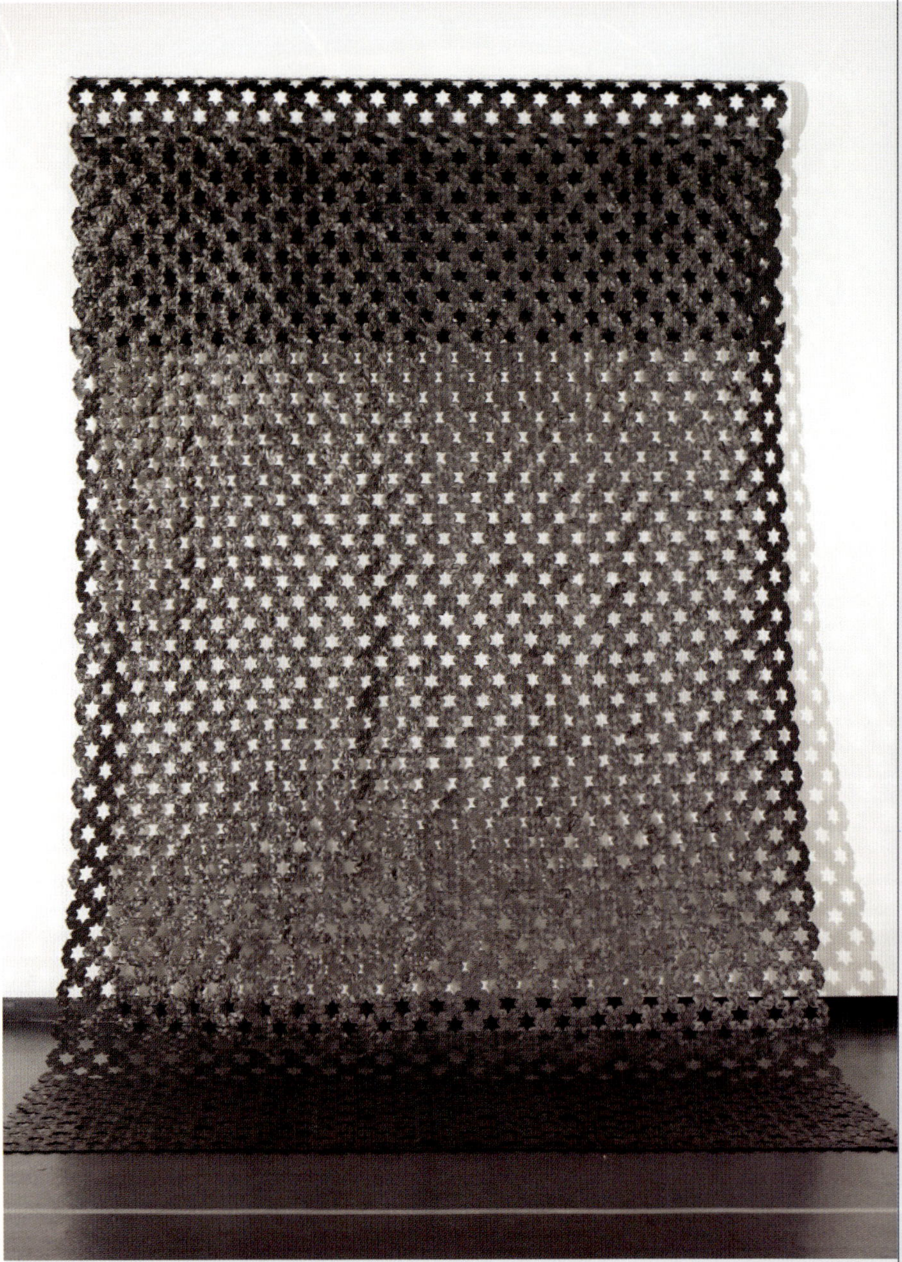

Figure 3.5 › Filipe Tohi, *Fakalava*, drawing, 2000. Photograph courtesy of the artist.

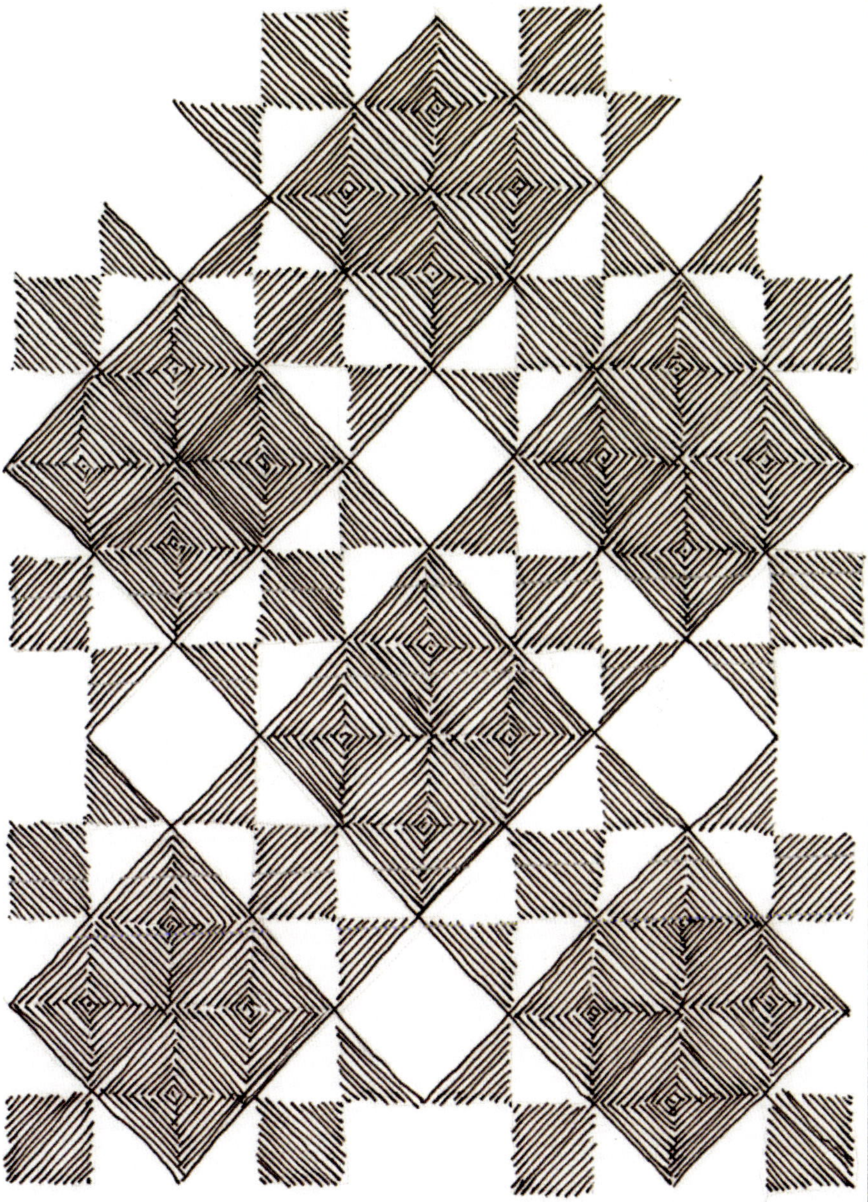

integrates the roles of both men and women, reinforcing the necessary balance found in Polynesian cultural traditions. The complexities of Tongan lashing design have become Tohi's cultural and artistic language. The depth of Tohi's knowledge of lalava can be observed in his works as the enormity of cultural knowledge associated with them is slowly and systematically revealed. Tohi believes the answers of the universe can be found in the patterns of lalava; they are, he says, the metaphor of DNA in modern times. Indeed, he defines lalava as the intersection of two strings as they spiral up and down, forming patterns. Without both strings (lines) there are no patterns and both must go together.[8] Clearly, lalava sits well within the concept of abstraction; but more importantly, the patterns created offer a view into the fourth dimension—they provide insight into the ways Pacific peoples conceptualised their world. Using models of the lalava designs (see *Fakalava* (front) **[figure 3.6]** and *Fakalava* (back) **[figure 3.7]**), Tohi expands the patterns into three dimensions, thus allowing his audience to see the geometric nature of the patterns and, more importantly, to see them from both sides. Moving around these models, we can see the tangle of two lines intermingled; and at once, both a complexity and simplicity is revealed.

Tohi provides a visual allusion to the cultural metaphor he depicts. Adrienne Kaeppler (2002: 293) noted that 'Tongan aesthetic philosophy [is] based on heliaki, to say one thing but mean another'. The use of metaphor and allusion enable the transference of cultural knowledge as context and meaning change. To fully understand these textile traditions one must understand 'the poetics and politics of Tongan verbal and visual modes of expression, the Tongan philosophy of aesthetics' (Kaeppler: 293). This is not just an artistic penchant, it is a philosophy, a way of life. As such, the utilisation of these patterns provides sustenance to a culture. Tohi believes that these patterns have been modelled into symbols of human interaction, so that the designs teach us how to live, to interact, to be. As the lashings were used on canoes, they often referenced navigational knowledge, knowledge transferred in the process of doing. The names of the patterns refer to guiding stars (the Pleiades, the Southern Cross, Venus), to fish and to conceptual knowledge. They reinforce the unspoken word; they make the invisible visible. This Polynesian way of speaking and learning through metaphor emphasises the importance of pattern—pattern as a mnemonic device of cultural knowledge.

The complexity of the design, and the pattern of the relationships between positive and negative space interact not only to reinforce the notion of balance but also the aesthetic, cultural and scientific knowledge of Pacific peoples. For Tohi, every pattern seen within the Pacific aesthetic can be found in lalava. Therefore, he recognises its importance culturally but, more importantly, recognises its potential as an aesthetic language. Just as languages are built through patterning, so is lalava. It is not a politicised language; it is not a critique: it is an aesthetic system that has enabled the transfer of cultural knowledge for millennia.

How people think; how they structure their language and their lives; how they make sense of their world—all these create a set of practices that becomes their culture. With the intervention of the West (through missionisation, colonisation and, most recently, migration) many aspects of Pacific cultures have been displaced. However, the core remains and the importance of language, abstract thought and belief systems have not been lost, but have in many instances merely become dormant. Some artists have been fortunate enough to receive traditional knowledge; others have gone in search of it. Both integrate it in their art practice.

The ideas associated with presence, narrative and oratory—embellished to make a point—provide an endless source of inspiration. Johnny Penisula explores 'the idea behind the story' (Panoho 1990: 32)—How did it come to be and why? This cultural questioning becomes the foundation of his practice and creates myriad interpretations for him to investigate. The questioning of one's environment, of one's surroundings—seeing things anew and reinterpreting them with contemporary eyes—affords an artist room to move and explore. In this way, Penisula creates work reflective of an idea or image. Many are reflective of his boyhood in Samoa; many are based in his relationship with water. Penisula remembers wondering how coral that was at one side of the lagoon grew in the sand on the other side. In *'Amu 'Amu* **[figure 3.8]** he plays with this idea, allowing the viewer to interpret his work as coral that is walking to its new home, or that it is standing still so as to let its roots grow in the sand.

Enabling the past to rest securely in the present is a fundamental principle in the artistic practice of Filipe Tohi. Working with stone, Tohi references the megalithic traditions of the Pacific, specifically the Ha'amonga 'a Maui Trilithon in Tonga. Work such as *Ha'amonga mata'a Maui* (1996) make reference to this Tongan monument,

Figure 3.6 › Filipe Tohi, *Fakalava*, front, 2000. Photograph courtesy of the artist.

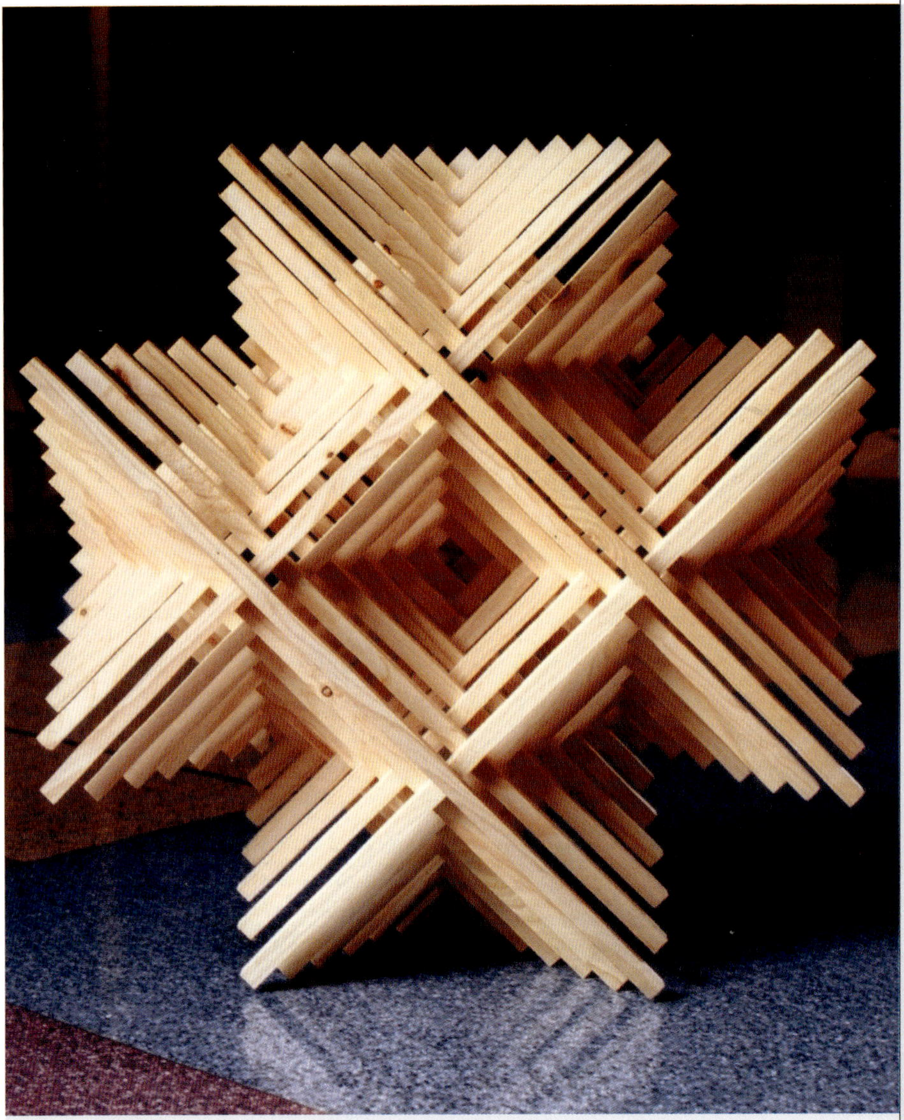

Figure 3.7 › Filipe Tohi, *Fakalava*, back, 2000. Photograph courtesy of the artist.

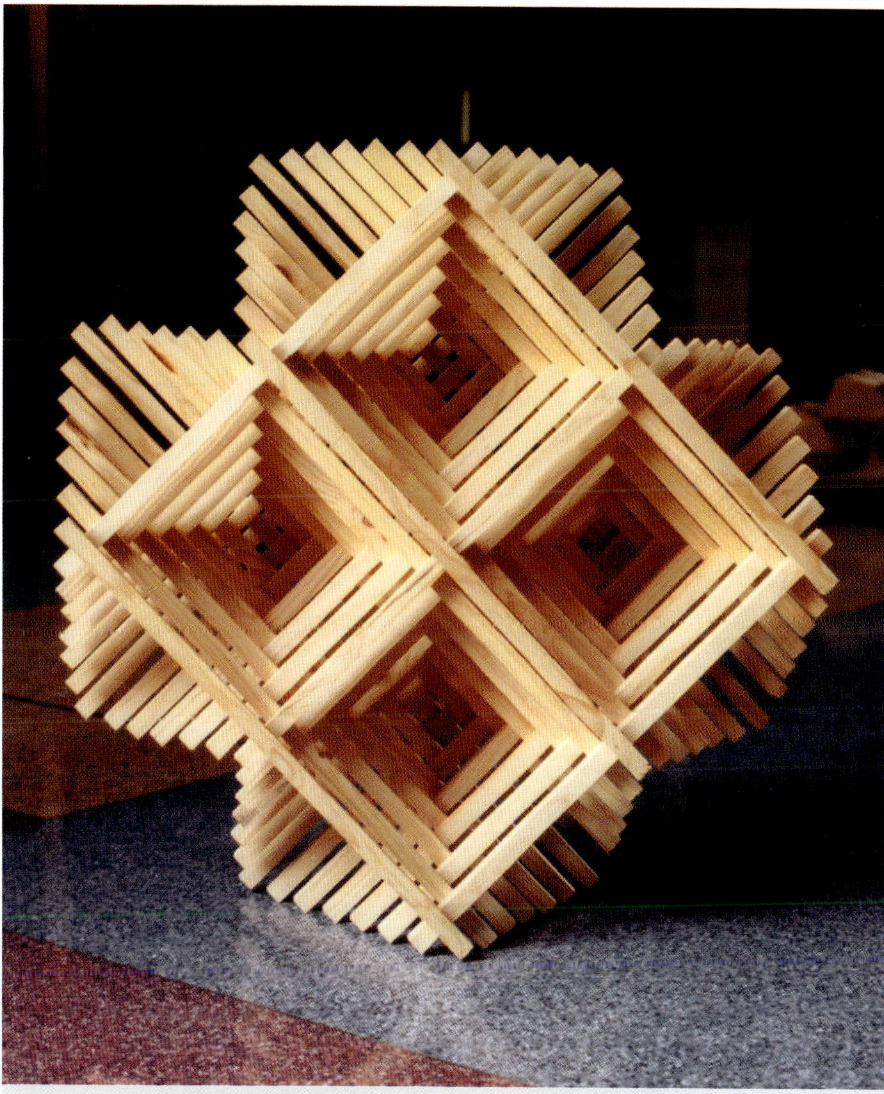

Figure 3.8 › Johnny Penisula, *'Amu 'Amu*, beef bone, 1985. Photograph courtesy of the artist.

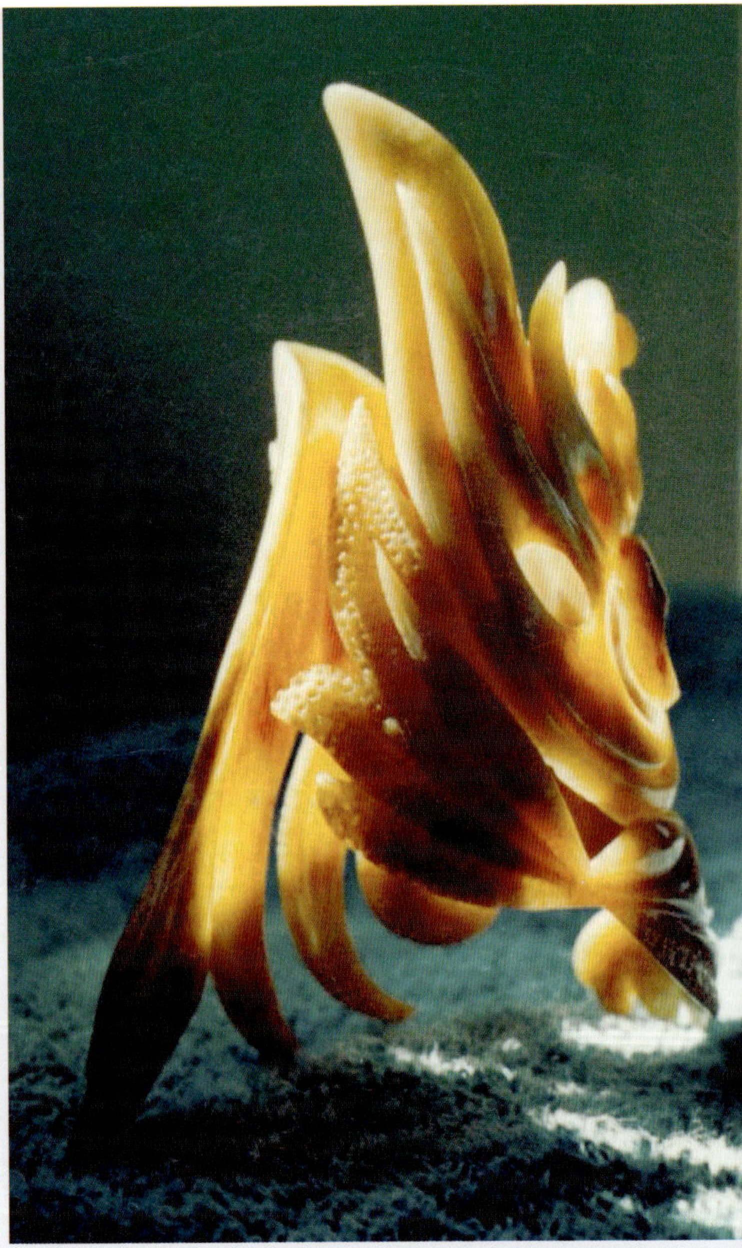

Figure 3.9 › Filipe Tohi, *Matamoana*, stone,1996. Photograph courtesy of the artist.

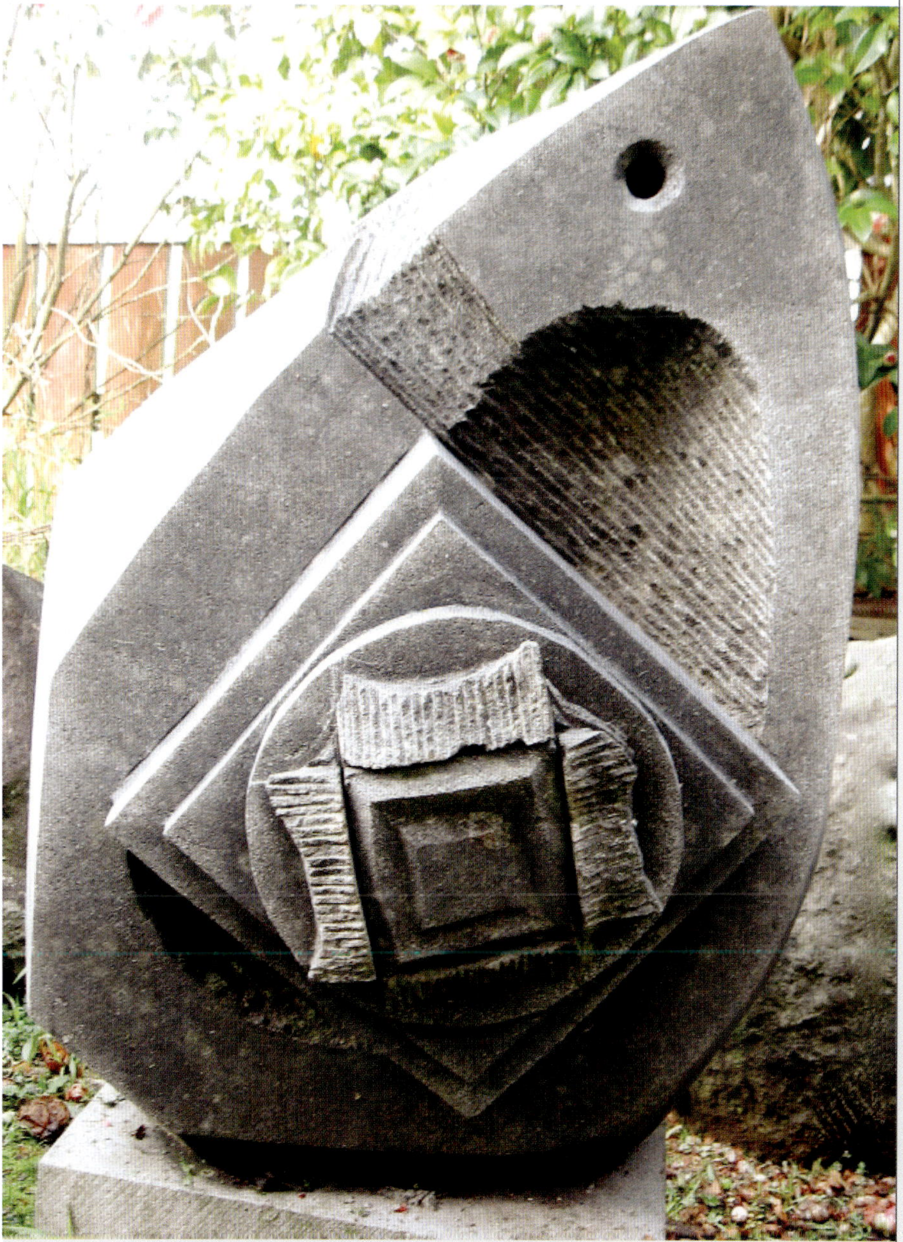

but Tohi also pushes this art form in new directions by cutting and lashing stone. Using a Pacific idiom, his works reference the ancestors, navigation and the sea. In *Matamoana* **[figure 3.9]** Tohi combines these elements in his depiction of a shark—an aumakua, a protector and guide.

Indigenous spirituality has become manifest in various ways in contemporary art practice. As Christianity has supplanted these beliefs, what remains are narratives associated with the spirit world, archaeological remains (megalithic sculpture and enclosures), drawings and descriptions of cultural practices from Cook's voyages (and from 20th century anthropologists), and an imagination that links these together. The importance of religion in the traditional Pacific is clear. Wanting to reinvest the next generation with traditional ideologies and knowledge, Pacific artists are inspired by the spiritual.

The gods are frequently drawn upon to make reference to a traditional past and to the loss of knowledge regarding an indigenous spirituality. Sometimes the gods are represented as a motif, sometimes as an abstract entity, but in all instances they provide the work with a Pacific character (see Chapter 2). In some cases this reads as an exploitation of a stereotype—indigenous spirituality relegated to a motif. On the other hand, these are entities and traditions associated with cultural knowledge and practices, and as such they play a large role in the work of contemporary Pacific artists.

Ian George, who works as both a painter and sculptor, frequently utilises motifs associated with Cook Islands belief systems. The staff god **[figure 3.10]** and Tangaroa are both used as key icons of Cook Islands belief and identity. Abstracting these already abstract images, George incorporates both within his practice. Utilising stories associated with Tangaroa and a knowledge base associated with the sea, George explores the relationships between the past and the present, and between the gods and men—as seen in *Te-Au-o-Tonga* **[figure 3.11]**. Traditionally, Cook Islanders benefited from their interaction with god images. Tangaroa was conceptualised as a fecund male. This creator god represented fertility, plenitude and well-being. The staff god, with its backbone of abstracted human figures, references the importance of genealogy and the passing of mana from the gods to men. These benign beings conjure sympathy towards indigenous life and a Cook Islands identity. Their incorporation in George's practice not only associates George with both the spiritual and physical realities of the Pacific, it firmly ties him to the Cook Islands.

Figure 3.10 › Cook Islands staff god, E150. 1055, Oldman Collection, Canterbury Museum.

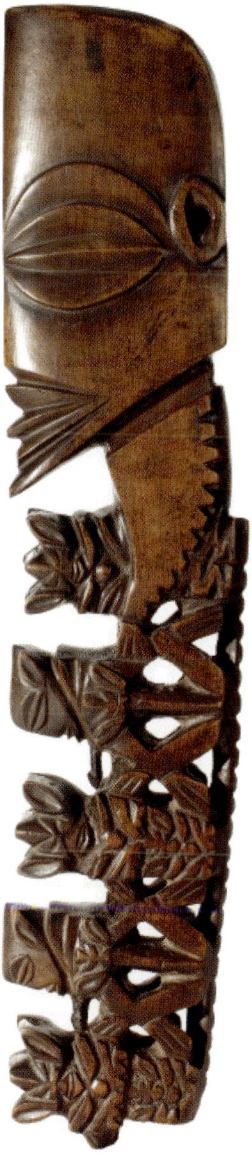

The importance of identity and positioning oneself alongside one's cultural heritage provides both a platform and a support system for one's practice. The emphasis on the traditional, on spirituality, on community and on strength provides the necessary balance within contemporary artistic traditions. As these elements combine, they create the relationship between an artistic practice and the artist's life. Language and knowledge are reinterpreted through figurative metaphor, creating the foundations of many art practices—foundations easily translated into the Western artistic canon as abstract expressionism. The strength associated with these traditions is reiterated in the work itself.

Fatu Feu'u creates sculpture that draw upon the Polynesian focus on the head (the seat of one's mana). *Tangaloa* **[figure 3.12]**, a three dimensional rendition of his mask motifs, asserts a presence and power associated with men, chiefs and orators. This presence or strength is also frequently incorporated into the work of Iosefa Leo. His sculptures portray a Samoan physicality and, in particular, a determined resolve, as witnessed by their posture and sensitivity of expression. Leo noted:

> First I look at the stone as it stands; the shape, and I concentrate, to feel the image, the meaning in the form of the stone. I refer to the stories of the bible, of Fa'aSamoa, the proverbs and the legendary people. I carve what I feel and perceive; all that is part of my life. (Panoho 1990: 21)

This strength is also depicted in Leo's *Fa'atalimo Molou Afio Mai (Waiting to Welcome You)* **[figure 3.13]**. Here it is an inner strength, held by women, that is epitomised (in this instance) by the enactment of a traditional greeting.

In contrast, Ioane Ioane has positioned his practice (which combines sculpture, installation, sound and performance) within a Western framework—a structure he frequently undermines with both piercing commentary and wit. He does not use the motifs of the Pacific, yet draws from within to create a conceptual space where 'magic may happen' (Mallon 2002: 98). Paying homage to Pacific spirituality, Ioane's practice also provides a sense of strength and purpose. The variety seen in his practice reflects not only his own journey as he has developed from painter to sculptor to installation artist, but the innovation and new technologies inherent in contemporary art practice. In 1990, Ioane (Panoho, 1990: 34) noted that he is

Figure 3.11 › Ian George, *Te-Au-o-Tonga*, acrylic on canvas, 1998. Photograph courtesy of the artist.

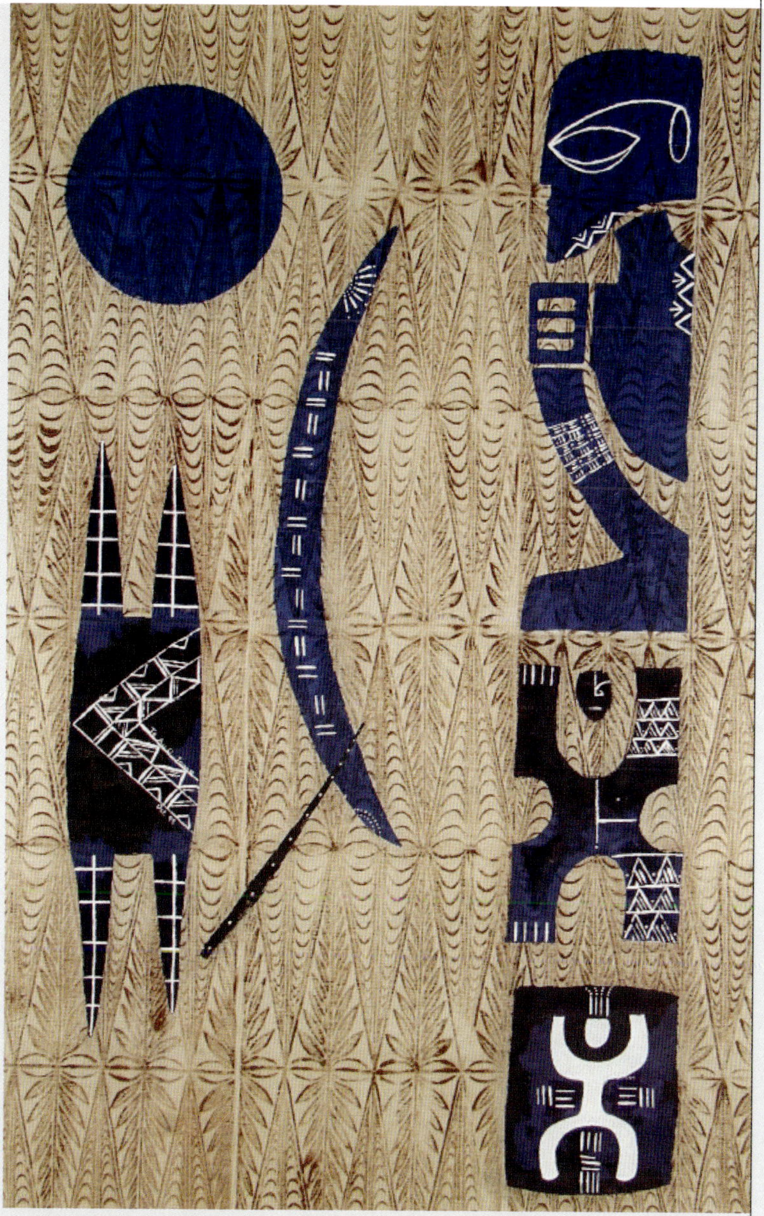

Figure 3.12 › Fatu Feu'u, *Tangaloa*, Hinerua stone, 1989. Photograph courtesy of the artist.

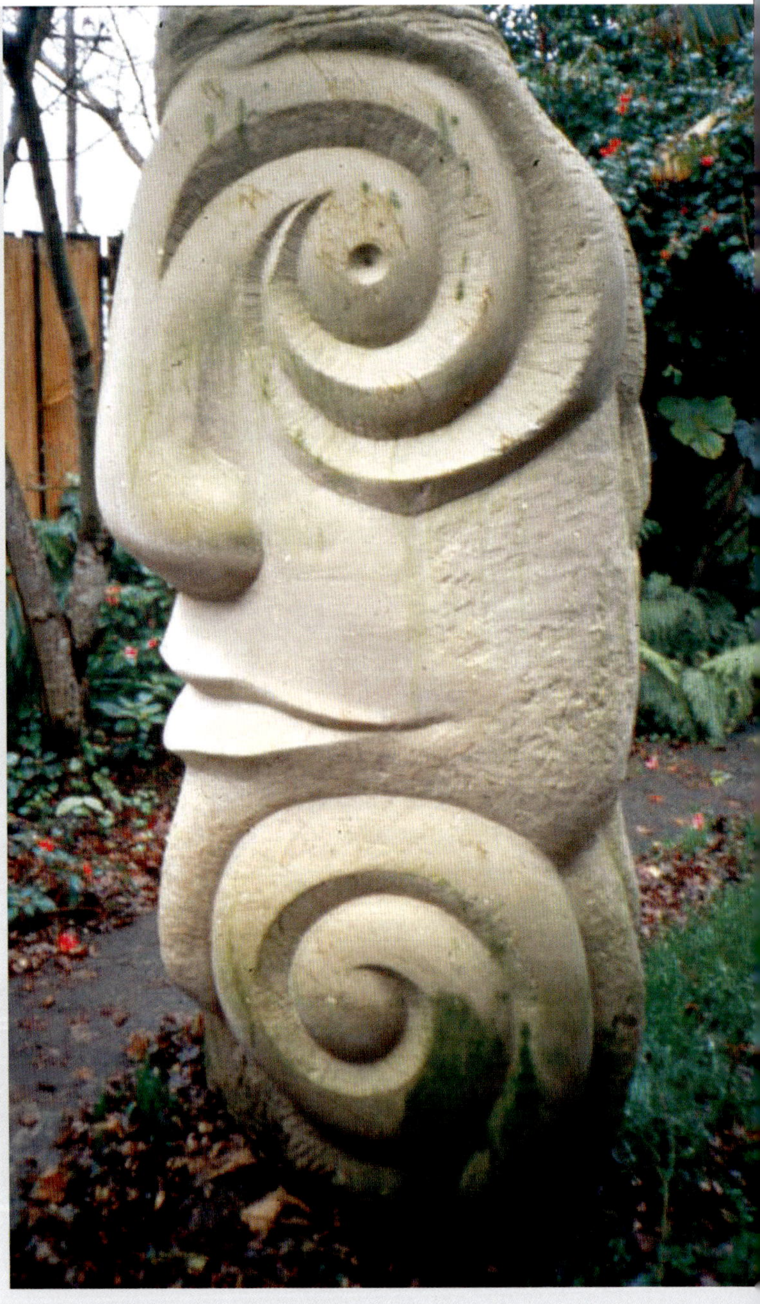

Figure 3.13 › Iosefa Leo, *Fa'atali Molou Afio Mai—Waiting to Welcome You*, Mt Somers limestone, 1997. Photograph courtesy of the artist.

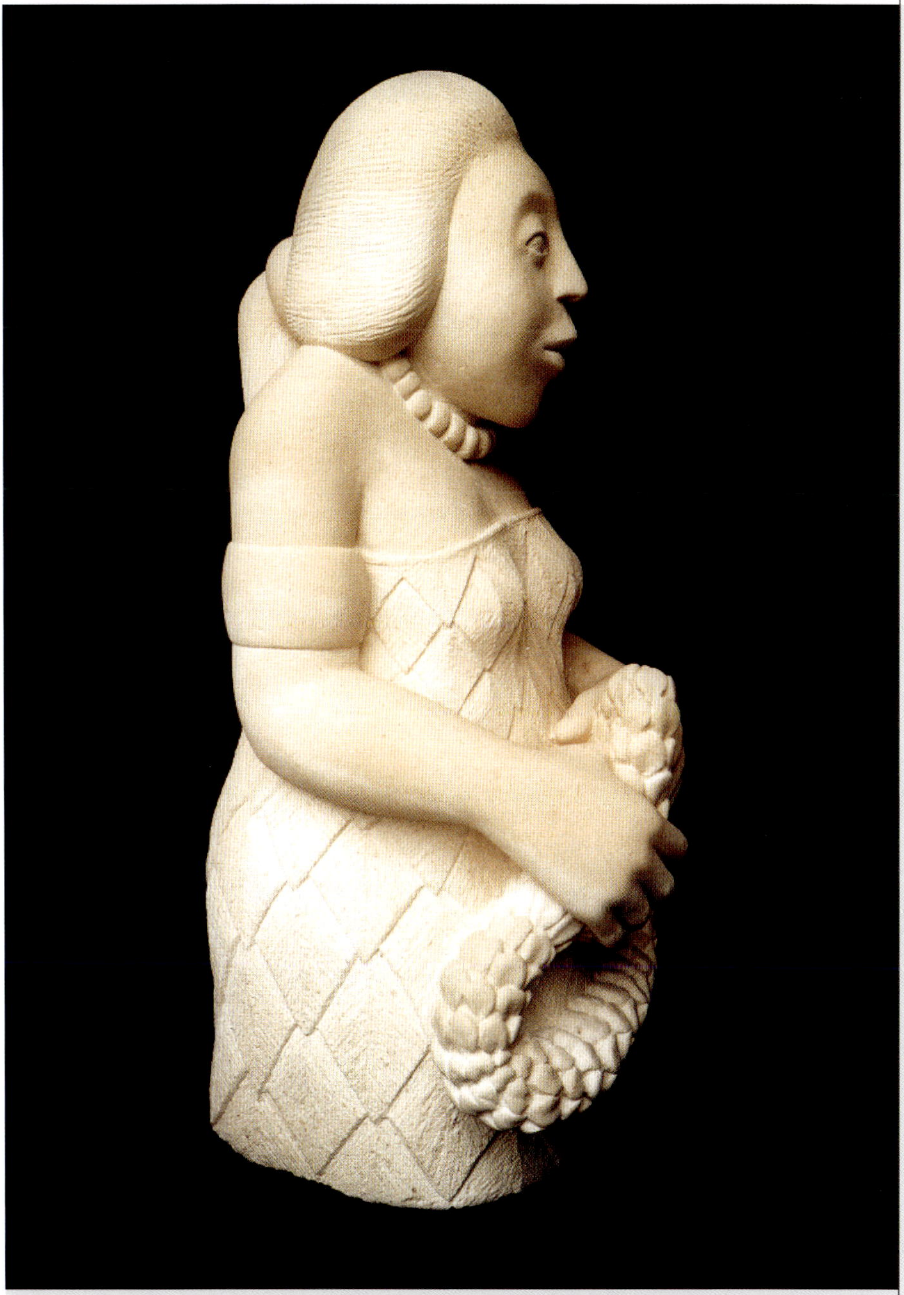

a student of materials, saying 'I don't really refer to our legends. I don't feel I'm competent enough to use the material to make figurative or symbolic images . . . I look at the materials, work with them, other things come later. I don't use the traditional symbols. I leave that to other artists'.

However, in such work as *Malosi* **[figure 3.14]** materials are coupled with ideas to reinforce a clarity of identity and the strength that this provides. Ioane looks to the natural world to reinforce the strength inherent within Pacific societies.

This arena of exploration enables contemporary artists to choose the tradition or characteristic that they feel embodies their interests. Richard Shortland Cooper's life revolves around family and the strength provided by community. It is these Pacific characteristics that sustain and support his work. Using the hibiscus as a symbol of a Pacific way of life, Cooper has also referenced women and their strength in his tivaevae work (see Chapter 5), as well as in *Te Aua Tiare* **[figure 3.15]**—an installation consisting of a garden of metal flowers lashed to manuka stems[9], which references not only the Pacific and its textile traditions, but also the underlying strength found in those communal practices (Cooper 1998).

Such practices are simultaneously incorporated and challenged by Lily Laita. Frequently working on black building paper and other domestic materials, she sidesteps the most obvious Pacific affinities. Yet, although there are no barkcloth or textile patterns and no hibiscus, she consciously places her work alongside the traditions of the Pacific. Her artistic practice has to do with creating a visual language that reflects the complexity of the oral traditions of the past. As one would slowly build images in the mind's eye, Laita creates images that reveal; but only after the viewer has truly looked. Language, people and images of cultural knowledge emerge from what appears to be an abstract canvas.

The link she has chosen to the past is language and the way in which cultural knowledge is passed from generation to generation. Other artists have chosen specific motifs that have served as mnemonic devices for centuries; Laita's work acknowledges the intuitive value of women and their role in the perpetuation of cultural traditions. *Vahine Pasifika* **[figure 3.16]** addresses the roles of contemporary Pacific women, combining historical facts (Samoan women on display at a German zoo, and the importance of grandmothers in the process of migration) with

Figure 3.14 › Ioane Ioane, *Malosi*, Douglas fir, Oregon pine, and slate, 1997. Auckland Art Gallery, Toi o Tāmaki.

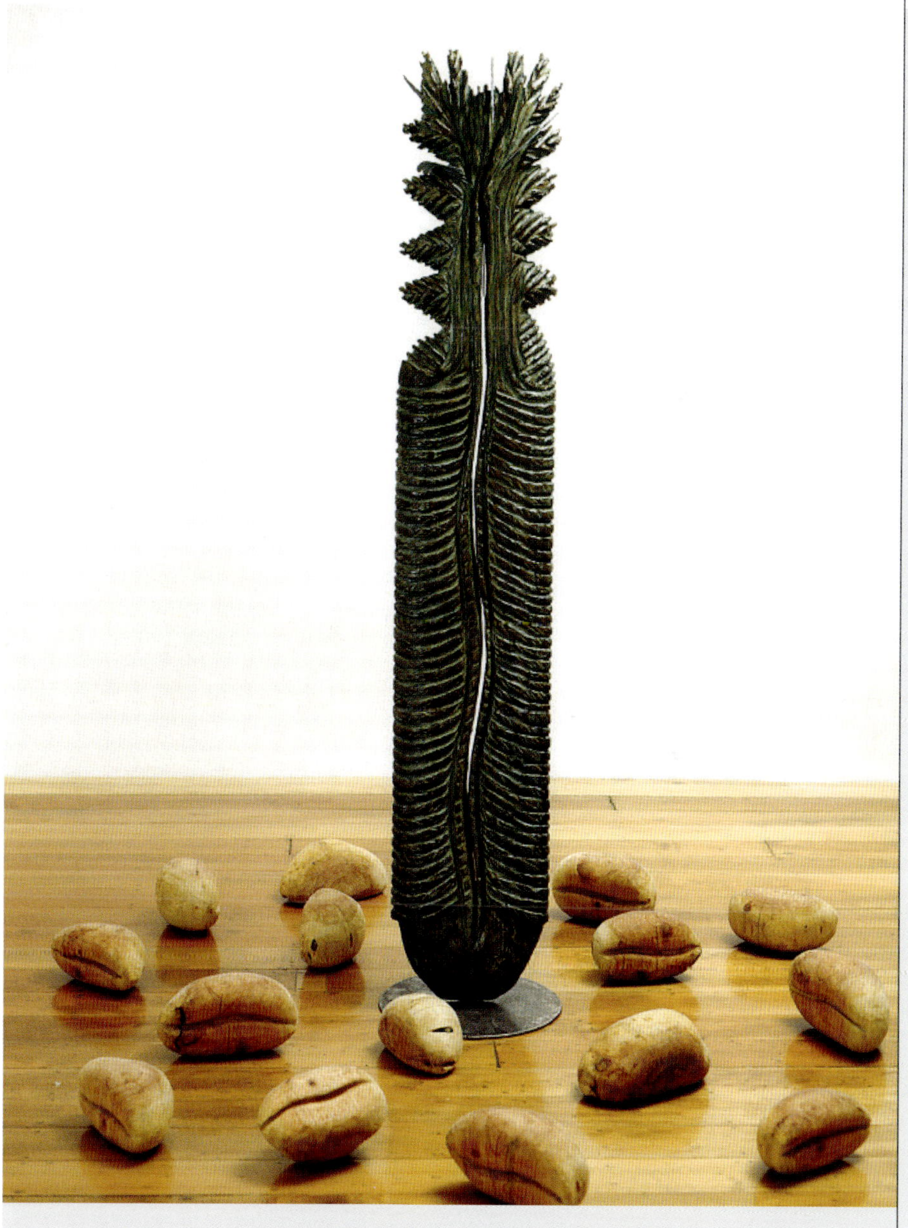

Figure 3.15 › Richard Shortland Cooper, *Te Aua Tiare*, sheet metal, manuka and flax, 1999. Photograph courtesy of Dr Richard S. Cooper.

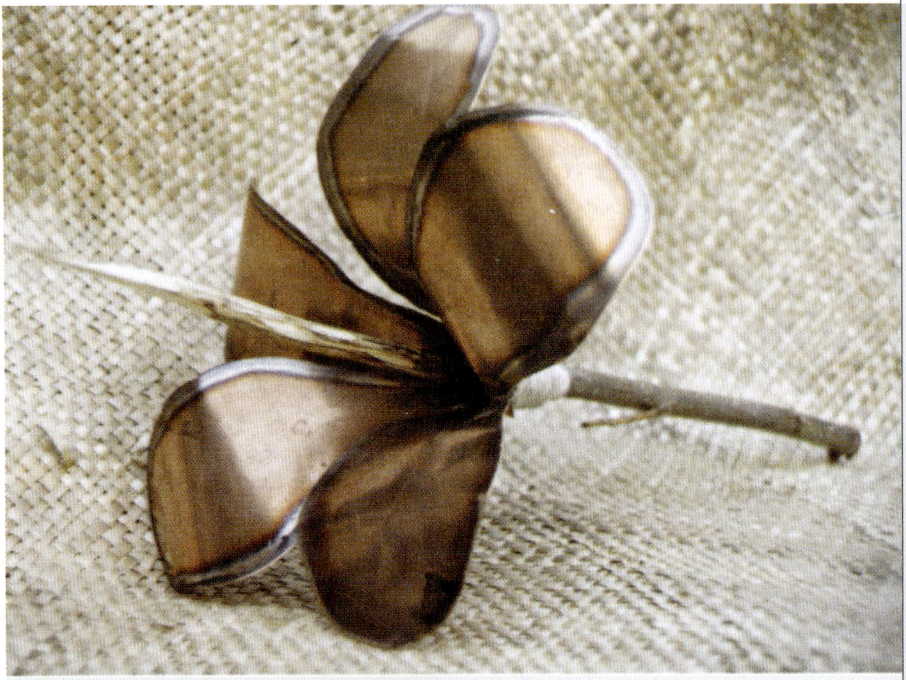

Figure 3.16 › Lily Laita, *Vahine Pasifika*, oil on builder's paper, 1998. Photograph courtesy of Chris Kitson.

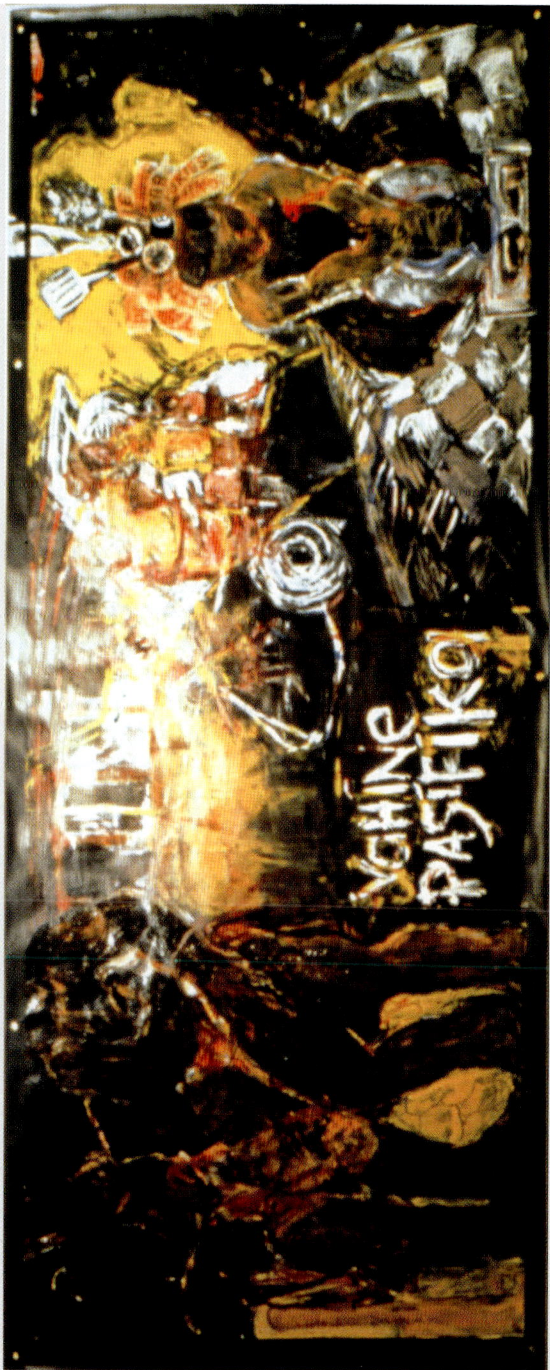

contemporary realities (the taupou's headdress includes elements of a contemporary stereotype—cleaning utensils and references to gambling). The grandmother holds this painting together—as many a grandmother has held her family together—by bridging the island and the urban, by transmitting cultural traditions and ideals to another generation. The inter-generational loss of knowledge is mitigated by her presence. In this way, Laita utilises her art practice to comment on both the histories and the modern realities of Pacific women. She feels that both knowing and understanding the past is important as a means of transferring knowledge. She is renegotiating tradition.

Change is constant. By drawing upon new ideas, materials and technologies, urban Polynesians have created new traditions—traditions that reaffirm the past. Abstraction—making the invisible visible—is the foundation of Pacific art practice. Utilising not only a Pacific way of visualising their world, but also traditional practices that have been developed over the millennia, contemporary Pacific artists in New Zealand have created vibrant new traditions. At the same time 'what Pacific island weavers make can be seen on the street on any day of the week, or at markets, Pacific festivals and island celebrations at any time of the year' (Pereira 2002: 77). The old and the new intertwine in a new island environment.

The balance of the old and the new is not only reflective of a Pacific mindset, it also enables an investigation into the dualities seen today. Working in various media, drawing upon both the traditions of the past and the present, Pacific art practitioners reflect the diversity of their genre. O'Neill paints with crocheted wool, but also combines performance and installation in her practice. George, Cooper, Leo, Penisula and Ioane demonstrate the diversity the field of sculpture has to offer. Tohi typically moves beyond the second dimension, creating lalava that intrigue regardless of their scale, and Laita incorporates the traditions of narrative and oratory with a new media: paint. Referencing a depth of cultural knowledge, a new Polynesian aesthetic has been created.

CHAPTER 04

Icons as Metaphor: Innovating Pacific Art

The ways in which the Pacific has been represented and the ways in which Pacific people often self-represent are frequently the same. In this era of taking back, the wearing of lavalava, flowers and bright colours signals cultural affirmation as well as cultural cliché. Throughout the 1970s and 1980s, as Pacific Islands became independent nations, identity became marked by cultural difference. As these nation states looked for symbols that could be representative of their fledgling countries, icons such as masks, drums, the canoe, tatau and barkcloth became symbols of Pacific identity (Keesing & Tonkinson 1982). Independence spurred on a cultural renaissance, and Pacific Islanders drew upon an inventory of visual manifestations of their cultural past. In so doing, they reinvented themselves as strong, independent entities. This process of drawing from within was also crucial to the development of contemporary Pacific art practice in New Zealand. The difference, however, was that in New Zealand these icons were being reinterpreted and incorporated into Western art forms as the wealth of island heritage was fused with a lived urban reality.[1]

Looking to the islands for inspiration, contemporary Pacific artists acknowledged these icons, which became markers of Pacific identity within a diaspora nation. However, this visual inventory quickly turned to stereotype, as the contemporary Pacific could not escape its mythological past—that of a paradise of island beauties and noble savages, of swaying palms and soft ocean breezes. This stereotype, however, was not one utilised by Pacific artists, for their art went beyond these clichés to address social, cultural and political realities in both their island homelands and in urban New Zealand. The stereotype did, nonetheless, provide a platform from which artists could assert their voice to innovate Pacific art. What may appear to be solely a rehash of Pacific icons, or just colourful marketing, has in fact affirmed a rich cultural heritage. As cliché glosses and generalises, the use of Pacific icons provides a complexity and depth to an art movement so often criticised as mere decoration (Stevenson 1999).

Stereotypes of the South Pacific—the notion of noble savages, beautiful maidens and an island paradise—quickly filled the European imagination upon Captain James Cook's return to England in the late 18th century. These ideas have been encouraged through literature, art and film ever since. Images of a smiling maiden garlanded with flowers and of a sturdy warrior marked with tatau come quickly to mind. The stereotype—the lei and tatau, as well as tapa and tiki—have become cultural icons. Yet the importance of these objects does not rest in the cliché, or in any meaning afforded them by Europeans. These cultural practices have remained integral to Pacific peoples for centuries. They reflect status, economic transactions and belief systems essential to these cultures. This is why they are icons; and it is this significance that provides meaning in their appropriation today.

This chapter focuses upon textiles and the lei as key icons of inspiration for contemporary Pacific artists. Addressing the notion that many painters draw upon barkcloth traditions, the importance of textiles is examined, as are their cultural implications both historically and today. Lei, a ubiquitous symbol within the Pacific, have been the muse for a number of artists, whose contemporary renditions provide a new audience for a traditional marker of status and identity. Both these icons are easily transformed to embrace metaphor. They reflect and assert the subtle acumen employed by Pacific women in their manipulation of status relationships. Unlike the canoe or tatau, whose meanings have not been reinvented but remain intact in their contemporary manifestations, textile traditions and lei epitomise the innovation found in contemporary Pacific art. In New Zealand this art form not only embraces these icons, it also reinterprets the stereotype to reinstate the convention to a meaningful position. To achieve this, contemporary Pacific artists draw heavily upon their island heritage, adding to it an urban edge. They use metaphor and wit to create this edge, which provides depth to their work, so moving it beyond the stereotype, beyond the cliché.

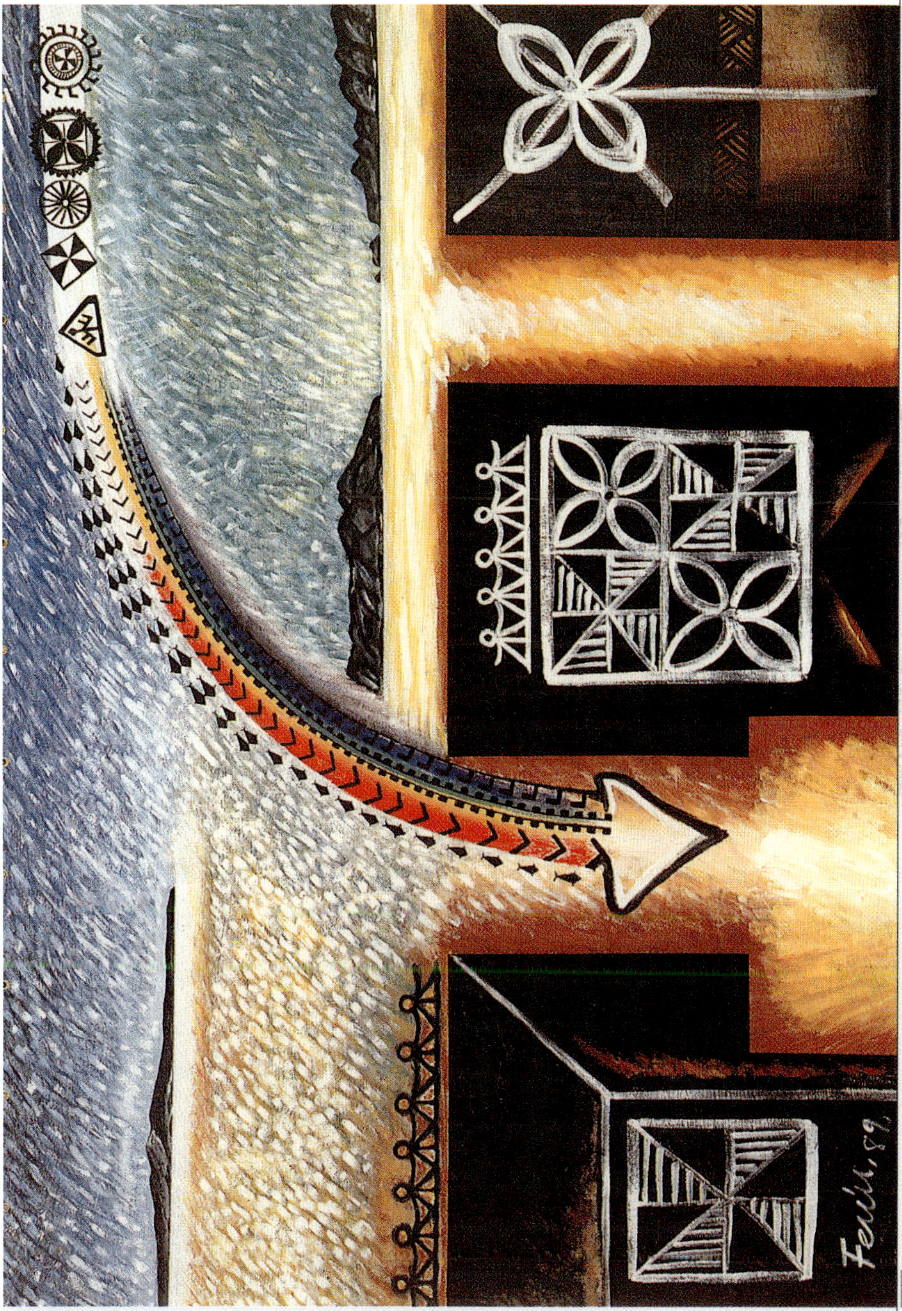

Figure 4.1 › Fatu Feu'u, *Nuanua Malama*, 1988. Photograph courtesy of the artist.

Much has been written, but little said, about the artwork of Fatu Feu'u. Inspired by his friendship with New Zealand artist Tony Fomison[2], Feu'u followed Fomison's suggestion of incorporating his cultural heritage in his art practice (Mallon & Pereira 1997: 16). In drawing upon the artistic traditions of the Lapita peoples as well as those of Samoa, Feu'u has sustained a vibrant arts practice. He combines motifs that were abstracted symbols of community, balance and social obligation. In this way he moves to the heart of a Polynesian aesthetic, which is both graphic and abstract. *Nuanua Malama* **[figure 4.1]** exemplifies the non-representational nature of Polynesian art, reinforcing both the spiritual and ideological basis of Polynesian cultures. Veiled meaning and metaphor prevail as objects and motifs become representative not only of a person or a position, but also of the ideologies and obligations those hold **[figure 2.8]**.

To say that Feu'u draws on barkcloth patterns as well as its grid offers no understanding of either his work or the traditions embodied in the barkcloth of Samoa **[figures In.5 and 2.6]**. Although barkcloth is a woman's art form, men are involved in aspects of its creation. There is a balance, socially, that is inherent in its production. This balance becomes explicit in the motifs that are painted on the cloth, which are representative of both men and women. They bring together the lineages of Samoa, as does the gifting of the cloth (which is its essential function). In addition, Feu'u uses motifs found within the tradition of tatau. When we trace these designs it becomes apparent that they too become entwined with barkcloth imagery. Both tatau and barkcloth motifs were utilised by the Lapita potters on their ceramic ware.

This body of work created by the Lapita potters does not, therefore, simply represent a refashioning of barkcloth imagery nor even an appropriation of a tradition. The motifs used address the concept of balance—the balance of social obligation, authority and power. It is fitting, therefore, that Feu'u often places these within a grid, as seen in *After the Rain* **[figure 4.2]**. The vane swastika (male) and Feu'u's frangipani (female) provide the foundation for this practice, creating a new art form that brings the past and present together. Feu'u exploits these patterns and images to reference fa'aSamoa, yet their contemporaneity announces the shift from the islands to the urban.

Figure 4.2 › Fatu Feu'u, *After the Rain*, oil stick on canvas, 1994. Photograph courtesy of the Wellington City Art Gallery.

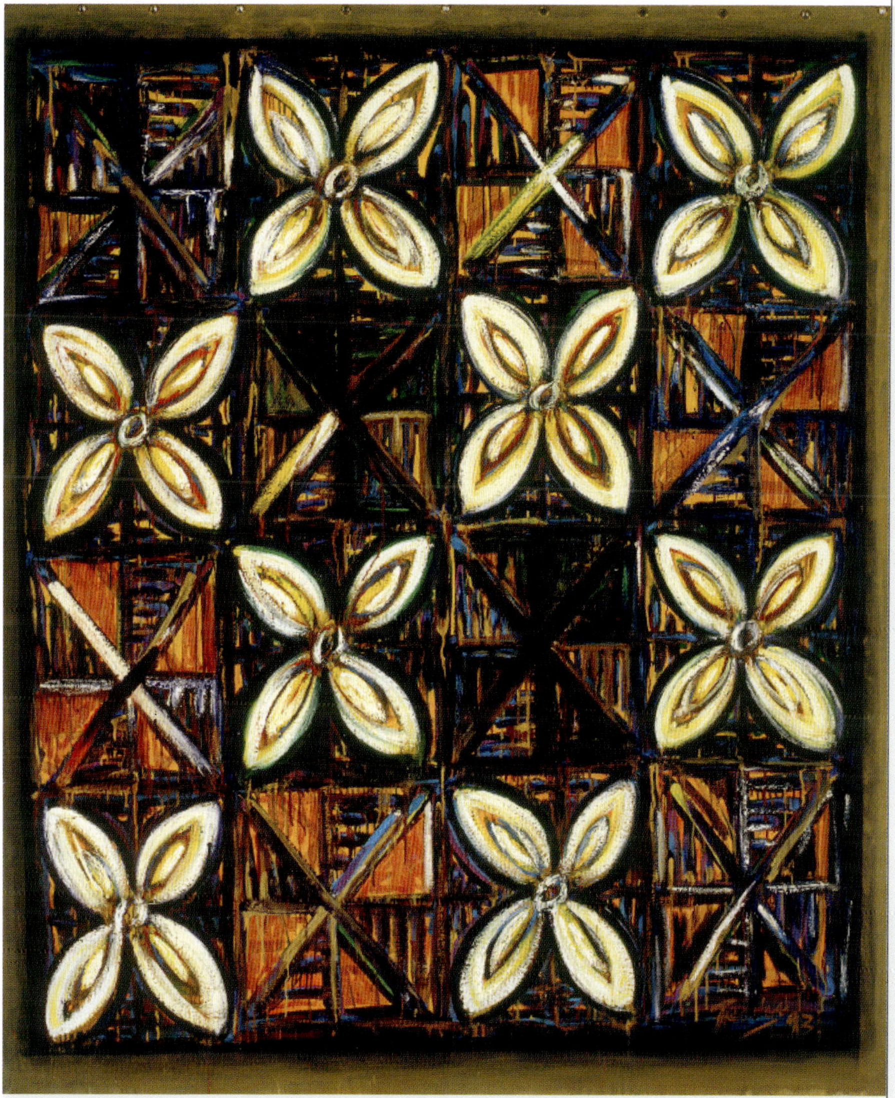

Feu'u, recognised as the father of Pacific art, has been criticised for the successful marketing of his work. Thomas (1995a: 204) noted that Feu'u 'has given consumer culture in New Zealand a distinctive Pacific accent'. His flat, yet vibrant, images were easily transposed to different media, which Feu'u marketed adeptly. His motifs became associated both with his own art practice, as well as that of every aspiring Pacific artist. This signature work quickly became cliché and the hallmark for the assessment of other Pacific artists.

However, Feu'u's work is more than a bright canvas with flowers and barkcloth designs that speaks of the Pacific. Even the frangipani that has so often become a cliché (because of its association with the islands, where it grows prolifically) is not a real frangipani. If we look at Feu'u's rendition, we find four petals, but frangipani has five. Therefore the motif combines the metaphor: the Samoan referent and the flower itself. Thus, Feu'u firmly positions his work as Pacific. At the same time our quick glance affords only the gloss; with it comes a false sense of understanding. As Feu'u commented:

> These things are deeply rooted in me . . . I looked at all the old symbols, and things that have meaning, like the headpiece of the tuiga, the headpiece of authority. Like the paddle for a canoe, when you turn it upside down it relates a message of survival . . . I believe that if you go back to the origin of things you find solutions. (Feu'u quoted in Mallon & Pereira 1997: 18)

Not surprisingly, Feu'u is very much dedicated to the promotion of Pacific art. He has continually created or tried to create opportunities for younger, lesser-known artists, frequently sharing gallery space with up-and-coming artists. This stems from the support that he himself was given, but also from the notion that 'part of our survival is our art. And if we don't [support each other], then we are lost. We are lost in another country, without an identity. Our art is very important. It's the heart and soul of every culture' (Mallon & Pereira 1997: 25).

It is also interesting that Feu'u has deliberately and successfully invented a contemporary pan-Polynesian art, a shared tradition rather than one specific to himself (Thomas 1999: 262). It is in this way that Feu'u responds to his reality of living in Auckland. Here, he finds the interactions between Pacific Islanders merge to

Figure 4.3 › Frances Palu, *Well if They Really Want to Hear Our Views, They Haven't Heard Nothing*, flax, recycled paper, raffia fibre, Indian ink, wool and sand, 1999. Photograph courtesy of the artist.

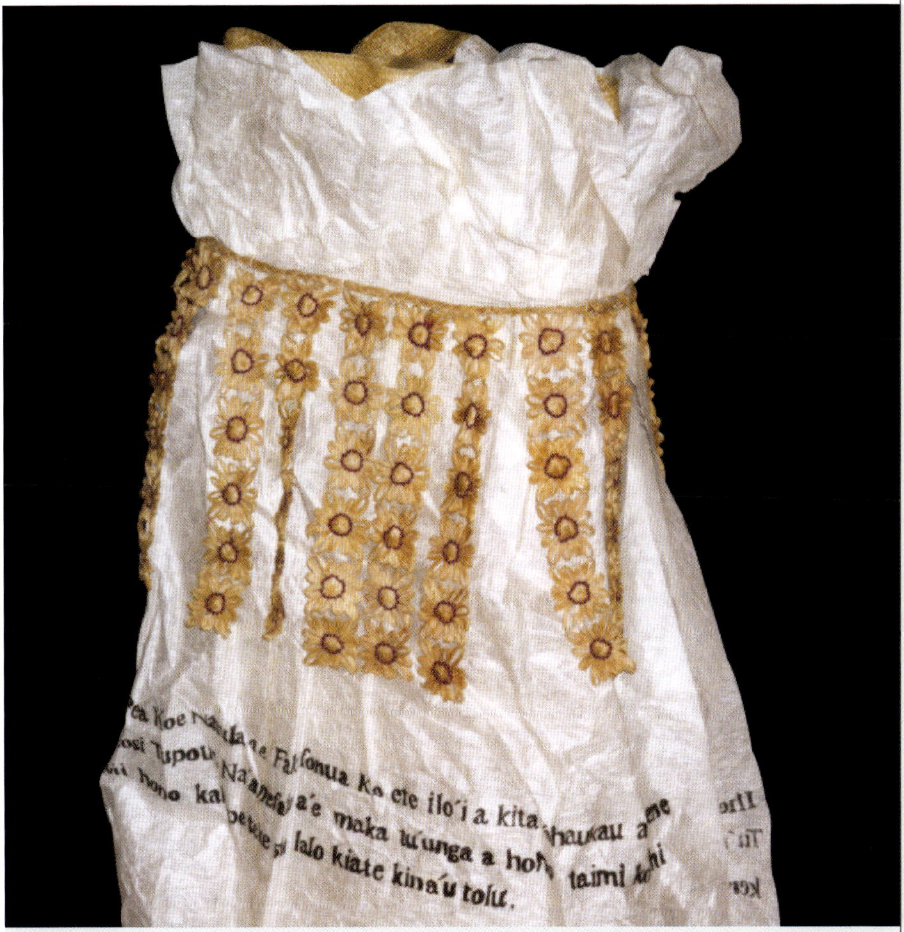

establish a vibrant culture. It is not the culture of his homeland, rather it is a blend of creative endeavours, a mix that enables a dynamic expression in the arts.

Feu'u utilises his art practice to both reaffirm Pacific identities and to bridge racial divides. His work combines a variety of Samoan and Polynesian motifs, each of which offer meaning to those knowledgeable about the culture. However, he also provides a glimpse into the Pacific, offering a connection of sorts to those without that cultural heritage. The use of motifs and icons associated with the Pacific offer a sense of understanding—a relationship to the Pacific for the viewer. Frances Palu, on the other hand, asserts that this sense of understanding, this glimpse into a cultural practice, does not represent true cultural understanding. In her *Well if They Really Want to Hear Our Views, They Haven't Heard Nothing* **[figure 4.3]** she both exhibits and conceals Tongan waist mats. Clearly a marker of Tongan identity and an important icon of Tongan culture, the wearing of mats can be seen as a cliché—that's what Tongans do—but can equally provide outsiders with a sense of understanding—oh, they are Tongan. Finding this notion ludicrous, Palu disallows this sense of recognition by concealing the mats. Thus, her work addresses the politics of cultural identity, asserting a unique position for Tongans within New Zealand.

The different island nations that are represented in New Zealand provide a unique variety of voices, histories and experiences. A bleak story of immigration rife with abuses (parental, spousal, alcohol) and petty crime, countered infrequently by positive family interactions, is recounted in the books of John Pule (*The Shark that Ate the Sun* and *Burn My Head in Heaven*). Pule's work often focuses on the notion of loss, particularly cultural loss at the hands of others, especially the church. The images vividly portrayed in his literary work are also apparent in his visual work. Pule's paintings and prints make reference to the 19th century Niuean barkcloth tradition **[figure 2.9]**, a tradition unlike that of Niue's neighbours and, sadly, a tradition that has also been lost.

Niuean barkcloth had, by the 19th century, moved beyond the grid. Innovative artists frequently incorporated floral motifs, along with historical commentary. They were maps or stories of interactions, as well as interventions. It is this combination of storytelling and visual art practice that has engaged Pule. Niuean barkcloth is different from most other Polynesian barkcloth in its design and its utilisation of

Figure 4.4 › John Pule, *Episode AA 9400935*, oil on canvas, 1995. Photograph courtesy of the Wellington City Art Gallery.

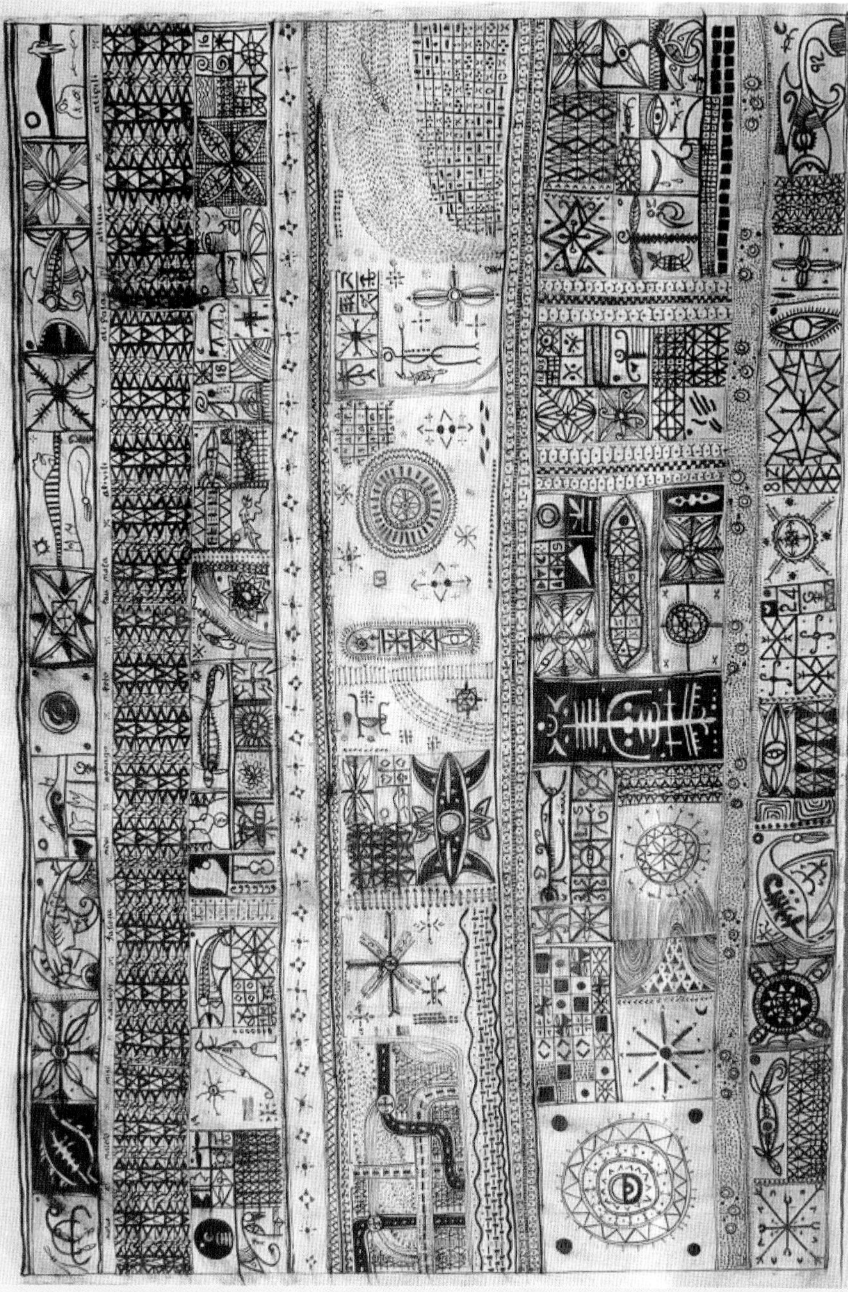

motifs. This enables Pule to create from a unique resource base. The icon is not the familiar Samoan/Tongan grid, but is frequently circular. Many imported motifs and figures occur, and the overall design is coherent due to the quality of line, not of pattern. *Episode AA 9400935*, as an example of Pule's hiapo, reflects this design aesthetic **[figure 4.4]**. Pule divides the overall design into smaller sections, creating vignettes, which together illustrate a map of cultural knowledge. Images reinforced by a visual language that is underscored by the spoken word become maps to ideas. The New Zealand state house, Liku, the shark and the church are all prominent elements in his visual language—a language, not unlike barkcloth motifs, that becomes repetitive, accessible and understandable. References to the grid can be reinterpreted as a map **[figure 2.10]**. Building blocks create foundations for places, houses, people and ideas.

> Pule reanimates these histories and stories like a shaman or poet conjuring up a vision grounded not in the present but somewhere in the distant past or the future—the poles of Arcadia and Utopia. He speaks with a tongue that twists, overwhelms and breaks words, allowing ancient creatures and spirits to escape from the confines of museums and books to haunt our imagination. (Refiti 2000)

Pule has created his own language—a personal iconography that is suggestive of myth without being literally connected with it (Thomas 1999: 267). His motifs include images of a sickly Christ, of lovers embracing, of fantastic animals with gaping mouths that seem to devour, or want to devour, one's soul. The shark is ever present, as are birds—constants in an island environment. But these, too, have taken on new meanings, have been reconfigured into a language representative of the Pacific, but not representing the Pacific.

Pule has stated that he collects metaphor.[3] This would suggest that his work finds its basis not in textiles, but in another Pacific art form—that of storytelling. His early painting, along with some recent work, incorporates poems—his poems, his expressive language **[figure 4.5]**. Through his art, poetry and other writing, he speaks of New Zealand as his homeland, while at the same time reaffirming the associations, memories and heritage of his spiritual homeland—Niue (Mallon & Pereira 1997: 86). This combination of present and past, of a highly developed sense of place and history, energises his work. The creation of an unhackneyed

Figure 4.5 › John Pule, *From the Bond of Time*, ink on paper, 1998. Photograph courtesy of Karen Stevenson.

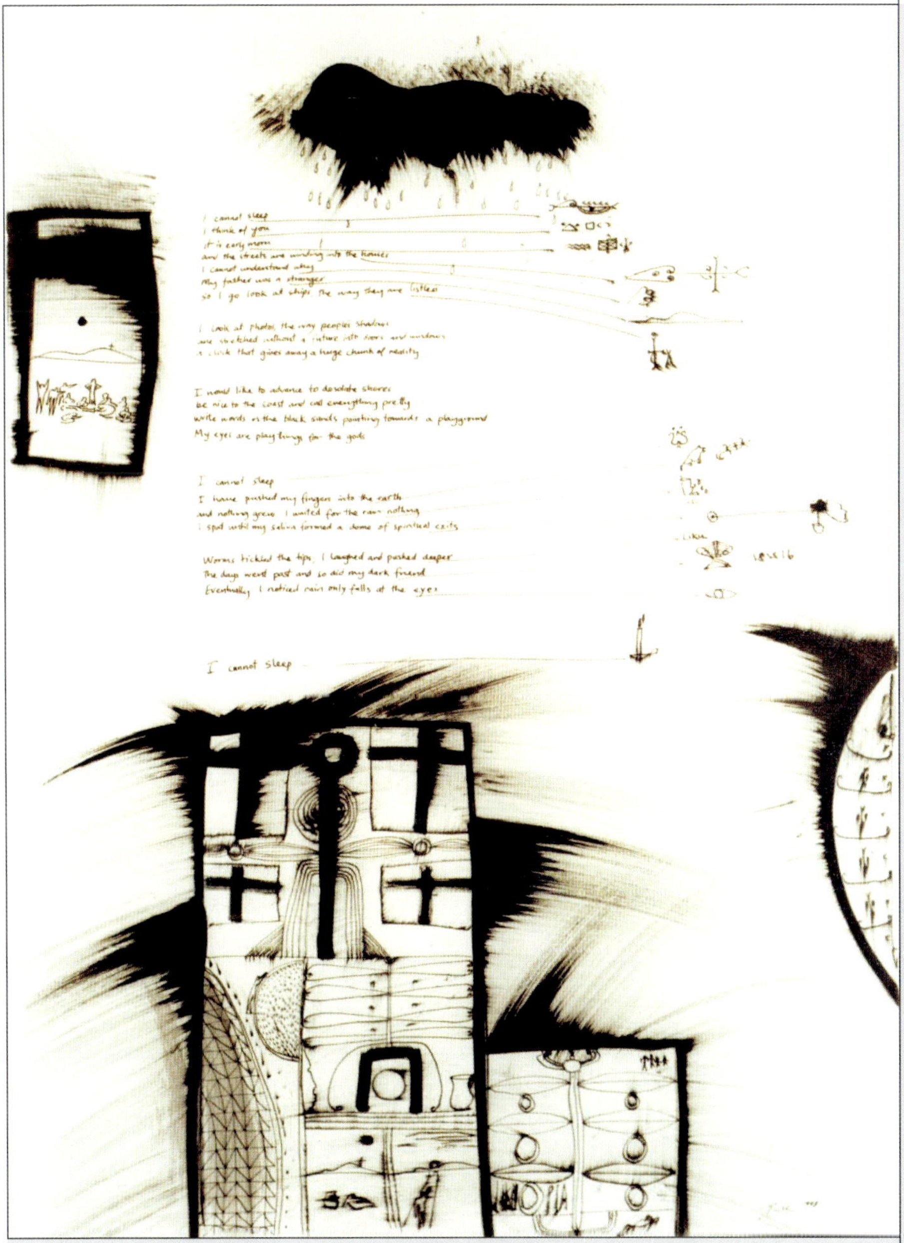

art form, referencing a past, speaks to the importance of contemporary Pacific art. It is completely different. As Thomas (1999: 269) noted, 'there is no deadening preoccupation with authenticity or tradition'.

Feu'u, Palu and Pule work quite distinctly. Each of these artists reference textiles as markers of specific identities. Therefore, each practice is read quite differently. Feu'u moves beyond the stereotype, being inclusive and embracing. Both Palu and Pule conceal—their work is easily read, but is it understood? In each case, these artists are refashioning an icon; they are creating anew. Feu'u is utilising a familiar object and infusing it with easily recognised motifs. In so doing, he is creating work that speaks not only of the Pacific, but also about the Pacific. It is a practice based upon the foundation of a Polynesian aesthetic, one that has continually transformed through migration and the interactions that migration provides. On the other hand, Palu and Pule create imagery from a personal inventory of ideas. The relationship to textiles—to the icon—enables the cultural mapping necessary for its reinterpretation in an urban landscape.

Ani O'Neill and Niki Hastings-McFall also draw upon the iconic and, in doing so, they allude to a variety of Pacific traditions, while still authentically replicating one that has no bearing in their work. Both artists are firmly ensconced in the urban lifestyles that they live and make no pretence of revitalising island traditions. They utilise the icon as a critique, commenting upon the stereotype embedded within the object, as well as its use in their urban environment.

O'Neill seems resolved to create a new island culture—one that is inspired in various senses by island origins, but not dependent on them (Thomas 1999: 266). In her Tangaroa series **[figure 1.7]** she confronts the audacity of an emasculated god being reinvented as a virile tourist icon. Tangaroa, the god of the seas and, for many, of creation, was the concern of men, not women. The missionaries emasculated this important god in their attempts to destroy him and the beliefs imbued in his image. By placing Tangaroa in a woman's forum, O'Neill is not attempting to reinstate the prowess of this fertile being, but is actually re-appropriating his image and simultaneously deriding the current sculptors of the Cook Islands who dogmatically decree that Tangaroa is *their* image, that women do not carve and that women may not appropriate this godly image. In re-creating these strict gender roles, they are also re-creating a past. It is quite fitting, therefore, that O'Neill incorporates an art

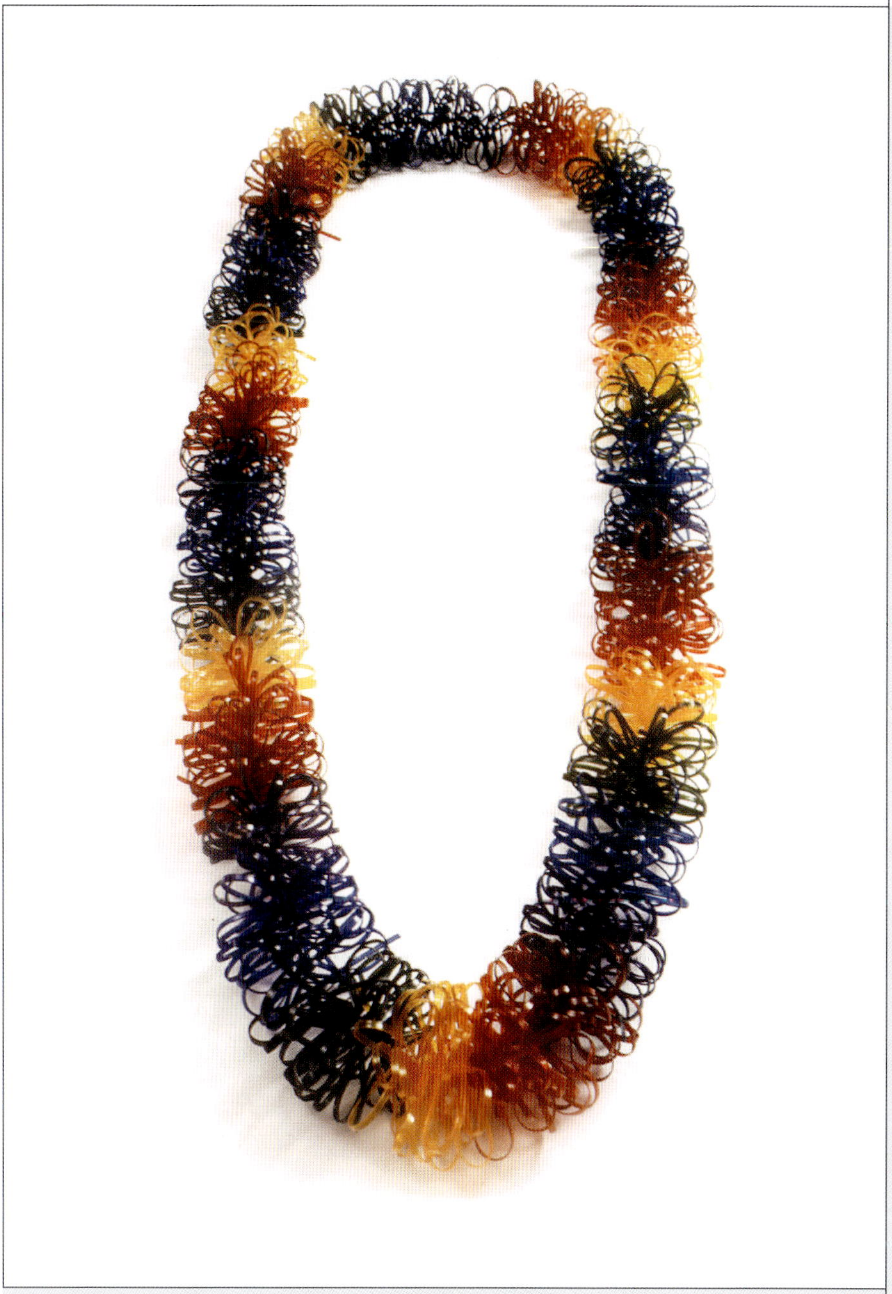

Figure 4.6 › Niki Hastings-McFall, *Urban Lei Series, Islander*, weedeater string, 1999. Photograph courtesy of the artist.

form taught by missionary women (embroidery) in her interpretation of this image. As with many Pacific works, the simplicity of her pieces belies the meaning and knowledge associated with them. Knowledge of the Cook Islands past and present is necessary to fully understand the joke. It becomes a representation of lived experience, of an outsider negotiating a position from which to speak.

Tangaroa is not the only icon that O'Neill has regenerated. Double entendre is her muse, and with works such as *Tropaks* (packaged hula girls) and *Sweet Rap* (candy lei) O'Neill has parodied these clichés that are so firmly embedded in a tourist reality. Even though these are tongue-in-cheek there is much respect for the artistic traditions and female authority that these images represent. What is being analysed is the cliché, as well as the ways that the West has characterised these art forms.

Tourist icons are ripe fodder for O'Neill's critique. However, the handwork of Cook Islands women is set apart. Again, there is no attempt to recreate or revive an art form (as these are vibrant in the islands), but rather the aim is to reinterpret and push its boundaries to new meanings within a new island environment. Firstly, the setting is an art gallery, not the home. But what O'Neill has done is open the gallery door to an artistic tradition that is often marginalised. Her tivaevae of plaited ribbon (*Star by Night* and *Kua Marino te Tai* **[figures 3.4 and 1.4]**) or crocheted paintings (*Rainbow Country*) **[figure 3.3]** offer an urban take on an island ideology (Stevenson 2001b). She incorporates technology and ideology in order to move beyond the stereotype and to assess the reality. The urban buzz is redirected via the coconut radio. Two lifestyles, both appreciated, are woven together to create the vibrant Pacific culture of New Zealand.

This combination of lifestyles is also seen in the work of Niki Hastings-McFall. Her icon of choice is the lei—something so benign, yet so integral to Pacific cultures. More than the cliché of flower garlands that greet one upon arrival in the islands, breast ornaments were significant reflectors of status. As adornment signalled one's position (single, married, elite, warrior), lei were markers of the socio-political hierarchies of the Pacific. Just as the lei takes on many guises, Hastings-McFall embraces this diversity and demonstrates both her wit and her desire to draw on her cultural heritage. In *Nuclei I* the use of dayglo plastic flowers represents the radiating glow associated with nuclear disaster—it is both a pun and a critique. With *Red Ula Rosary* (red feathers and rosary beads) she combines the mana of red feathers with rosary

Figure 4.7 › Chris Charteris, Niki Hastings-McFall, Sofia Tekela-Smith, invitation to *1 Noble Savage 2 Dusky Maidens*, 2000. Photograph courtesy of Niki Hastings-McFall.

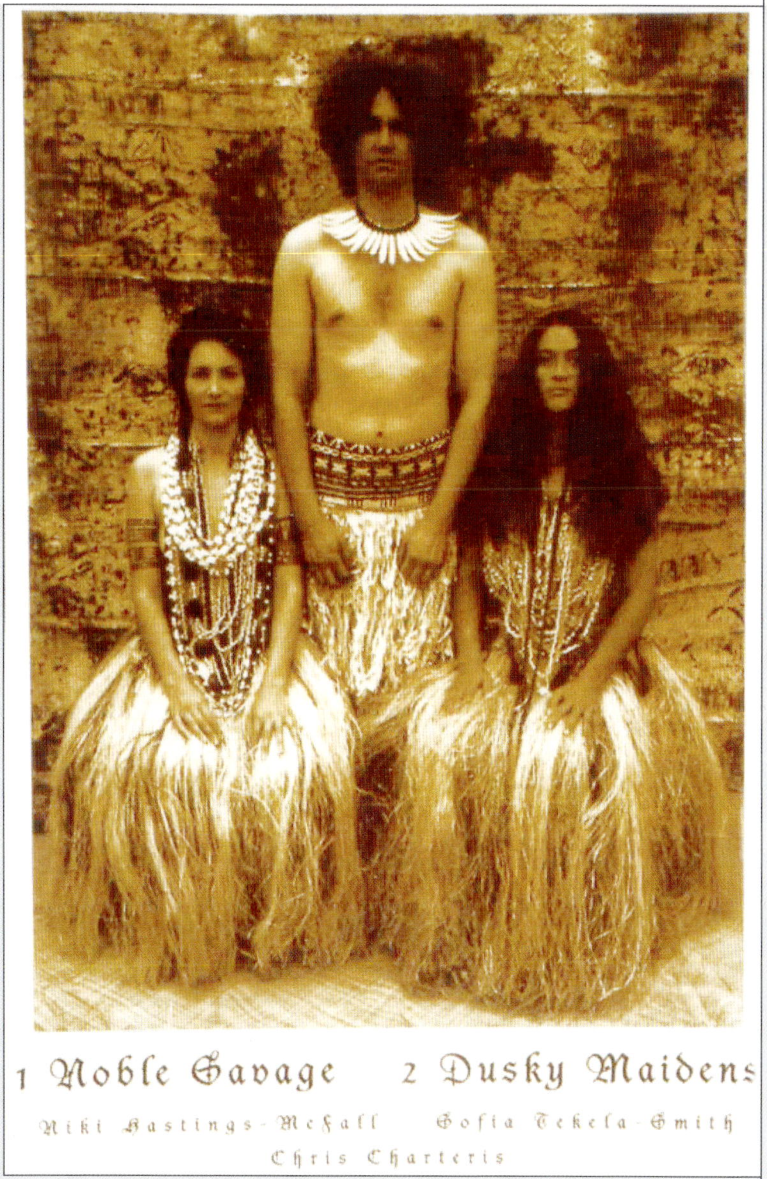

beads, offering the viewer a different access to the gods: each is representative of her multicultural heritage. Interweaving humour with layers of cultural meanings give these mundane and familiar body adornments a modern twist (Timms 2000).

Like O'Neill, Hastings-McFall finds much to parody in the contemporary lives of Pacific Islanders as they counter the stereotypes of the Western gaze. Hastings-McFall's humour is the basis and inspiration for her *Urban Lei Series*. Using McDonalds' throwaways (*Maclei*), curtain nets (*Nosy Neighbour Lei*), weedeater nylon (*Islander*) **[figure 4.6]** and soy sauce containers (*Too Much Sushi Lei*), Hastings-McFall addresses the lived island and urban realities of New Zealand.

> The game consists simply of constructing objects that look traditional but using the most unlikely modern components . . . a delightfully delicate little necklace is painstakingly put together from tiny squares of filmstock, or a pearl-shell breastplate is made not from shell but a computer disc. (Timms 2000)

The allure of the dusky maiden is also referenced via the lei, and as such it intermingles with the cultural politics of representation. What one finds is the utilisation of the icon to question and, at the same time, reflect aspects of contemporary Pacific life. On the one hand, the reference is to times past, to a reinstatement of the prestige associated with the lei. On the other, there is a critique of the cliché, of the ways in which the islands and their people are represented. Posing in such a way as to recreate the ethnographic photograph, Chris Charteris, Niki Hastings-McFall and Sofia Tekela-Smith became *1 Noble Savage 2 Dusky Maidens* **[figure 4.7]**. The critique of this cliché balanced their respect for a cultural heritage with their reinterpretation of the Western stereotype.

So easily parodied, the cliché provided the construct for an exhibition of contemporary Pacific jewellery. Niki Hastings-McFall and Sofia Tekela-Smith have reinterpreted the kapkap (a suspended breast ornament found in the Solomon Islands and the Marquesas) in a variety of ways. Traditionally made of mother-of-pearl shell with tortoiseshell filigree, Hastings-McFall brought together such seemingly peculiar combinations as gold and computer disks, or mother-of-pearl and stainless steel. In *Breastplate Masi* **[figure 4.8]** Hastings-McFall combines mother-of-pearl with sterling silver patterns derivative of Fijian barkcloth. This combination reflects a

Figure 4.8 › Niki Hastings-McFall, *Breastplate Masi*, mother-of-pearl and sterling silver. 1998. Photograph courtesy of the artist.

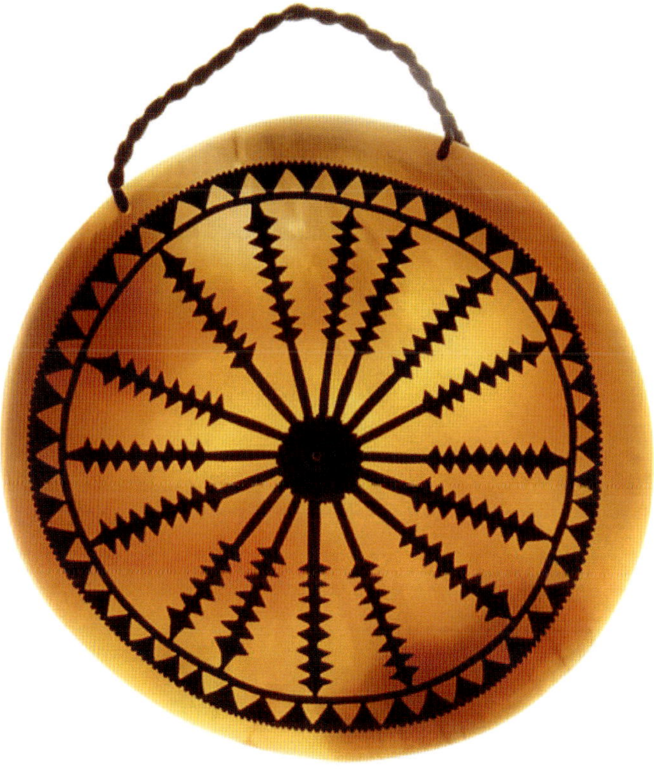

Figure 4.9 › Lonnie Hutchinson, *Malanga*, recycled wood, 1996. Photograph courtesy of Karen Stevenson.

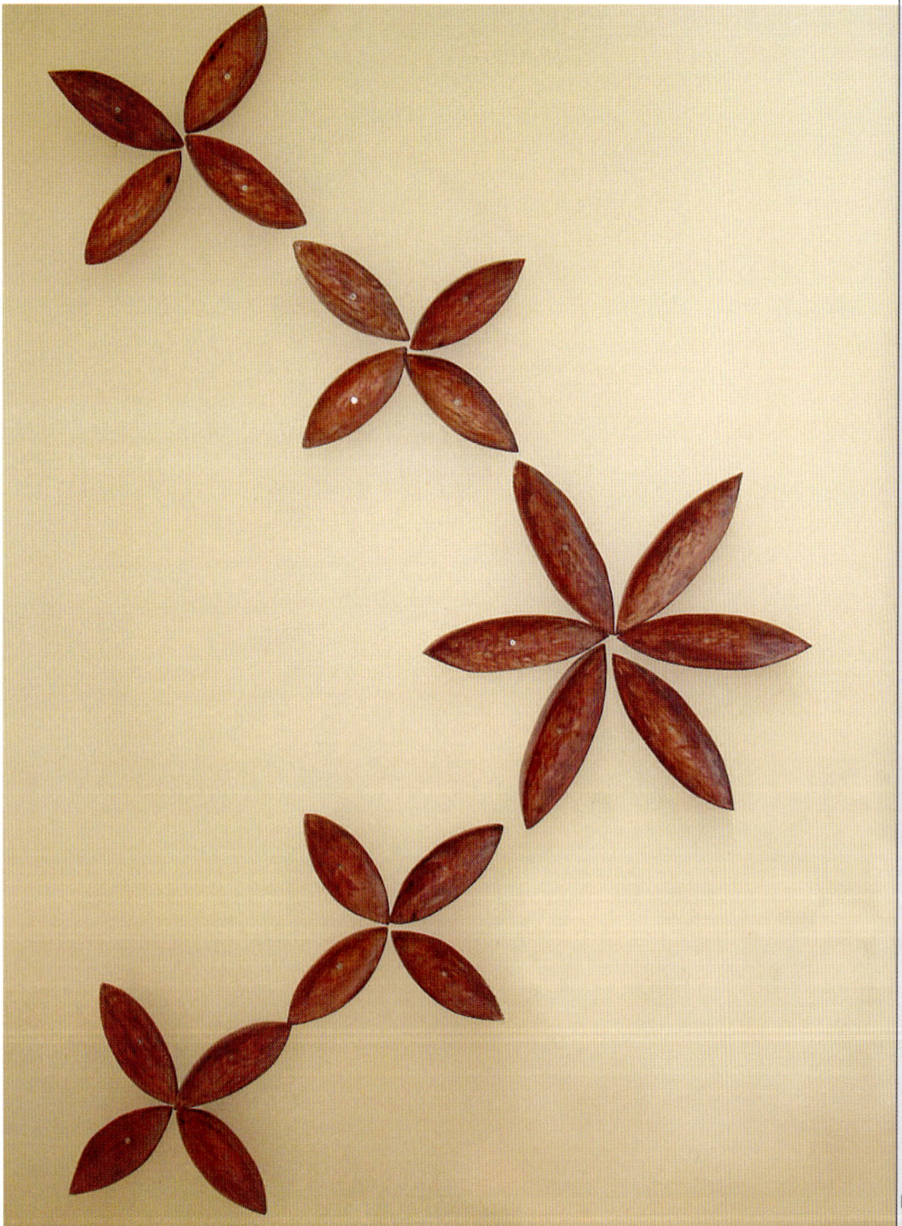

Figure 4.10 › Dagmar Dyck, *Knochen-halskettle*, screen print, 1995. Photograph courtesy of the artist.

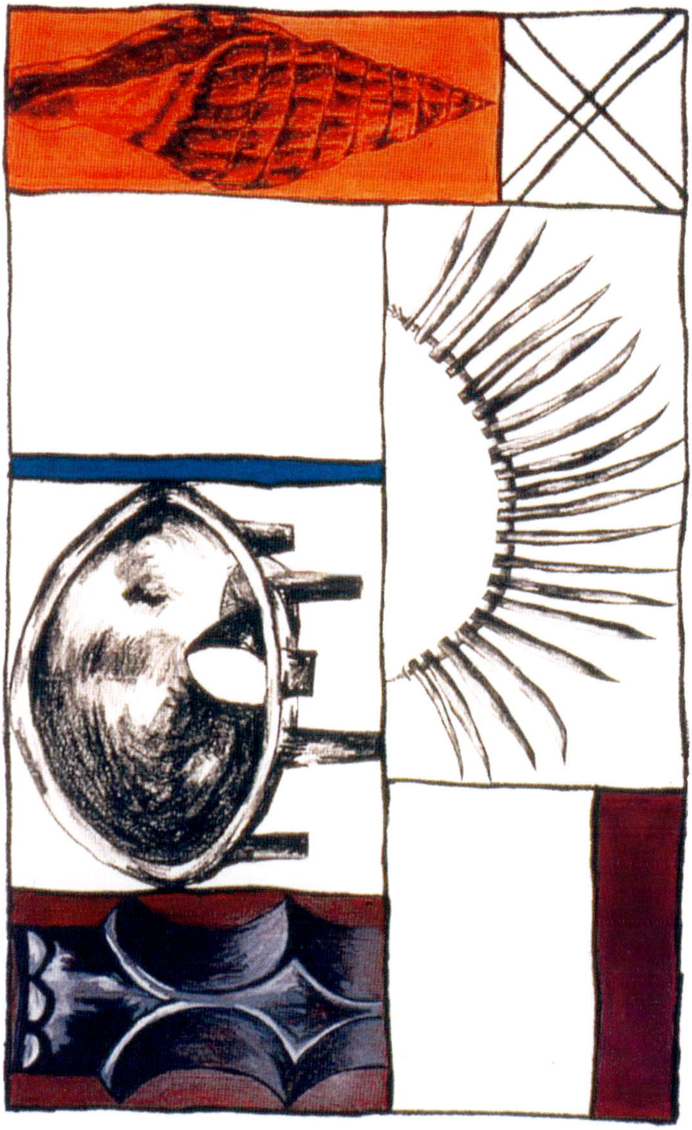

modern set of valued items in the same ways that the traditional materials did. Sofia Tekela-Smith has also drawn upon the kapkap, investing it with contemporary meaning. By creating jewellery that reflects the status relationships of historical Pacific societies, she allows an association with a Pacific heritage that is reinforced by a contemporary identity. Using materials such as jade, pearl shell, seeds and shells, Tekela-Smith creates pieces imbued with identity for urban Pacific people.

In contrast, Lonnie Hutchinson in *Malanga* **[figure 4.9]** has taken the idea of the lei, but moved it beyond the realm of personal adornment to a statement of Pacific identity. The carved lei comprises numerous pods, referencing seeds, coconuts and canoes. When combined, these become floral motifs that read as a string of flowers—a lei. This reference to Pacific icons, either metaphorically or realistically, reinforces their importance to a new generation. This is also seen in the work of Dagmar Dyck. *Knocken-halskettle* **[figure 4.10]** combines objects of Tongan material culture that at one and the same time reinforce a Pacific identity and reiterate the cultural importance of these objects. Evotia Tamua has also captured the importance of lei in her photograph *Mama and Papa Tariu* **[figure 4.11]**. Taken in the Cook Islands, this image demonstrates the contemporary use of lei to both honour and memorialise the past. Although no longer objects of status and prestige within the Pacific, these icons offer a glimpse of the artistry of status and status relationships, which were the foundations of Pacific art and culture.

Artists are recreating and reinterpreting the old in new media, thereby moving the cliché into a contemporary world where Pacific Islanders are repositioning themselves. These textiles, lei and objects of adornment—symbols of cultural identity—are redirected to provide a position from which to take back, rather than to attract a tourist gaze. The practices of these artists are emanating from the traditional in innovative and unconventional ways. Metaphor and cliché are addressed through the juxtaposition of various cultural readings of similar icons and symbols. These often afford a relationship to histories, genealogies, stories and memories, all of which reinforce strength of identity today. The looseness with which these artists commandeer the icon allows them the space to play, to create anew, to move the past into the present and the icon into metaphor.

Figure 4.11 › Evotia Tamua, *Mama and Papa Tariu*, 1995. Photograph courtesy of the artist.

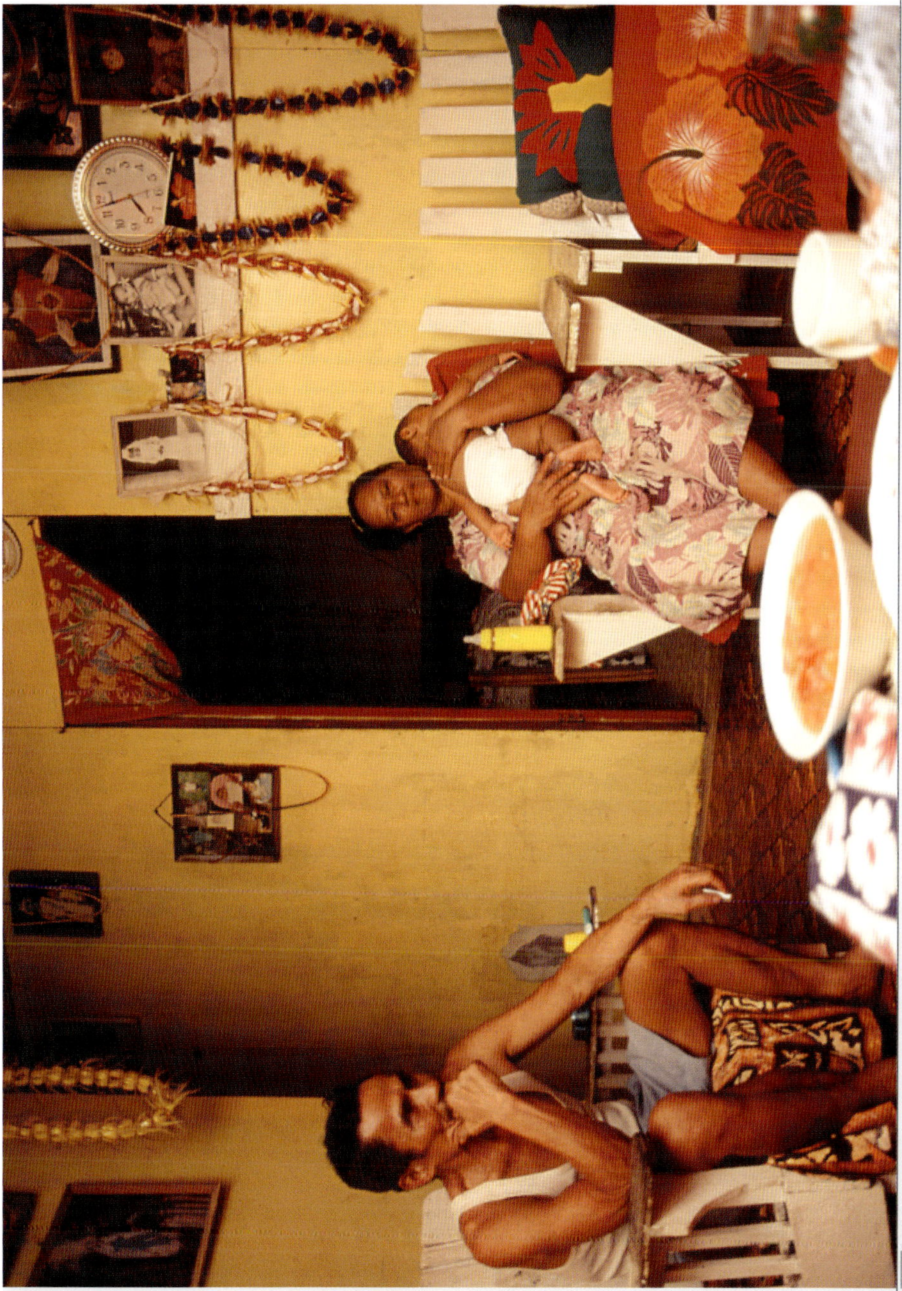

CHAPTER

05

Dusky Maidens and Noble Savages: Re-presenting 'Selves

The Pacific and its traditions are seen as other, as exotic—a tourist destination, a souvenir. The clichés of the happy islander, of sun-drenched beaches, of beautiful maidens and of savage men complete the myth. Post-modern theorists talk about taking back and renegotiating; but what happens to cultural traditions once they have moved from the island to the urban, once they have hit the public domain? In New Zealand, artists are currently drawing upon their traditions, creating new ones, asserting their voice, re-presenting themselves and demanding the viewer re-evaluate their perceptions of the Pacific.

The number of artists referencing a Pacific identity is steadily growing. The media that they work with is as diverse as they are. Most of the artists have navigated institutional art education and are creating traditions that bridge the differences between the world of their ancestors and their own urban reality. It is this reality that reinforces the social and political agendas of their work. Firmly based in New Zealand, these artists are telling their stories—stories that address cultural and social conflict; stories of suicide and of a necessary balance; stories that enable the assertion of their own identity. As Tai Mulitalo (2001: frontispiece) wrote:

this Samoan me
God-bronzed
gene-baked
trap me not in cliché
but set me free my friend
judge me not and let me be
my own shade of brown

This chapter considers the artistic practices that draw upon the issues surrounding the conflicts and realities of being a Pacific Islander in New Zealand. In particular the work of Anderson (Andy) Leleisi'uao, Sima Urale, Pacific Underground, Tai Mulitalo and John Pule demonstrate the need to balance expectations, obligations and stereotype with one's personal wants and desires—an important issue addressed by a number of Pacific artists in their arts practice. Identities are constructed that not only refute the stereotype, but also assert their Pacific identity. A social consciousness—a need to tell their stories as well as to provide a voice for others—is drawn from the conflicting demands that create their lives.

Andy Leleisi'uao, John Pule and Sima Urale bring the social and economic realities that embody New Zealand clearly into focus. Leleisi'uao's critique highlights the constant struggle for Samoans (working to remit money back to the islands for the church or for their children's education) and the contradictions between fa'aSamoa and New Zealand life. Both the economic and cultural obligations, which leave Pacific Islanders drained, blatantly negate the stereotype of the happy islander. The migrant expectation of a land of milk and honey is critiqued in Leleisi'uao's *I Miss My Polynesian Me* **[figure 5.1]**. This work critiques the dream, dispels the myth and speaks to the reality—the challenges, the dispossession and the desperation felt by those entrenched in an urban lifestyle. Suggesting the conflict between being Polynesian and fitting into New Zealand society, the viewer is confronted by a man torn between the past (represented by traditional motifs) and the present. He sees himself vacantly staring into a mirror, his blue reflection referencing his blue-collar job. He has lost himself in his urban reality. *You Make Me Nobody* **[figure In.7]** continues this critique: a factory worker with a zipper over his mouth illustrates both the numbness that these workers feel, as well as their lack of voice. Leleisi'uao offers a voice to this silent and submissive workforce—a workforce that struggles to be heard, seen and valued. In these works, Leleisi'uao captures the hopelessness, despair and anger experienced by Pacific blue-collar workers, who are destined to toil in factories and other menial jobs.

The same themes are found in the written work of John Pule. In *The Shark that Ate the Sun* (1992) Pule expertly weaves tales of migration, dispossession, drinking and loss. There is a violent aspect to these stories—of children afraid of their father, yet wanting to please. There is also another reality—that of children rebelling from their family or culture as they find their own way on the streets. Petty crime, fighting and underage drinking are just some of the social issues that Pule addresses. Loss, not only of a cultural nature, but also of dignity, strikes deep when the factory, the pub and violence rule your life.

The migrant reality is also addressed in Sima Urale's film, *O Tamaiti* (*The Children*) **[figure 5.2]**. She constructs an image—not of bright colours and hibiscus, but of a childhood lost to parental demands. The film begins with the arrival of a baby, creating a family with six children. Tino, the eldest, must look after his siblings, must do the shopping, cook meals, and oversee baths and bedtimes. The parental and cultural desire to get ahead necessitates multiple jobs, and so, with the extended family left behind in the islands, children have to fend for themselves. They strive to maintain equilibrium, to feast with weekend parents. Here, Urale's focus is on the children. Like the silenced factory workers, children are also ignored. Trying desperately to maintain a balance—to meet all expectations, yet stay out of the way—raises questions concerning cultural obligations and fa'aSamoa.

These issues are also brought to light in the photography of Evotia Tamua. With *The Choir Master* **[figure 5.3]** Tamua captures the essence of the Pacific church, its focus on the traditional and its reinforcement of Pacific values. Here, as well as in *O Tamaiti* and *The Shark that Ate the Sun*, we see the lives of Pacific peoples unravelling through the eyes of children. The stresses of parenthood, of wanting the best for their children, come to the fore as social, cultural and economic obligations (tithing to the church and sending money home) impede their progress towards the immigrant dream. As a result, a generation of Pacific Islanders see the issues surrounding culture in a different light from their parents. Seeds of discontent germinate, developing into issues of identity as they grow.

Figure 5.1 › Andy Leleisi'uao, *I Miss My Polynesian Me*, acrylic on canvas, 1994. Photograph courtesy of the artist.

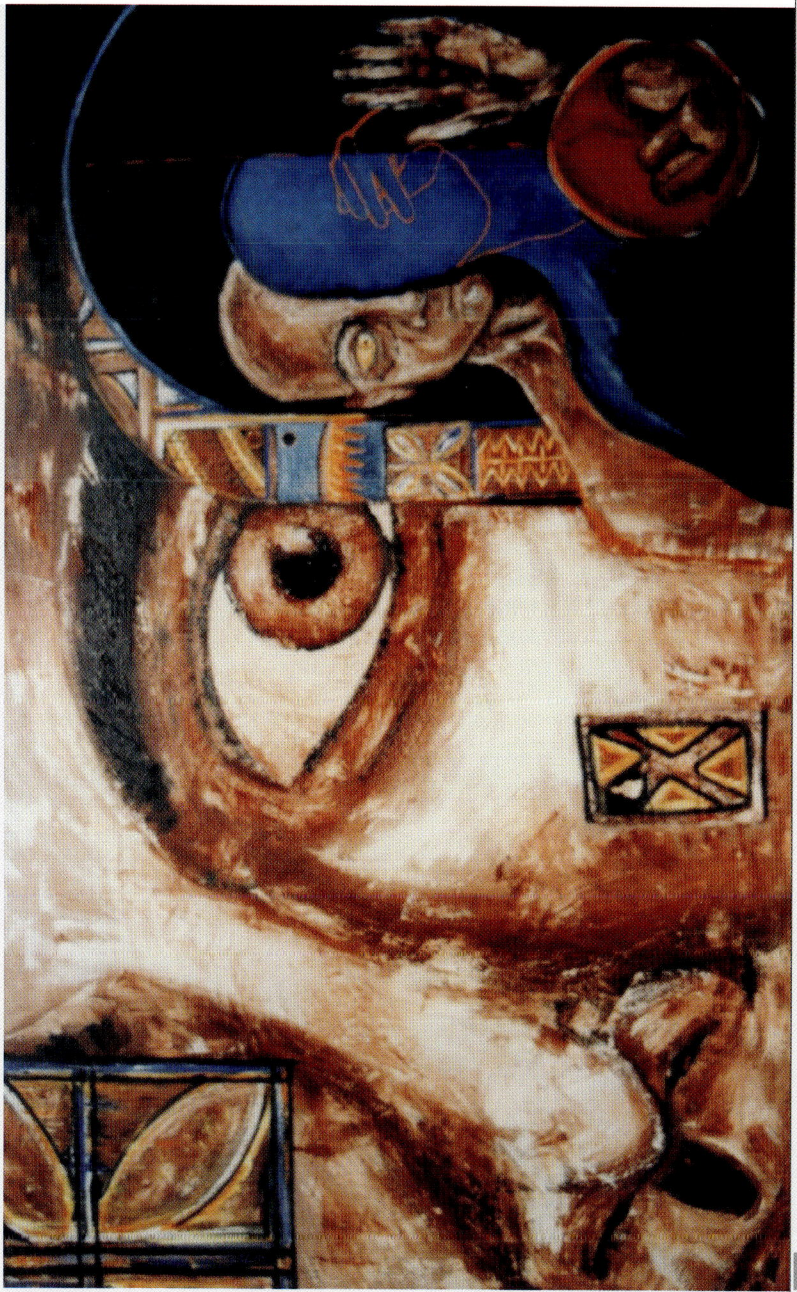

Figure 5.2 › Sima Urale, *O Tamaiti*. Photograph courtesy of the New Zealand Film Commission.

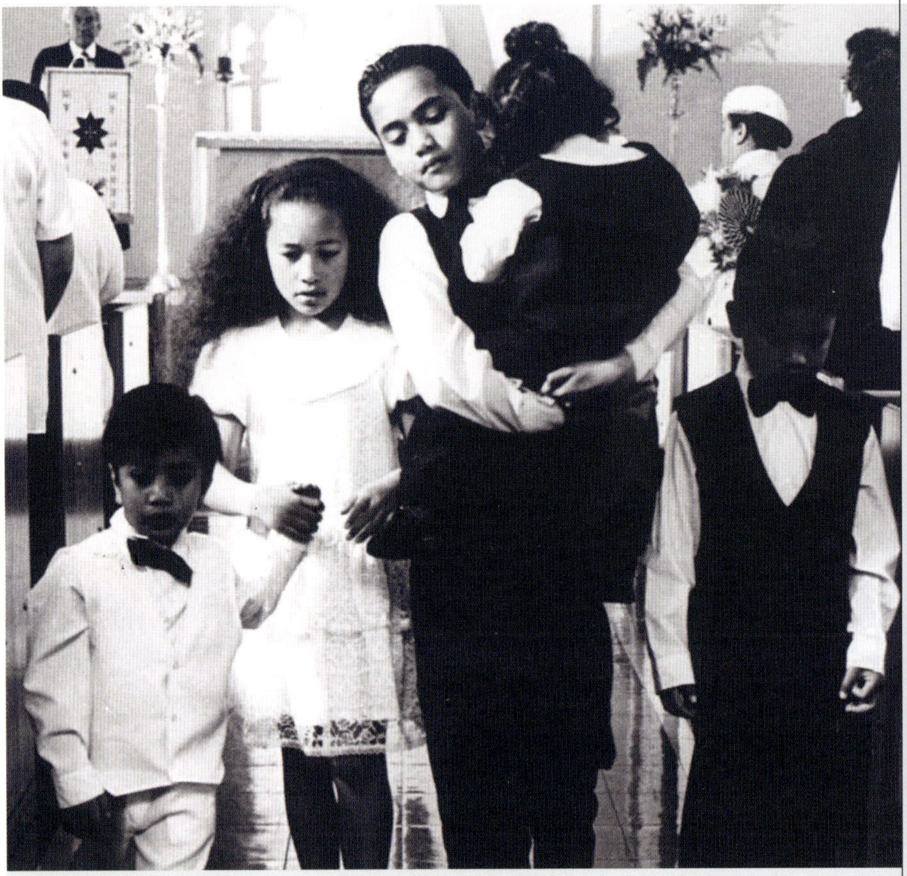

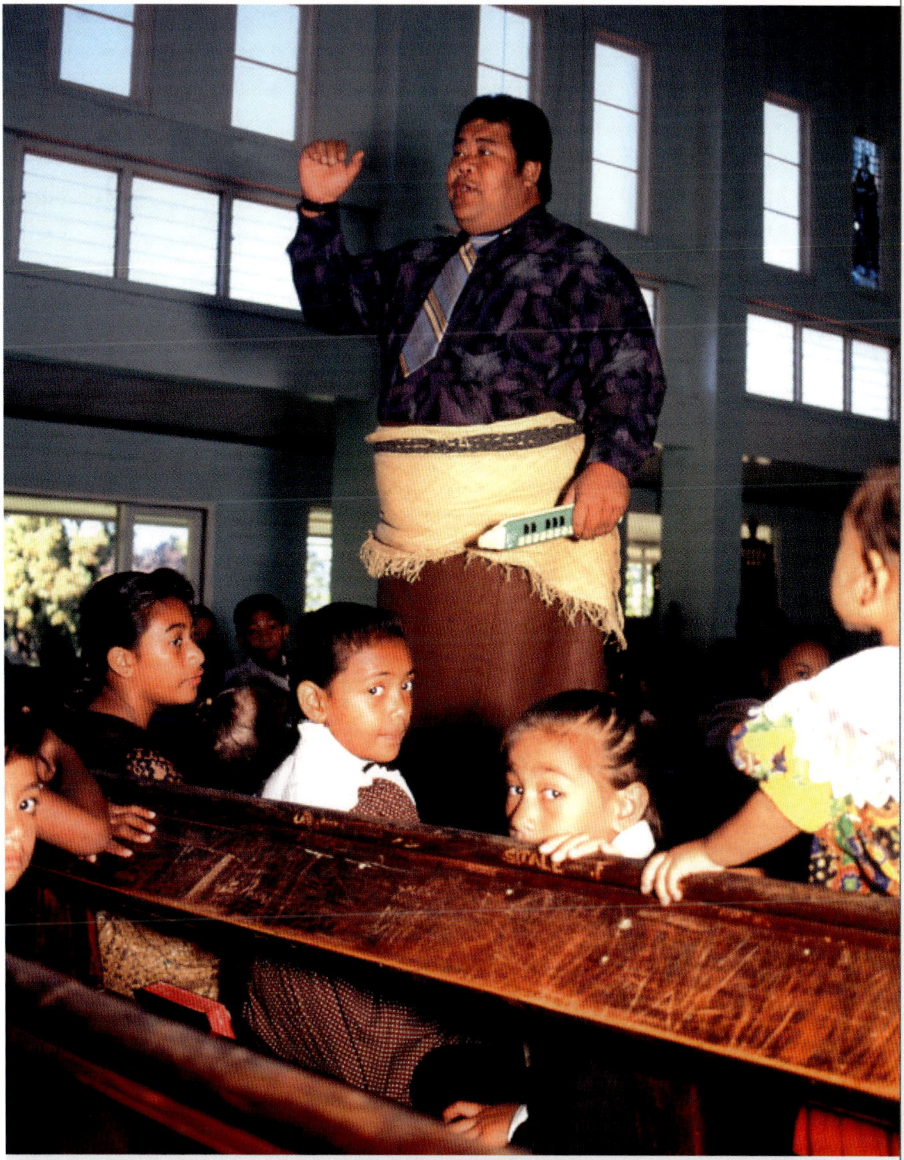

Figure 5.3 › Evotia Tamua, *The Choir Master*, 1995. Photograph courtesy of the artist.

Identity and strength of conviction are often hard to find when parental role models are blurred with apprehension. This line of questioning one's identity is apparent in a series of photographs (combined with personal statements) by Tai Mulitalo. In black and white, the colourful gloss frequently associated with Pacific peoples is sidelined, and this enables us to direct our attention to the people themselves, not the stereotype. *My own Shade of Brown* (2000) 'is an expression of cultural identity' (Mulitalo 2001). In this work Mulitalo combined her photography with the stories of six Samoan men and women, so as to explore the diversity of the Samoan experience in New Zealand. She stated (2001: backcover) that 'not only are there many different ways of connecting to one's culture; different ways of existing as a Samoan, there are differences in the ways individual Samoan people adapt to the challenge of living in an overwhelmingly Palagi environment'.

Sofia **[figure 5.4]** exemplifies the spirit of these individuals as they live: at work, at home, in church and at play. We hear their voices as they create their own representation. These stories speak of the challenges Samoan peoples face in their attempts to integrate into New Zealand society; in the process they discuss interracial marriage, defying and returning to the church, the importance of language, balancing cultures and being accepted for who they are.

> There is no room for growth in shadows. I wanted my independence. It was important to me that I did not offend my parents, but it was also important that I had psychological freedom. At university I was exposed to a different set of rules and cultural behaviour. University encouraged independent thinking and the need to question everything, whereas at home my father's word was law. (Mulitalo 2001: 14–15)

Balance is not always easy to come by, and the social problems that have arisen within migrant communities underlie the work of Andy Leleisi'uao. As his own culture's critic, Andy exposes not only the statistics, but also the repercussions of suicide and domestic violence, together with the silencing of any discussion of these issues within the Samoan community. *Relief Tied to a Tree* **[figure 5.5]** is a haunting acknowledgement of suicide—an escape from the struggle and demands of balancing the island and the urban. *Taroman* addresses violence against women, and *Honest to God* **[figure 5.6]** makes a strong statement about the role of the church in Samoan life.[1] The church has created a village setting within the community (the minister

Figure 5.4 › Tai Mulitalo, *Sofia*, 2000. Photograph courtesy of the artist.

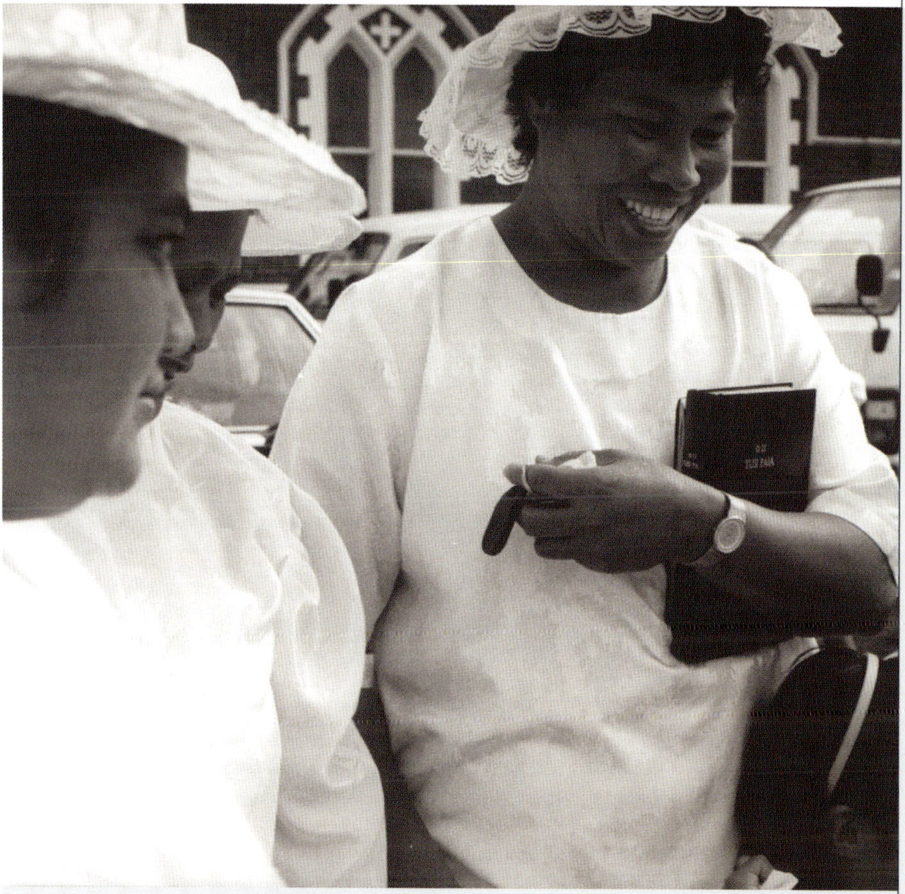

taking on the role of chief). Within this framework, immigrants know how to act, they know their role; it is the familiar in an unfamiliar setting. Leleisi'uao critiques this structure, which hides many of the social problems within the community—a lack of voice, suicide, domestic violence and hypocrisy. He brings these social problems into the open, demanding that they be revealed. Employing caricature is a way of engaging with difficult subject matter such as domestic violence and suicide. This is not to deny the importance of these issues, but to present them in a genre familiar to children, in a traditional way—using humour as critique.[2] Leleisi'uao also works in a bold and graphic style to reinforce his position on these issues. These bold and abrupt pieces deliver Leleisi'uao's message.

Bringing issues to public view also underlies the performance piece *Can You See Me?* **[figure 5.7]** by Lonnie Hutchinson. Enveloped in brown packaging tape, Lonnie positioned herself—a brown figure—in public places in Auckland. The performance posed the question 'Can you see me?' The response, for the most part, was 'No'! She was ignored and literally walked over. In this simultaneously subtle *and* bold performance piece, she questioned the position of Pacific Islanders in the world's largest Polynesian city, and their relationship with their palagi compatriots.

These personal and collective conflicts are well known within the Pacific community, and have become the foundation for a series of plays written and performed by Pacific Underground, a Christchurch based theatre collective.[3] These plays told the stories of an immigrant generation and their families, while at the same time questioning and highlighting a perception (or rather a misconception) of Pacific peoples in New Zealand. *Fresh off the Boat* (1994) **[figure 5.8]** addressed the cultural conflict between the island and the urban, demonstrating diverging points of view within the Pacific community. Through humour and stereotype, island values are posited as old-fashioned and out of place in the New Zealand environment. Anxiety mounts as women find a voice and men assert their dominance, as people change in their struggle to integrate into New Zealand society and as cultures change. The problems associated with the need to balance constant and diverse demands provide the audience with opportunities for cultural understanding. Humour offers balance to this poignant story.

Traditionally, Pacific cultures drew upon humour to critique and comment upon public issues. Pacific Underground uses this trait to address cultural differences

Figure 5.5 › Andy Leleisi'uao, *Relief Tied to a Tree*, acrylic on canvas, 1997. Photograph courtesy of the artist.

Figure 5.6 › Andy Leleisi'uao, *Honest to God*, acrylic on canvas, 1998. Photograph courtesy of the artist.

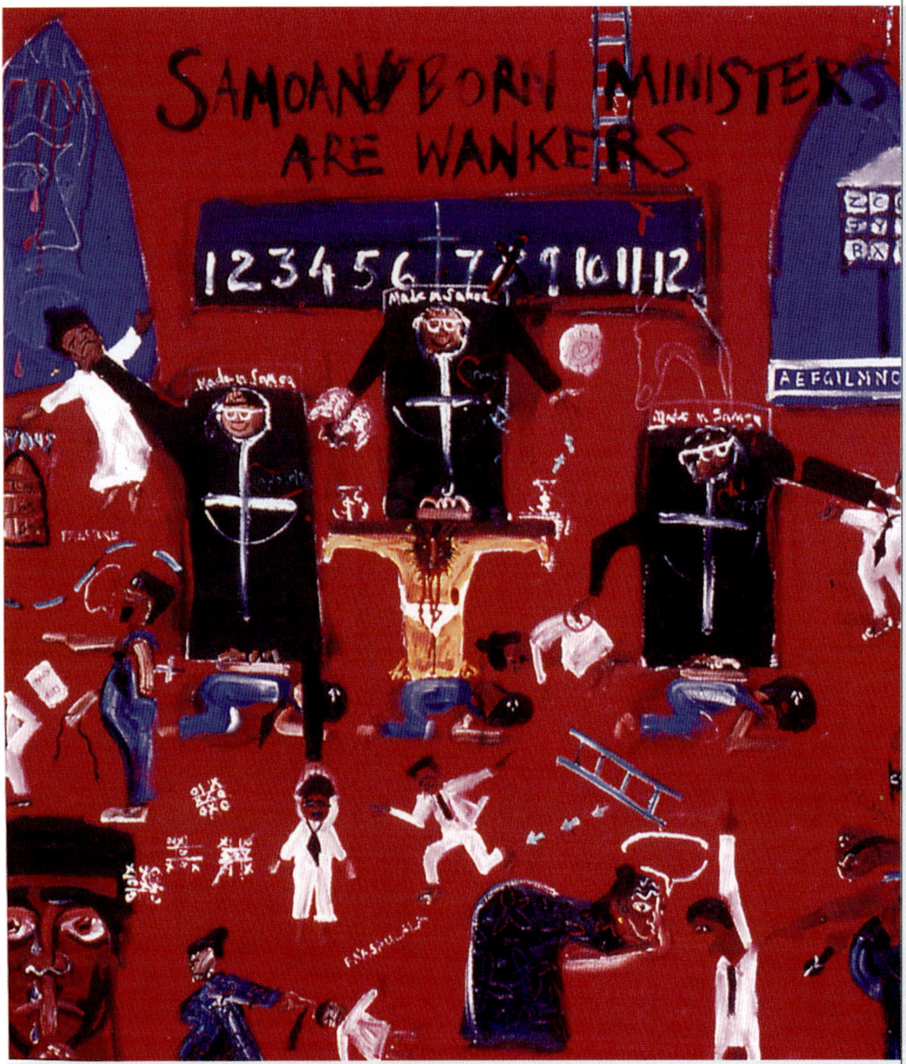

Figure 5.7 › Lonnie Hutchinson, *Can You See Me?*, 1998. Photograph courtesy of the artist.

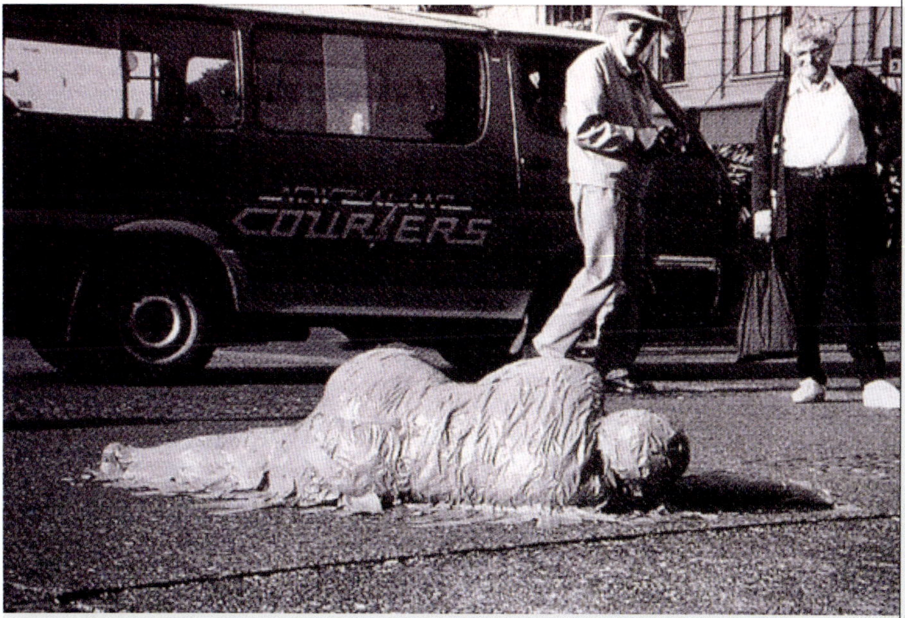

and to bridge cultural boundaries. This is clearly seen in *Romeo and Tusi* (1997), where cultural misunderstandings abound. A New Zealand version of the famous Shakespearean story of two feuding families, *Romeo and Tusi* draws upon every stereotype of both Māori and Pacific Islanders. By accentuating these stereotypes, the playwright forces the audience to realise the limitations and the impediments to cultural understanding that these stereotypes cause. This play was originally performed in schools as a means of exposing Pacific peoples to the issue. Anton Carter noted:

> We were one of the few Pacific island theatre groups that was touring, so for schools it was probably the only exposure that they ever get of brown people on stage being brown people and being positive and good. So our school and community performances were really an effort to say to the parents of the kids, 'hey look these young kids have skills and it's about a job and if they want to act they can act. Don't force them into factories, don't force them into things that you know about'. (Carter quoted in Mallon 2002:143)

The theatre pieces *When the Frigate Bird Sings* (1996), *Tatau* (1996) *and Dawn Raids* (1997) are more dramatic and offer insight into cultural practices, again highlighting the conflicts found in Pacific peoples as they strive to be both who they are and who their parents want them to be. *When the Frigate Bird Sings* comments upon the role of the fa'afafine in Samoan life. The eldest son, a fa'afafine, is torn between his obligations and duties as eldest son and the conflict this brings with his younger brother, who both understands and refuses to acknowledge his older brother's position. Obligation and multiple layers of cultural practice are also at the heart of *Tatau,* which teases out the many preconceived notions associated with getting and wearing a tatau, what it means and the process that one must undergo to understand the obligations associated with what, to many, is a fashion statement. *Dawn Raids* **[figure 5.9]** revisited a period of social unrest and humiliation in the 1970s when race relations were strained over immigration policy. Again a family like many others is the focus. A father's set of values (of discipline, respect and honour) is placed in opposition to his family. Choosing to abide by the laws of a new homeland, prioritising them over his family, he sees his decisions destroy the family he was trying to save.

Figure 5.8 › Pacific Underground, *Fresh off the Boat*, production poster, 1994. Photograph courtesy of Pacific Underground.

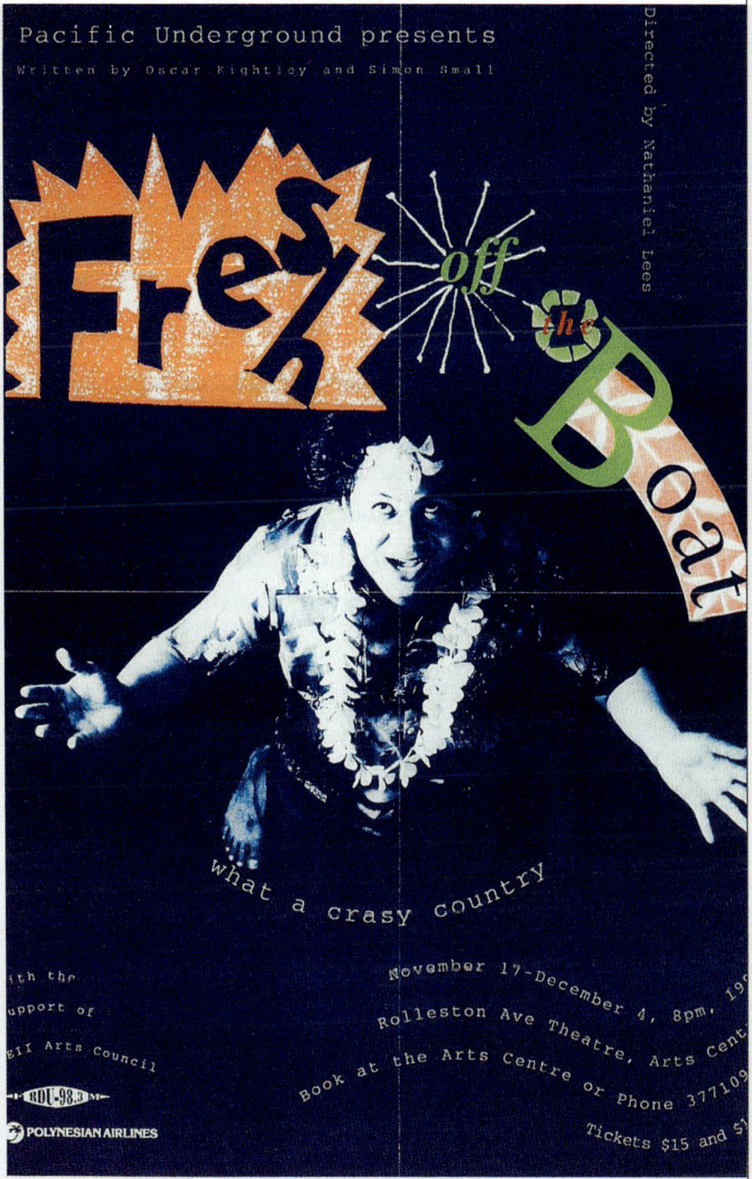

All of these plays demonstrate the creative abilities of their writers and the prominent position Pacific Underground played in Pacific theatre in New Zealand. They also provide insight into the diversity and the depth of Pacific peoples' cultural values and practices, which are often overlooked as a thin layer of stereotype. Anton Carter (2002: 149) noted '. . . self-determination and definition have been important themes of theatre work by Pacific peoples. In rewriting and challenging stereotypes there is a necessity to create characters that truly represent a Pacific Island perspective'.

This body of work has provided New Zealand with the opportunity to look at itself, to reflect upon the joy and pains these stories present, and to acknowledge their significance. Theatre and literature play an important role in providing new interpretations of past oral traditions. Pacific Underground, Sima Urale and John Pule provide a continuum of a Pacific story telling tradition—one where social criticism and critique is the foundation.[4]

These artists are building bridges of cultural understanding. The power in these works comes from their ability to examine the process of change, and to assert their voice and identity as both unique and a part of a cultural whole. Change is not new. The acquisition and conveyance of knowledge has allowed cultures to develop for millennia. Oral traditions and imagery (patterns as mnemonic devices) offer a foundation to reinterpret and recreate the traditional past. This legacy, inspired by the assertion of identity, enables New Zealand born Pacific islanders to negotiate between the perceived ideal (the islands) and their reality as the other's other.

In order to position themselves as versed in their culture—as able to pass knowledge to the next generation or to their younger siblings—they are learning language, learning about their history and learning about their culture's traditional beliefs so as to understand the pre-Christian ideology of their ancestors. They regard this knowledge that they have chosen to learn out of interest (not something imposed on them by a school curriculum) as knowledge they have been denied by missionisation, colonisation and migration.

John Pule is an example of this desire to learn. He continues to develop his knowledge of the Niuean language and his understanding of his cultural past. As a writer, his tools are language and knowledge. As a painter, he creates his own language—a language of metaphor, which draws from traditional mythology, history and what

Figure 5.9 › Pacific Underground, *Dawn Raids*, production poster, 1997. Photograph courtesy of Pacific Underground.

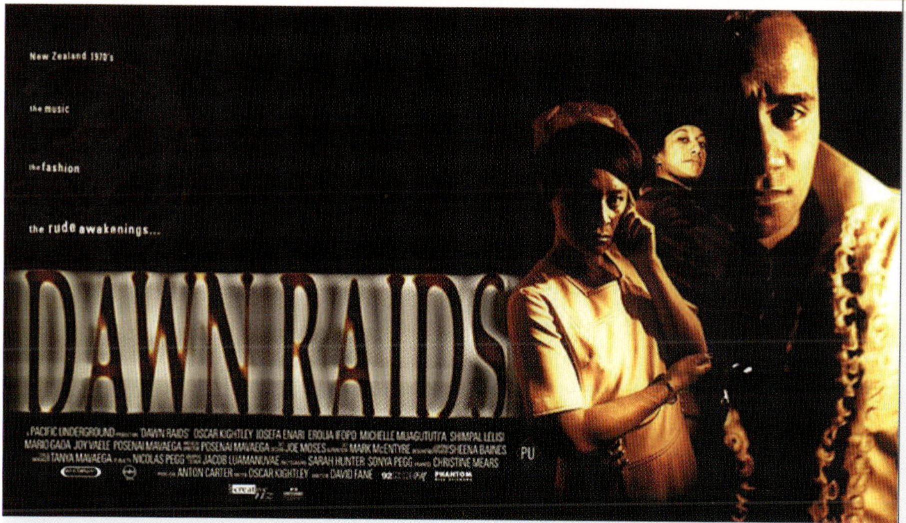

remains of his culture—a culture ravaged at the hands of the West **[figures 2.10 and 4.4]**. Pule employs these tools in his artwork and in his writing, combining the two in a series titled *From the Bond of Time* (1998) **[figure 4.5]**. Excerpts from his novel *Burn my Head in Heaven* (1998) are also the foundation from which motifs spring, adding visual energy to the text. The canoe, church, cross and animals (especially the shark)—the consistent motifs in his work—intermingle with the stories in his novel: stories that reference oral traditions, stories created anew, stories often compartmentalised and complex. Pule's imagery is contemporary. However, the novel weaves together the past and the present, so enabling his characters to assert a Niuean identity—to acknowledge their heritage. Pule further addresses the loss of language, culture and belief systems—all are played out in the work.

Balancing the traditional, the island and the urban often creates contradictions that Pacific artists must face in their art practice. The result is that they consciously embrace particular aspects of their heritage which enable them to exemplify their position within contemporary practice. Using the familiar to critique the stereotype, and (ideally) to demand a second look is a tactic used by many. However, using the icon to destroy the myth seems a complex method to reinforce an idea; there is always the danger that the viewer will not understand. Sima Urale explores the cliché of the pliant Polynesian female in *Velvet Dreams* (1997). The film focuses on the work of Charlie McPhee, a painter of Pacific women on velvet. Using a film noir format, Urale sends her narrator in search of the girl of his dreams—his velvet, dusky maiden. The format is key because it offers both a time frame for the practice of painting on velvet (the 1930s and 1940s) and also enables an appreciation of this kitsch/retro tradition.[5] While outlining the history of velvet painting in the Pacific, Urale unveils the concept of the dusky maiden, showing the representation of Pacific women as little more than objects of lust to be a white-male construct. The elusiveness of the beautiful maiden, however, both critiques and challenges this cultural construct. As the narrator-detective stumbles over the clues (clichés and stereotypes), the search for the dusky maiden is described in a humorous manner. Urale undermines the cultural construct by questioning the standard representation of Pacific women. The pliant female, as well as the savage male, are clichés of the West—stereotypes perpetuated as the myth of the Pacific endures. Countering these perceptions is easy; changing them is a different story.

Figure 5.10 › Riki Tangaroa, *Avarua Church*, 1995. Photograph courtesy of the artist.

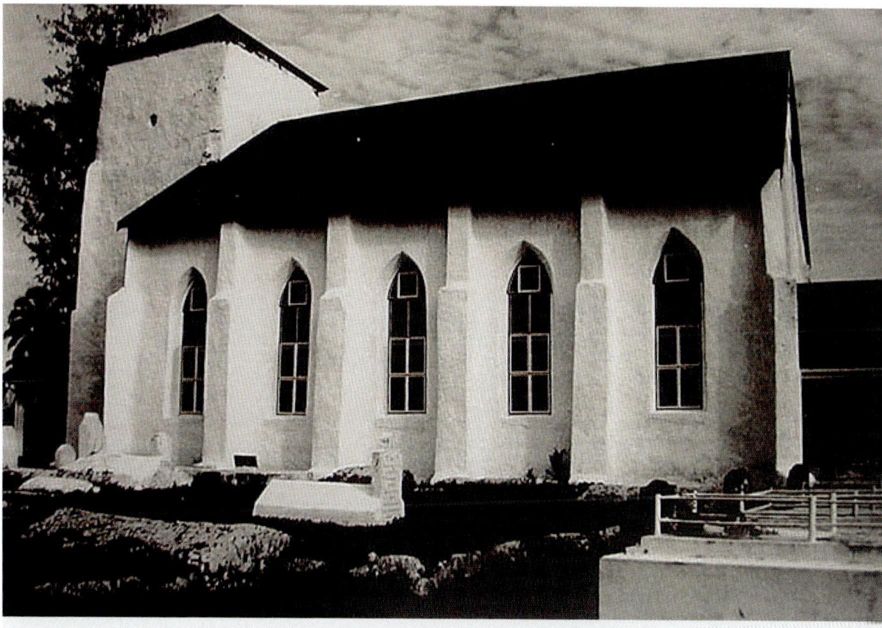

Chris Charteris, Niki Hastings-McFall and Sofia Tekela-Smith have contested this stereotype in *1 Noble Savage 2 Dusky Maidens* **[figure 4.7]**. Recreating an ethnographic photograph, they re-present themselves, thereby owning the stereotype. Dressed in a traditional manner, they emulate the photographs taken in Samoa in the 1890s—photographs that were sold for Western consumption and that created the stereotype. *1 Noble Savage 2 Dusky Maidens* uses the stereotype, therefore, to demonstrate its lack of authenticity. The perceived truth becomes a fiction, and in the process the stereotype is re-presented.

Riki Tangaroa has also looked at the ethnographic photograph, and in a series of her own photographs, taken in the Cook Islands, she comments upon the Western ownership of representations of the Pacific, as well as the myth of a culture caught in a bell jar—a representation of a dream. *Avarua Church* **[figure 5.10]** announces the accomplishments of the early missionaries. It also suggests timelessness, as both the church and Avarua remain frozen in the 19th century.

Pacific artists in New Zealand must recognise both the geographical and social reality which continue to position the Pacific as popular culture, as stereotype. The islands are still a dream (even to some of these artists). They are still marketed as a tourist destination. Pacific peoples and Pacific culture, however, are not for sale. Colonial governments have been replaced by sovereign nations. It is necessary, therefore, to express the cultural practices, both traditional and contemporary, which comment upon and critique this stereotype. Michel Tuffery believes that the representation of Pacific Islanders as entertainers (just one of many stereotypes) has long outlived its purpose.[6] It is time for artists to focus upon issues that raise the stakes and that assert their voice.

As Pacific culture becomes a vital element within the New Zealand context, urban New Zealand born Pacific artists create an art of their own, using their own traditions, which are derived from the cultural and ideological practices of the islands. For some, telling "real" stories and exposing cultural flaws creates negative stereotypes. For others, however, these artists are positioning themselves as real—they own their image, they are telling their stories, and in the process they are asserting both an individual as well as a cultural identity.

Figure 5.11 › Richard Shortland Cooper. *Tivaevae Rakau*, recycled rimu weatherboards and domestic materials, 1999. Photograph courtesy of Dr Richard Shortland Cooper.

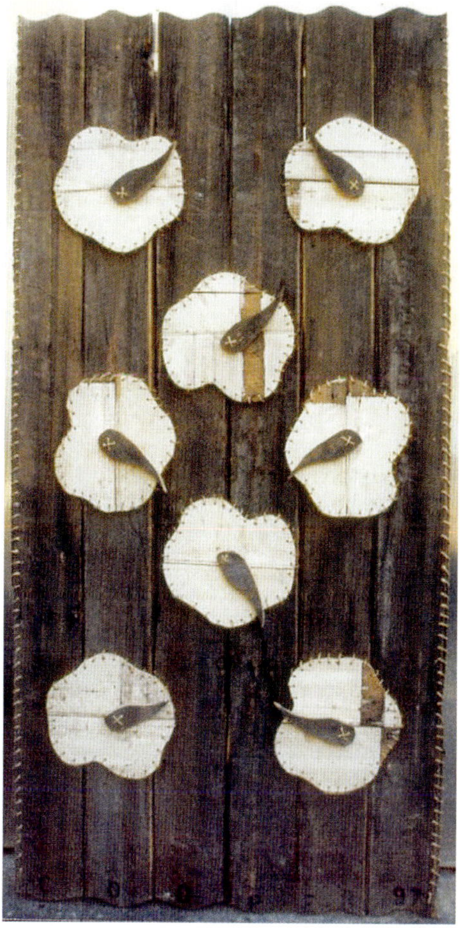

Figure 5.12 › Michel Tuffery, *Hibiscus and Mo'o*, paint and wood, 1998. Photograph courtesy of the artist.

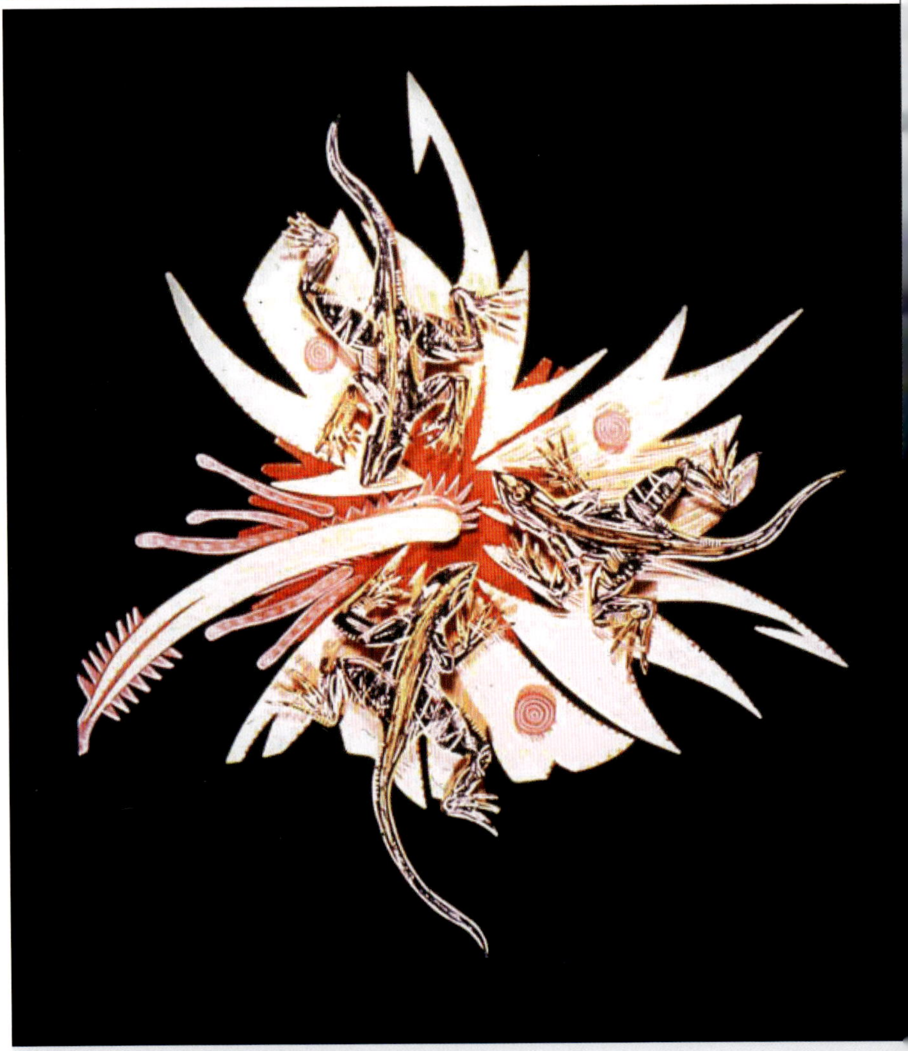

Figure 5.13 › Niki Hastings-McFall, *Brooch Siapo II*, silver, titanium, and niobium, 1998. Photograph courtesy of the artist.

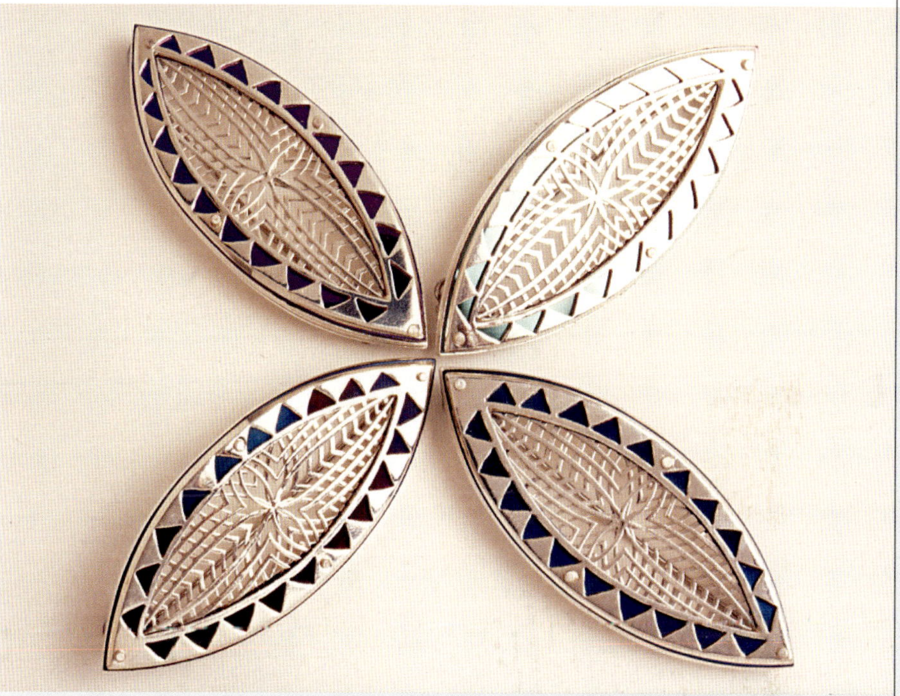

Perhaps more than any other motif, the frangipani remains a stumbling block for many artists. I use this flower as a gloss for all Pacific flowers (including hibiscus, tiare Tahiti and ginger) that reference their island homes, particularly the colour and fragile nature of those homes. Many artists utilise the flower as a referent to cultural traditions; others use it as a key trope in the West's view of the Pacific. Fatu Feu'u incorporates "his" frangipani into his practice **[figure In.5]** as a symbol of women and their importance within a Polynesian concept of balance. Richard Shortland Cooper has referenced the hibiscus in *Tivaevae Rakau* **[figure 5.11]** to acknowledge his Cook Islands ancestry and the artistic traditions of women. Michel Tuffery also pays homage to Samoan women in *Hibiscus and Mo'o* **[figure 5.12]**. Utilising the hibiscus as a symbol of the Pacific and women, he adds to this his reinterpretation of the upeti board (a board carved by men and used in the embellishment of barkcloth by women). Again, balance becomes apparent as both sides of that artistic tradition are acknowledged.

In contrast, Niki Hastings-McFall and Graham Fletcher employ the floral motif as an assertion of identity—as a signifier of Pacific. Hastings-McFall's *Brooch Siapo II* **[figure 5.13]** incorporates barkcloth and tatau motifs as embellishments of her frangipani. In doing so, she does not critique the image, but utilises it to assert a Pacific identity. Graham Fletcher, on the other hand, questions the stereotype in his *Stigma* series **[figure 5.14]**. Dubbed the 'Andy Warhol of the Pacific' (McAloon 2005: 5), Fletcher's work addressed the repetitive, mass-produced images associated with the Pacific. Hung with pins, the works in the *Stigma* series also comment on the notion of the Pacific as a specimen—something to be scrutinised by the West. By blurring the edges of his images, he also suggests the fragility of the flower as a symbol of Pacific cultures. This negotiation between the island and the urban—the cliché and lived realities—enables multiple readings of these works, reflective of the identities and issues being asserted.

The social realities of immigrant communities are not always pleasant, but they are no different from those experienced by other communities in the "host" nation. What many of these artists are suggesting is that their world is no different from the palagi world: getting ahead, dreaming about the future for yourself and your children, worrying about violence—these desires and concerns are universal. However, these common goals do not fit the stereotype of Pacific communities. The

Figure 5.14 › Graham Fletcher, *Stigma*, enamel on aluminium, 1999. Photograph courtesy of the artist.

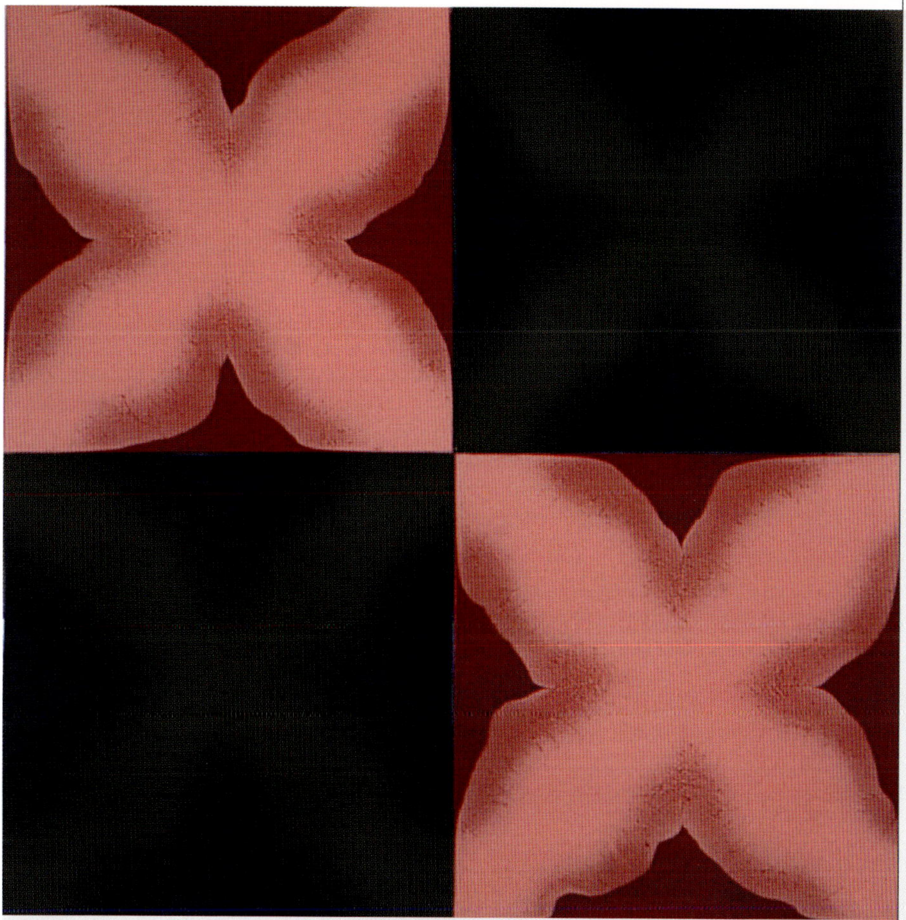

Figure 5.15 › Dagmar Dyck, *Folau Tahi II (Voyage)*, mixed media on tapa and canvas, 1999. Photograph courtesy of the artist.

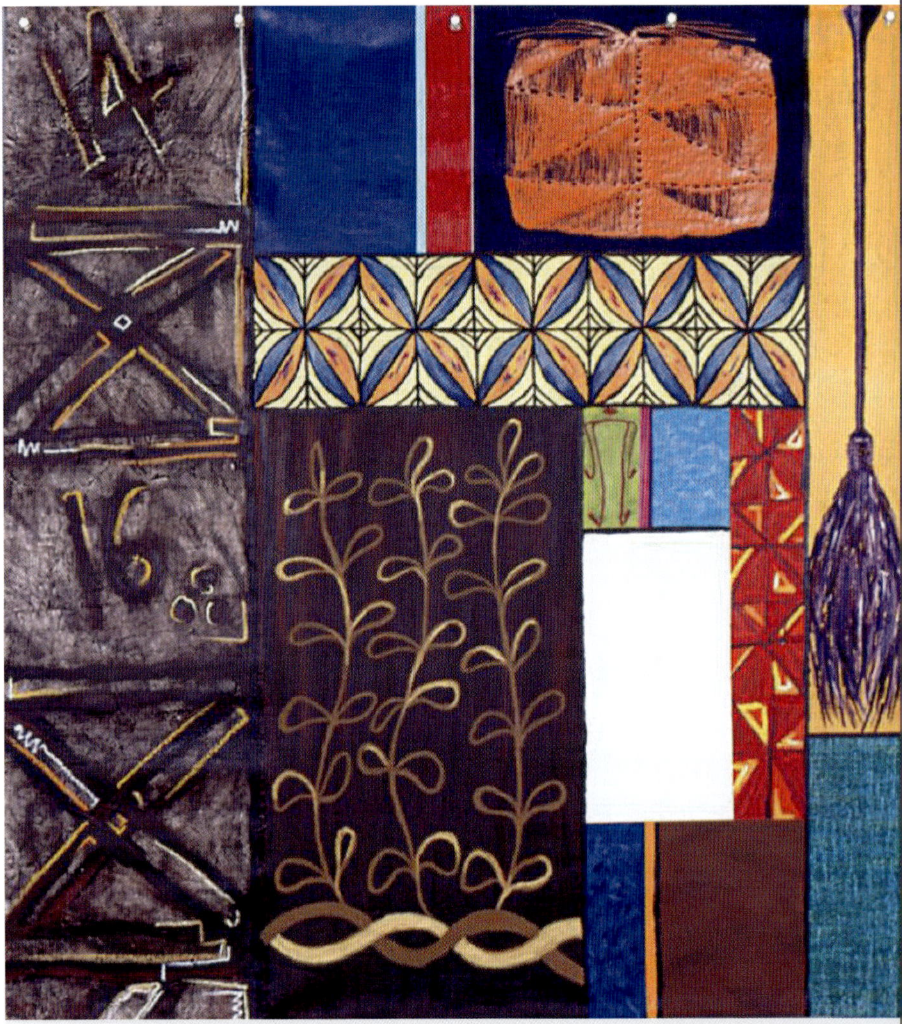

Figure 5.16 › Iosefa Leo, *Afio Mai, Welcome*, walnut, 2000. Photograph courtesy of the artist.

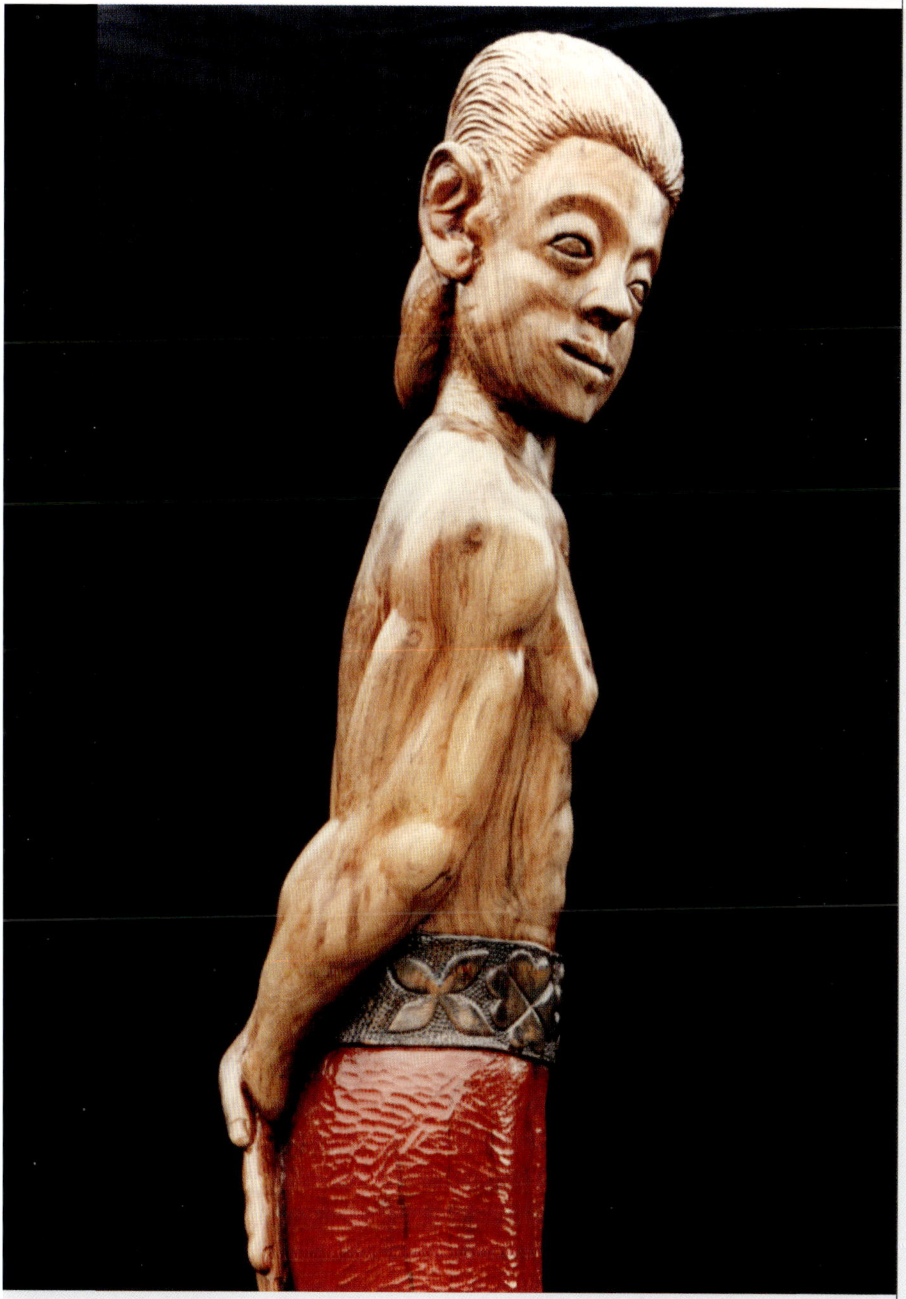

challenges of integrating into a new society, learning not only a new language but also a new culture, are the root causes of misunderstanding.

Some social realities, such as domestic violence and drunkenness, are creeping into and challenging the stereotype of the happy islander. Bringing these issues to the fore is complex. Yet, when this is balanced with work emulating and honouring the traditional past—offering a pride of place—a positive cultural identity can be created. Dagmar Dyck does just this in her practice. In *Folau Tahi II (Voyage)* **[figure 5.15]** Dyck references objects of Tonga's past—barkcloth, objects of adornment, status objects and weapons—in order to reiterate the strength of those cultural traditions. The notion of strength, of standing strong and proud, also reveals itself in the work of Iosefa Leo. In *Afio Mai, Welcome* **[figure 5.16]** a matai waits to welcome guests. Portrayed with monumental hands, a well-developed torso and a sincere expression, he embodies a chiefly persona. The link to the past is the foundation for the future.

By incorporating ideals of the past, artists are not sacrificing their culture, but addressing issues that provide the opportunity to move beyond the stereotype. These artists are neither offering just a bit of colour, spice or the exotic, nor are they riding a wave of fashion; they are critiquing it. As they move beyond the stereotype, they are demanding recognition of their position—one based in New Zealand, not in the myth, not in the cliché. It is this position of knowledge, offered through notions of identity, which propels contemporary Pacific art into its own. This new approach is both conscious and politicised. Based on social, cultural and economic realities, it focuses on the artist's own identity—an identity that is urban, global and island based. Pacific artists uniquely offer a voice for both the young and the old, for the past and the future. This will, ideally, bridge the gap between islands and cities, between language and ideologies, between myths and the church. In so doing, it will create a new myth, neither traditional nor Pacific, but one firmly ensconced in the urban realities of New Zealand.

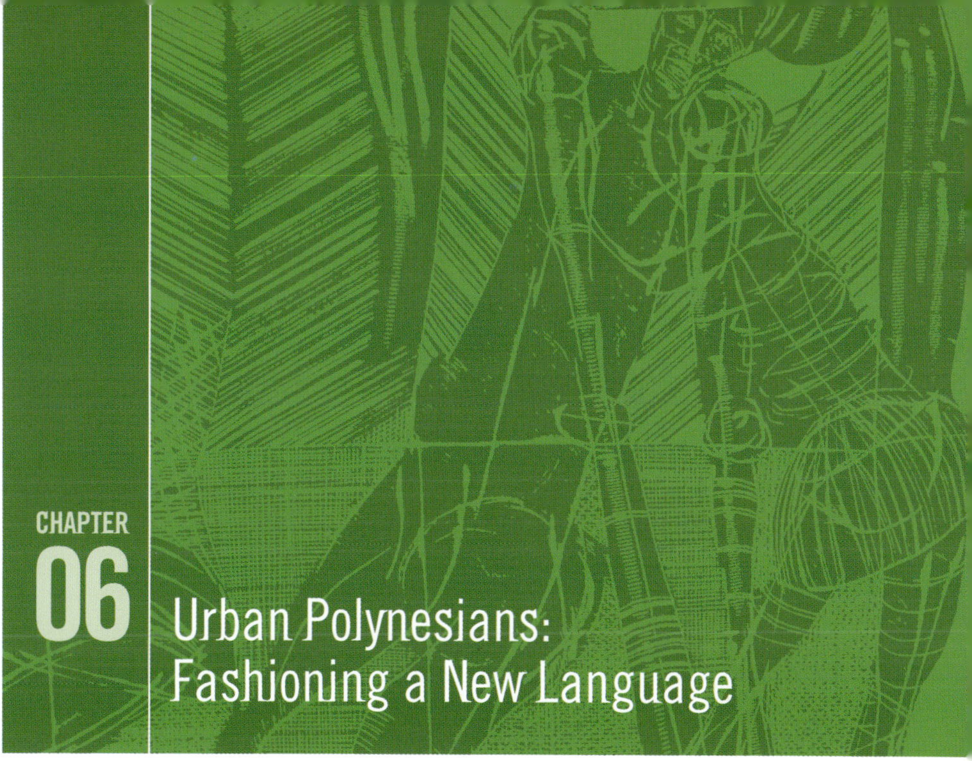

CHAPTER 06

Urban Polynesians: Fashioning a New Language

In the past twenty years, academic discourse has filtered into popular culture, and popular culture has become part of academic discourse. This dialogue draws upon academic language for its vocabulary, reinterpreting it to signify concepts relevant to a specific agenda at a historically specific time. That language may become overused, both within educational circles and on its fringes, often transmuting to satisfy a particular assertion. "Hybrid" is one such word—it now has a variety of meanings, depending on the context in which it is used. This multiplicity of meanings can lead to misinterpretation.

Hybrid, as an academic term within the specific agenda of addressing issues of colonialism within the post-colonial for a specific group of people, came into being in the 1980s (Bhabha 1984, 1985). As a scientific term, it defines the blending of species; as a sociological term, it defines the blending of cultures. Today, within the discourse of indigenous studies, the expression is employed in a combined fashion that enables speakers to mould it to their own agenda. To some, it offers a sense of empowerment; to others, it is offensive.

In the Pacific, the post-colonial does not exist. One can see independent nations, but they rely on first world nations for their economic survival. As such, many consider that the concept of the post-colonial (which suggests that the colonial relationship has ended) is insulting. Furthermore, suggesting that indigenous peoples are not authentic because they have succeeded within the Western educational system or use Western materials raises the ire of many.[1] However, if one looks at some of the tenets of these discussions, the debate offers more than this—in particular, it offers the importance of a voice and the rewriting of histories that had disappeared from many texts.[2]

Bhabha (1984: 132) utilised the term hybrid in relation to his ideas of mimicry—indigenous peoples mimicking the dominant culture as a means of survival. Working within that system the hybrid becomes "not quite/not white". Young (1990: 148) commented 'if the effect of colonial power is to produce "hybridisation", this undermines colonial authority because it repeats it differently'. The gaze of the discriminated is turned back upon the colonial power. Thus, the hybrid can become a source of resistance.

Addressing the ways in which hybridity is taken on by a number of Pacific artists, it becomes clear that their ownership of the term enables them to both subvert and conquer the West. As Linda Smith (1999: 14) noted, Pacific Islanders 'have a presence in the Western imagination, in its fibre and texture, in its sense of itself, in its language, in its silences and shadows, its margins and intersection'. Utilising icons of their cultural heritage to give voice to histories, ideas and social injustices that are frequently ignored, Pacific artists not only engage in the debate of hybridity, they own it.

In the 1990s Pacific artists were positioned as the other's other. At the same time they were asserting their voice in order to establish themselves as players in New Zealand's cultural landscape. Pasifika, founded in the urban street culture of Auckland, quickly moved throughout New Zealand. Reflecting a Pacific place in New Zealand society, Pasifika combined fashion, music, journalism, photography, dance, theatre, film, literature and the visual arts, thereby ensuring not only a presence but also a voice that could assert a Pacific identity. This has enabled what Albert Wendt (1995: 3) called the 'indigenising of Western art forms'. This is clearly seen in literature, where different story telling styles are being used, but it can be seen in other art forms, too. Black Grace (a dance troupe based in Auckland) often incorporated traditional dance moves within their modern choreography, and musicians frequently included traditional rhythms, together with indigenous language, in their songs. Drawing inspiration from the past and the present, as well as from the island and the urban, Pacific artists have created Pasifika.

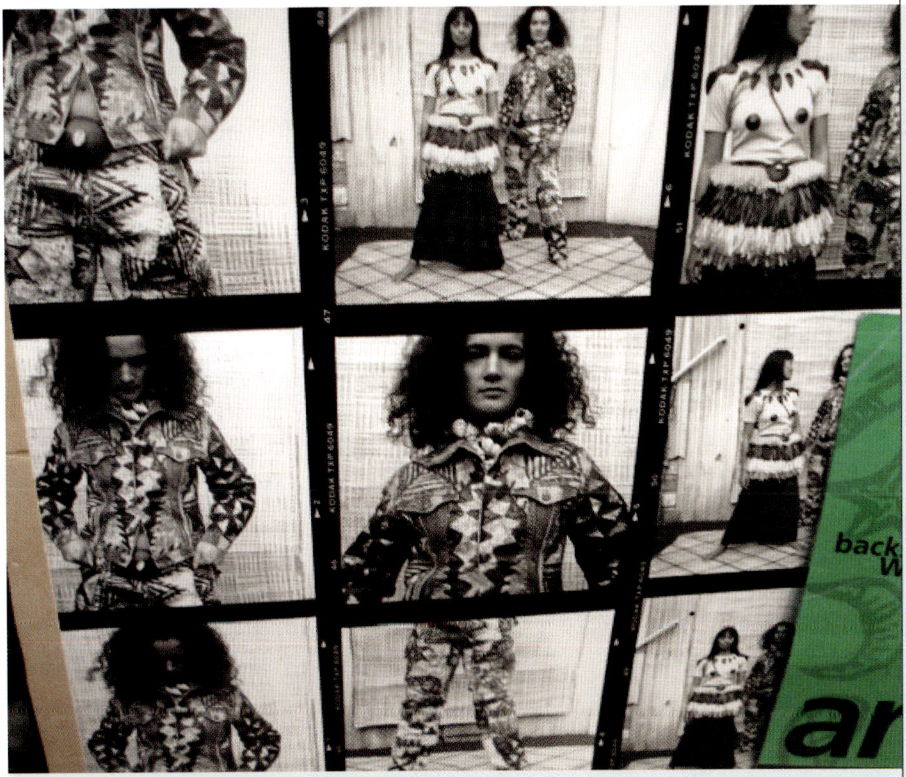

Figure 6.1 › Greg Semu, proof sheet from fashion shoot, 1996. Photograph incorporated into *Eyeland Part 2: Welcome 2 da K'lub*, 2006. Photograph courtesy of Rosanna Raymond.

As such, Pasifika comprises a variety of art forms formerly seen to be dominated by either the West or the East, but not the Pacific.[3] Opera, modern dance, theatre and contemporary art have not been recognised as indigenous art forms, even though song, dance and art have always been a part of Pacific cultures. In 1999, *Classical Polynesia* was created and staged under the direction of Iosefa Enari. Calling upon the talents of Pacific singers and dancers, this opera, in which historical Polynesian songs were reworked to the opera genre, celebrated a Pacific heritage tied to the islands along with a Pacific identity in New Zealand.

Creating the opportunity for Pacific expression was essential, and providing Pacific actors with the opportunity to play Pacific roles became the foundation of Pacific theatre. Paul and Justine Simei-Barton re-situated well-known stories, placing them in the Pacific. These included *Romeo and Juliet*, which was set in Samoa and came to the stage in 1987. The use of Pacific settings in turn led to the telling of Pacific stories. *Fresh off the Boat* **[figure 5.8]** in 1993 was a strong beginning. Theatre was an art form that created a platform to develop and present the skills of Pacific actors and writers. Anton Carter commented:

> Theatre in New Zealand has now become a powerful medium of expression for people of Pacific Island heritage. It is used to educate, raise awareness of important issues, experiment artistically, and just to purely entertain. Only by looking back over time, and particularly the past ten years, can the breadth and diversity of what is termed in New Zealand 'Pacific Theatre' be fully appreciated. (Carter 2002: 147)

Nathaniel Lees, a Samoan actor who spent years playing Māori roles, was delighted to read and eventually act in "Pacific" theatre. In reference to John Kneubuhl's *Think of a Garden*, Lees (quoted in Carter 2002: 149) observed 'it was such a joy to read about ourselves and our language, . . . we knew it would reach whoever came to see us'. The success of Pacific theatre has come from the strength of its stories, of creating real dialogue and talking about real people. It was another platform to tell the stories of family, of the previous generation, of issues cultural and social that shaped their lives. The characters became people that we knew. Pacific Underground pioneered this new playwriting genre, but it was one quickly taken on by others—in particular Makerita Urale, Victor Rodger and Toa Fraser. Each of these writers has offered another point of view, another voice.

Figure 6.2 › Frances Palu, *Ta'ovala*, linen suit, muslin shirt, green feather trim and crocheted, green raffia vest, 1997. Photograph courtesy of Giles Peterson.

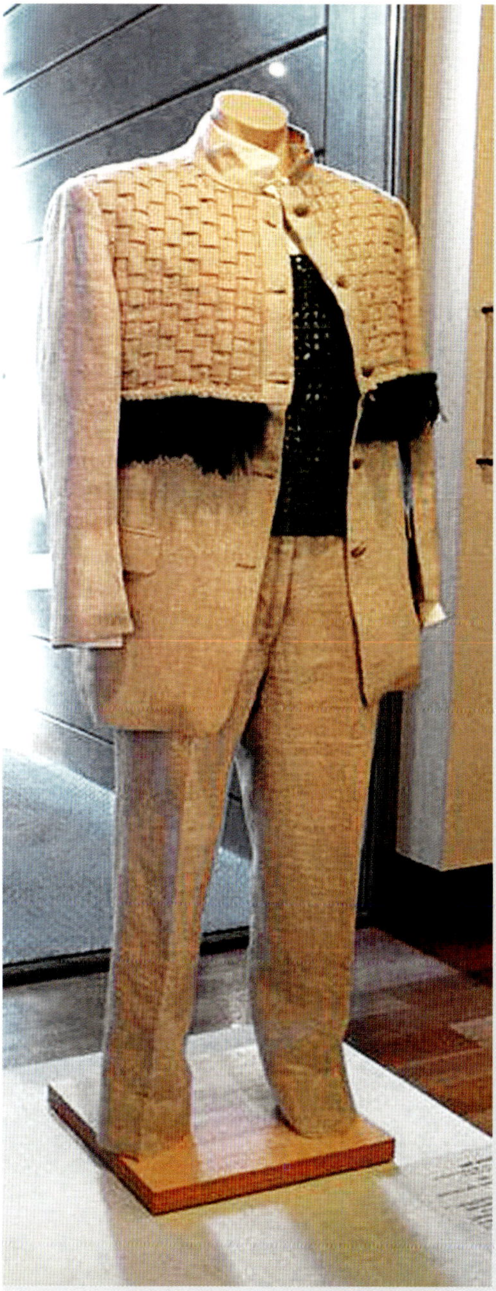

The predominance of Pacific Underground gave Pacific theatre a Samoan and, quite frequently, a male focus. Toa Fraser's *No.2*, however, provided insight into Fijian family life, enabling audiences to value a diversity of life experiences for Pacific peoples in New Zealand. *Frangipani Perfume*, in contrast, gave us a woman's voice. Written by Makerita Urale, directed by Erolia Ifopo and employing the talents of three women actors (Sima Urale, Dianna Fuemana and Joy Vaele), it was a play 'pulsating with sassy energy' (Welsh 1998). The play offered a woman's perspective through the conversations of three sisters—all cleaners—as they speak of their dreams and aspirations. As their stories unfold the listener is invited into their lives; as they banter, offer up social criticism, and reveal their hearts and lives, the audience can't help but recognise and embrace their humanity. At the same time, the insight of these intelligent and vibrant women as they come to grips with their lives refutes the stereotype of Pacific women as voiceless and as "merely cleaners".

Similarly, stereotypes are shattered by modern Pacific dance. No longer entertainment for the tourist, dance has also taken on the West. Incorporating the Pacific's stories and modern dance has created innovative and abstract movements, which blend with a siva beat, making it Pacific. New Zealand has been fortunate to have two Pacific dance collectives—Black Grace and Mau. Both of these groups have indigenised modern dance. Lemi Ponifasio commented that:

> Being a dancer is not only a pursuit of an artistic expression but it is also an existential choice of life and living as a body . . . Here in the Pacific, the notion of the va is the lived and cognisant body relationship with the world. The va or the body's intentionality is the foundation of all expression, including dance. (Ponifasio quoted in Taouma 2002: 140)

Mau creates dance productions, events and performances that focus on movement—on the body as art. Combining the Bhuto tradition with his own sense of movement, Ponifasio creates dance that combines not only the East and the West, but also the Pacific.

Neil Ieremia's Black Grace moved Pacific dance into another realm—not just traditional, not just modern—creating the opportunity to explore the boundaries of the modern dance genre. Ieremia (quoted in Taouma 2002: 138) in describing his company, said 'Black Grace, an all-male Polynesian dance group who identify as

Figure 6.3 › Rosanna Raymond, *G'nang G'near*, Levi's and barkcloth, 1992–1997. Photograph courtesy of the artist.

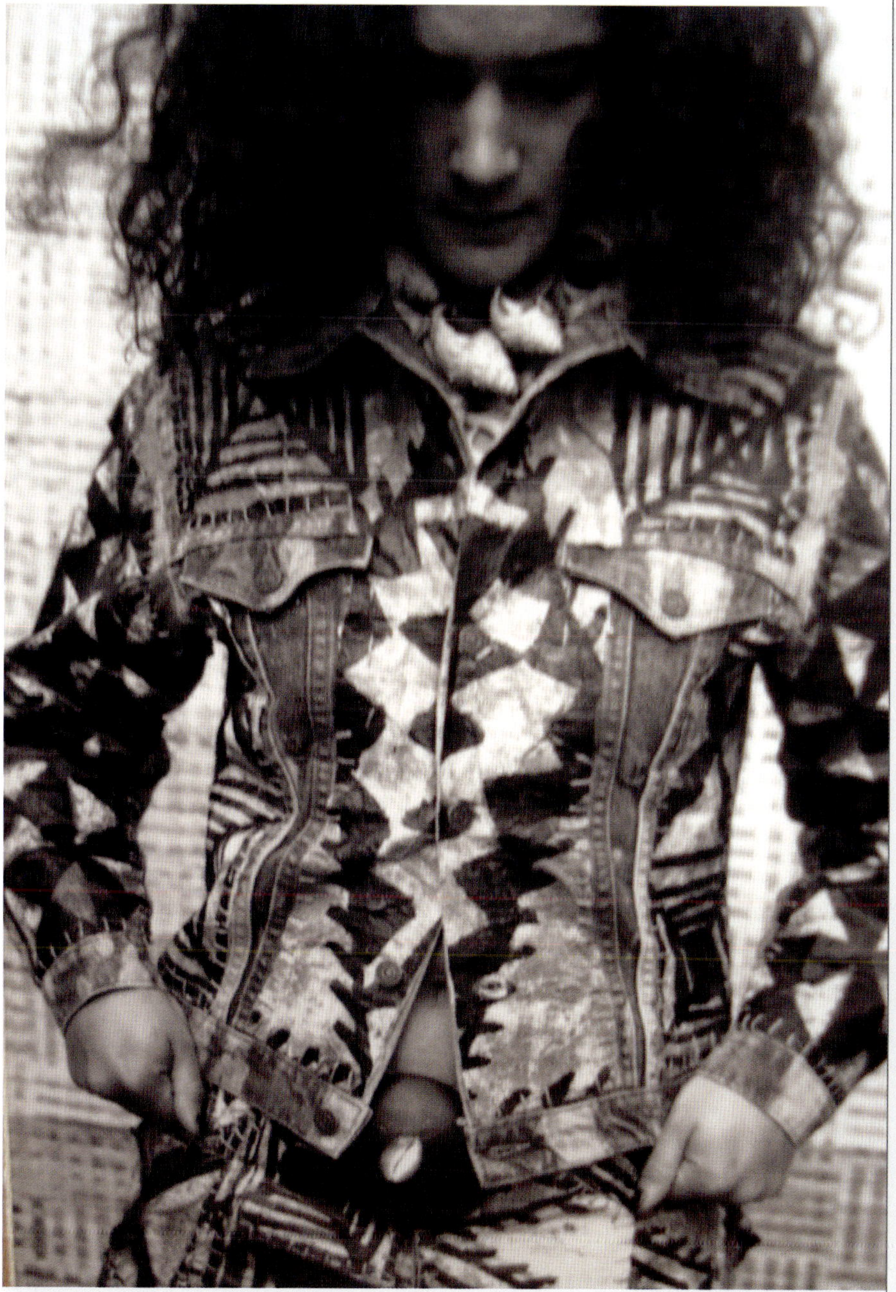

"contemporary", have performed . . . varied themes which have at times included rugby, male stereotypes in the dance world, and Pacific cultural issues'.

In combination with these explorations, Ieremia incorporated traditional Pacific dance motions, as well as a percussive element into his choreography. Narrative was also a factor, enabling his dancers to tell stories—Pacific stories that were both traditional and contemporary. This type of narrative, or movement as metaphor, has always been inherent in Pacific dance traditions. Adrienne Kaeppler (2002) noted that Tongan dance is metaphor in movement—it becomes a means of relaying information. The abstract nature of modern dance is, therefore, quite reflective of the abstract nature of traditional Polynesian dance. This enables a current audience (both Pacific and non-Pacific) to understand the art form—both audiences can read it.

Enacting the notion of indigenising the West is possible because of the role that Auckland (as the largest Pacific city) and New Zealand play in contemporary Pacific society. The concept of an urban Polynesian is one frequently used in New Zealand. The combination of an urban lifestyle with a Polynesian mindset is the reality for many as they forge an integrated, yet distinctly different, life. The village has morphed into a city. Factories and universities have replaced the plantation. New technologies and experiences combine to create the vibrant and distinct cultural lives that the diaspora produces. The hybrid of resistance remains even as indigenous peoples embrace Western materials and education. Makarita Urale commented 'it doesn't matter what tools we use, it matters what's in our minds'. [4]

This assertion supports Smith's belief that 'many indigenous intellectuals actively resist participating in any discussion within the discourses of post-coloniality. This is because post-colonialism is viewed as the convenient invention of Western intellectuals which reinscribes their power to define the world' (Smith 1999:14). One must, however, look at that fine line between actively participating in and subverting the dialogue. Pacific art practices work to negate the notion of hybrid by adopting it on their own terms. Using the technologies and education systems of the West, Pacific artists empower themselves with information and tools that enable them to innovate and create.

Hand in hand with the blossoming of the performing and visual arts in New Zealand was the growth of a street culture that not only infused energy into New Zealand's

Figure 6.4 › Pacific Sisters performing at the Seventh Festival of Pacific Arts , Samoa, 1996. Photograph courtesy of Karen Stevenson.

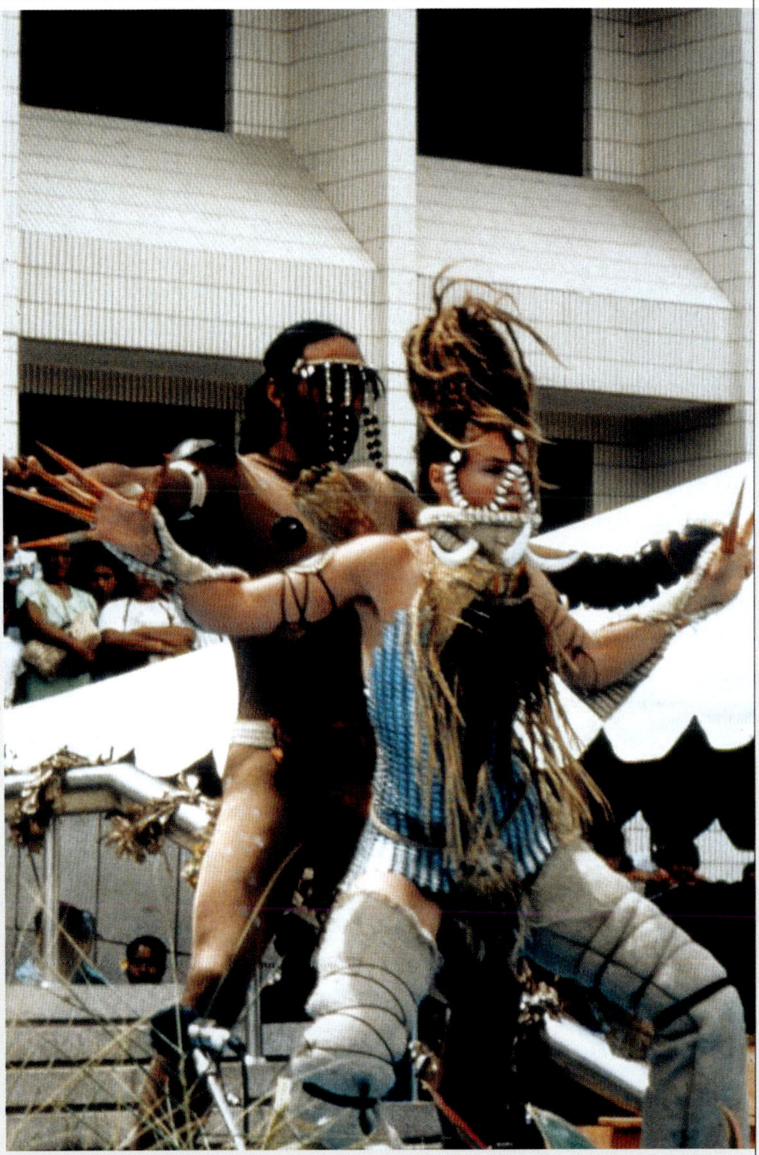

culture, but also created a symbiotic relationship between and amongst Pacific artists. At a time when academics were debating tradition and authenticity, and politicians were styling national identities, Pasifika was coming into its own. Music, hip hop, fashion, journalism, film, design and the visual arts combined to create events and cooperatives that would change the face of New Zealand art. Stacey Gregg summarised it: 'There's a new feeling abroad in this land. It's fresh. It's vibrant. And it's ours. Nobody else's. It's that Pacific sort of feeling'.[5]

Pasifika Festival, Pasifika Fashion Week, The Pacific Sisters, Pacific Underground, Pacific Theatre, Tahotahi ma Uo, the Tautai Contemporary Pacific Arts Trust—a new generation was creating a place for themselves. Theirs was a combined synergy—urban, raw, fresh—that moved beyond the traditions and cultural foundations offered by their parents: they were urban Polynesians. This is seen in a variety of art forms, perhaps most obviously in fashion, theatre, music and the visual arts. Pasifika fashion grew from a personal style amongst Pacific Islanders in Auckland. Lavalavas and jeans, cultural tattoos and Pacific inspired jewellery were combined to create a new style. This look, first seen in clubs, became known through pop culture media, in particular *Planet* magazine. Through the photography of Greg Semu **[figure 6.1]** and the styling of Rosanna Raymond, urban Pacific style became codified. Raymond noted:

> The clothing brands Standard Issue and Street Life were some other brave souls thinking outside the square . . . it was all so shocking then. But Planet was a great vehicle for us, putting them on the covers, doing stories on the artists, exposing a more positive picture of Polynesian culture to the mainstream—not just overstayer and machete stories. (Raymond 2002: 96)

Pacific youth began to see themselves and their culture in print. Combining fashion with an urban Polynesian look, Raymond created shows that brought together the talents of several fashion designers, artists and musicians to move this club energy onto the catwalk. Raymond (2002: 96) explained 'I would watch gangs of youth come to town from my window on Fridays from out South wearing lavalava around their jeans, or as bandannas—influenced by the new gangster rap thing which had been "Polyafied". They wore their jeans baggy and wore their dads' steel-capped boots . . . Pacific Island youth were considered leaders of style'.

Figure 6.5 › Rosanna Raymond, *La'a La'a Le Luga Fanua o Le Mata (A Walk in My Eyelands) —An Urban Excessification Installation for Open Skies Divided Horizons at Auckland Art Gallery Toi o Tāmaki*, 1997. Photograph courtesy of the artist.

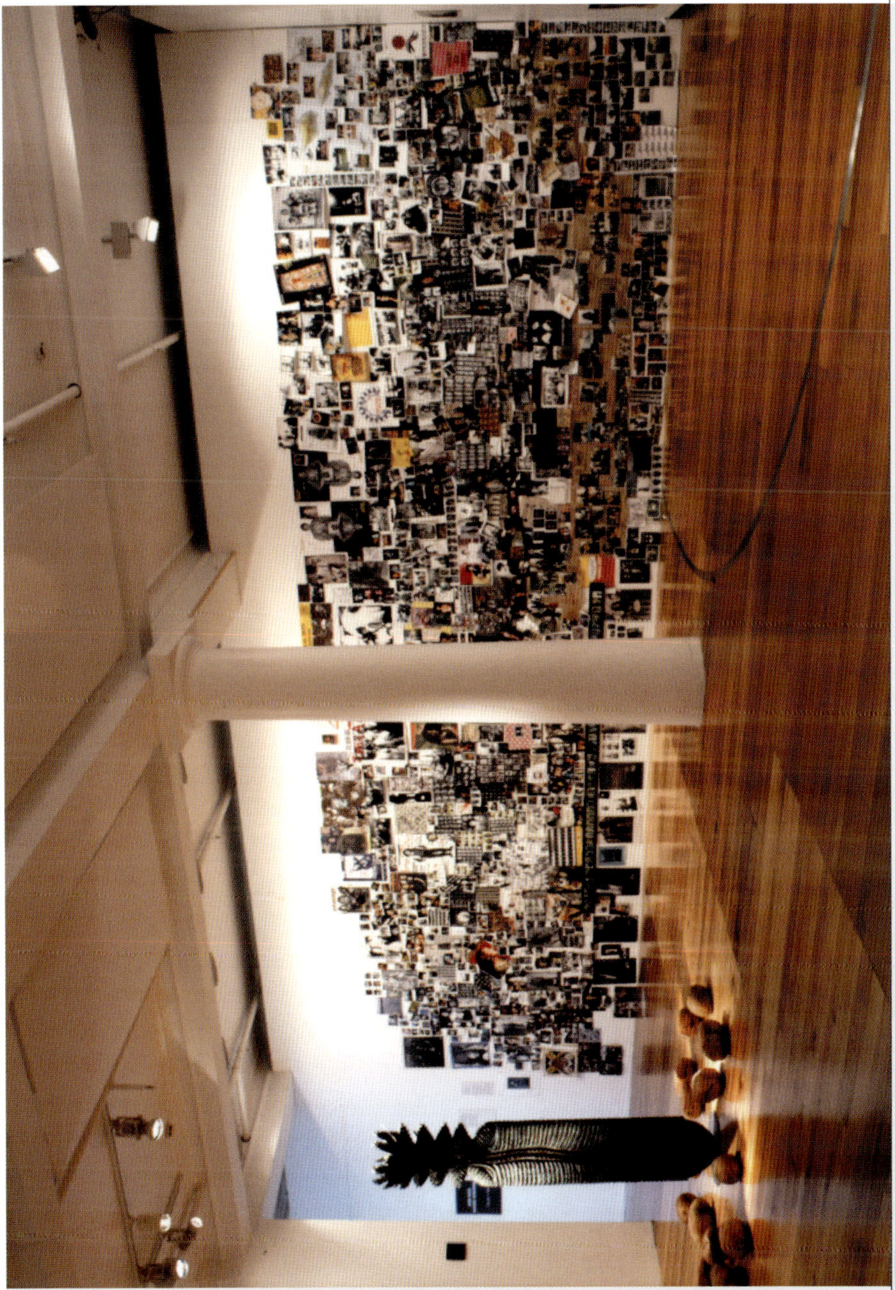

Designers such as Paula Chan-Cheuk, Janine Clarkson, Louis Fesola'i and Frances Palu created garments that were clearly Pacific, but nothing the Pacific had ever seen before. Not quite fashion, not white fashion—Pasifika. Drawing upon traditional designs and motifs (from tattoo, barkcloth and tivaevae), costume and adornment, they created for a new generation. The fashion industry, inspired by what was happening, instituted Pasifika (in 1993) as part of New Zealand Fashion Week. The introduction of categories such as bridal wear, evening wear and traditionally inspired, urban Pasifika streetwear created opportunities for designers to be both recognised for and supported in their endeavours.[6]

Fashion Week became the platform for designers to trial their Pasifika ideas. They focused their attention either on urban streetwear or on creating from a more traditional base.[7] Louis Fesola'i combined the formal Samoan/Tongan lavalava into a new line of menswear, while Paula Chan-Cheuk created a wedding dress from barkcloth. Frances Palu's linen suit, *Ta'ovala* **[figure 6.2]** incorporated a plaited (mat) design and feathers into the jacket, while the vest was made of crocheted raffia. The combination of streetwear, fashion, items of chiefly status and Pacific textile traditions created an interesting blend of the island and the urban. Drawing upon textile traditions, yet reinventing them for urban youth, Rosanna Raymond created *G'nang G'near* **[figure 6.3]**. Starting with a pair of Levi's and customising them with barkcloth, Raymond was asserting a visible Polynesian presence.[8] She comments, 'I was interested in making something . . . whole . . . from scraps . . . somewhat like my cultural makeup . . . repatriating the culture back to me . . . not recreating the past but using the past to make a relevant future for me, making my Polynesian heritage relevant to me as an urban NZ born islander'.[9] *G'nang G'near*, which was inspired by a group of artists working in Polynesian jewellery and clothing, was the first costume Raymond created for The Pacific Sisters.[10]

As a collective that included artists, photographers, designers, models and helpers, Pacific Sisters utilised the fashion show concept as a springboard for their performances. Traditional costumes were their initial inspiration, but then these artists let their imaginations run as they created ensembles that combined traditional materials (such as barkcloth, feathers and shells) with modern (such as metals, fish net stockings, video tape and op shop clothing) **[figure 6.4]**. Added to the visual explosion of these costumes were the sounds of the nightclubs—hip hop, reggae and rap—and a flamboyant showmanship often associated with drag shows. The Sisters created

Figure 6.6 › Rosanna Raymond, detail of *La'a La'a Le Luga Fanua o Le Mata (A Walk in My Eyelands)—An Urban Excessification Installation for Open Skies Divided Horizons at Auckland Art Gallery Toi o Tāmaki*, 1997. Photograph courtesy of the artist.

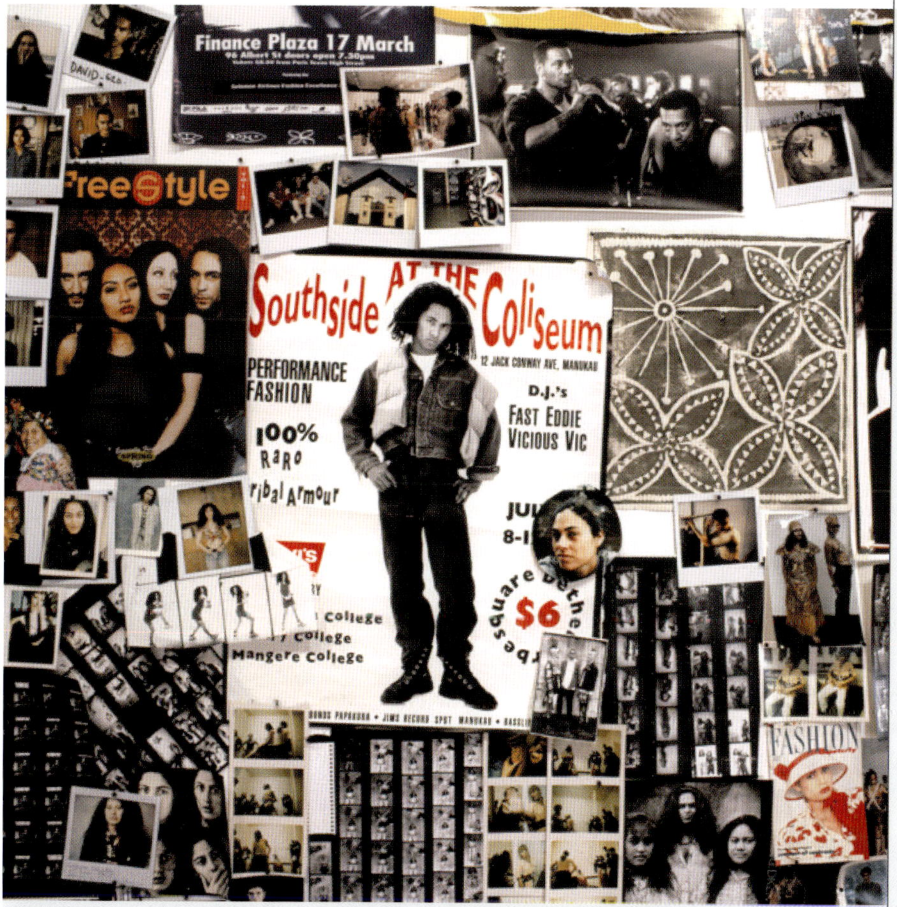

performances that reflected their heritage and, more importantly, mirrored their urban nights out. The energy created was contagious; the mainstream was dazzled.

The club scene became art. In 1997 Raymond brought together photo shoots, magazine covers, advertisements and photographs, 'the flotsam and jetsam of my life'[11] to create *La'a La'a Luga Le Fanua o Le Mata (A Walk in My Eyelands)* **[figures 6.5 and 6.6]**. This accumulation of urban imagery acknowledged the importance of Pasifika as new and as being vital to an urban Pacific identity. It also claimed Raymond's place positing a 'particular brand of eyeland cult'ya' (island culture).[12]

The energy of the urban Pacific, of youth culture and nightclubs was also buoyed by the music industry—by raves, DJ'ing and the hip hop phenomenon. Hip hop, reggae and rap were firmly embraced by Pacific musicians and DJs, who came to dominate the industry in the 1990s.[13] A key to hip hop development is the role of the producer and the creation of battles (where DJs compete against each other). As such, Phil Fuemana, K.O.S., Brother D and Pacific Underground played a large role in the growth of the industry at both the club level as well as through the creation and promotion of albums.

Phil Fuemana was instrumental in the development of Pacific hip hop. In 1994, he managed the *Proud: An Urban Pacific Streetsoul* tour (accompanied by a compilation CD), which included, amongst others, the Pacifikan Descendants, OMC and Sisters Underground. Although *Proud* is often cited as the beginning of Pacific hip hop, Fuemana observed that 'it didn't set the benchmark . . . all of us were already on that journey' (Fuemana quoted in Shute 2004: 45). Pacific hip hop hit the big time with OMC and their single *How Bizarre* (1996). Produced by Alan Jannson, who also produced the *Proud* tour and compilation, it combined Pauly Fuemana's Niuean background, a Pacific Island guitar style and hip hop beats to create a 'uniquely Polynesian sound with the current feel' (Shute 2004: 48). This was followed by Che Fu with *2 B S-Pacific* (1998) and *Urban Pacifika: Pioneers of a Pacifikan Frontier*, a 1999 compilation CD that included Dei Hamo, AKA Brown, Moizna, Lost Tribe and Bobby Owen. Sane Sagala (quoted in Shute 2004: 55) commented 'when he wasn't at the helm of Urban Pasifika Records, pushing all the artists, they just kinda folded, which proved that he was really the driving force behind most of the groups'.

Figure 6.7 › Brother D, *Brother D and the Dawn Raid Family, Element of Surprise*, 2007. Album artwork by Paul Jeffcoat & Andy Murnane. Photograph courtesy of Dawn Raid Entertainment. This compilation CD is titled 'Villijah Nation vol. 1' and includes a number of artists who use re-worked negative language to assert their Polynesian identity.

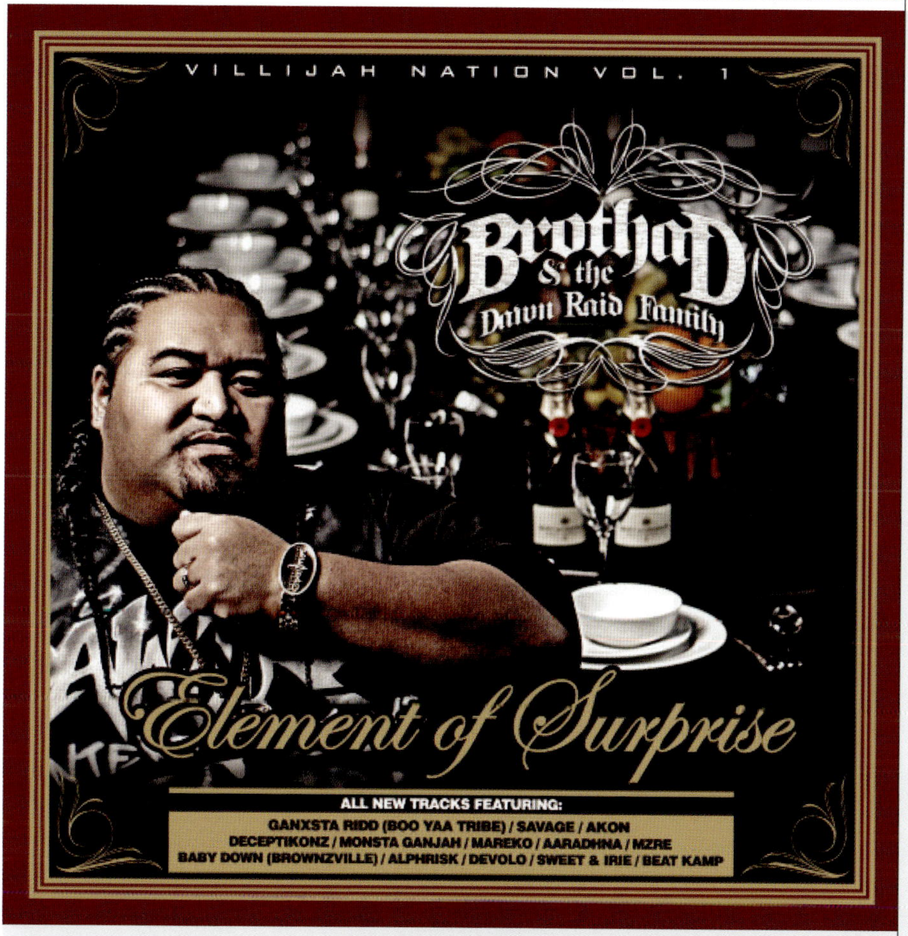

Some were critical of the move into the mainstream that these CDs represented; however, they also enabled the continued growth of the industry—an industry, which for the most part, supported club battles and young crews. Zemke-White (2002: 128) commented that 'this creative engagement has produced a dazzling array of singers, songs, dancers, mixes, rappers, fans, and events, allaying fears of homogenisation or loss, and making Aotearoa and the world a much richer place. Pacific pop music of all styles can be seen to represent resistance through revitalisation, interface, and remembrance'.

Hip hop was another vehicle for Pacific Islanders in New Zealand to make assertions about their identity. Names—a key aspect of DJ'ing—were important. The Pasifikans, Dei Hamo (they are Samoan), AKA Brown, Dam Native, Gifted and Brown, Overstayers, Token Village and Savage all make reference to a cultural heritage or a stereotype that they could own **[figure 6.7]**.[14] Using the stereotype and racial slurs enabled them to make positive statements about who they were and where they lived.

From the start the group was focused on presenting their perspective on life in Aotearoa from a Polynesian point of view. The name Lost Tribe was used to represent migrants who were unsure about where they fitted in contemporary society in Aotearoa, and the group saw themselves as representing these people, promoting unity among them and expressing the new culture they were developing (Shute 2004: 51).

King Kapisi (Bill Urale) did much the same, making his stories—Samoan stories—relevant to New Zealand.

Nonetheless, there is cultural critique in this genre. Often associated with gangsta rap from the United States, these artists address their realities in New Zealand. Urale believes that a culture needs to be addressed, not forgotten. Therefore, although the artists are buying into the music machine of the West, their underlying desire is to create a sound that evokes the needs, desires and future for Pacific peoples in New Zealand. Kristen Zemke-White (2002: 120) acknowledged that 'the Pacific personae and imagery of the music, as well as its community presence, demonstrate that it can be used to reflect and perpetuate modern Pacific identities, acknowledging a Pacific past, a New Zealand present, and a globally connected future.'

Figure 6.8 › Dawn Raid Entertainment, Cocoland T-shirt sampler. Photograph courtesy of Dawn Raid Entertainment.

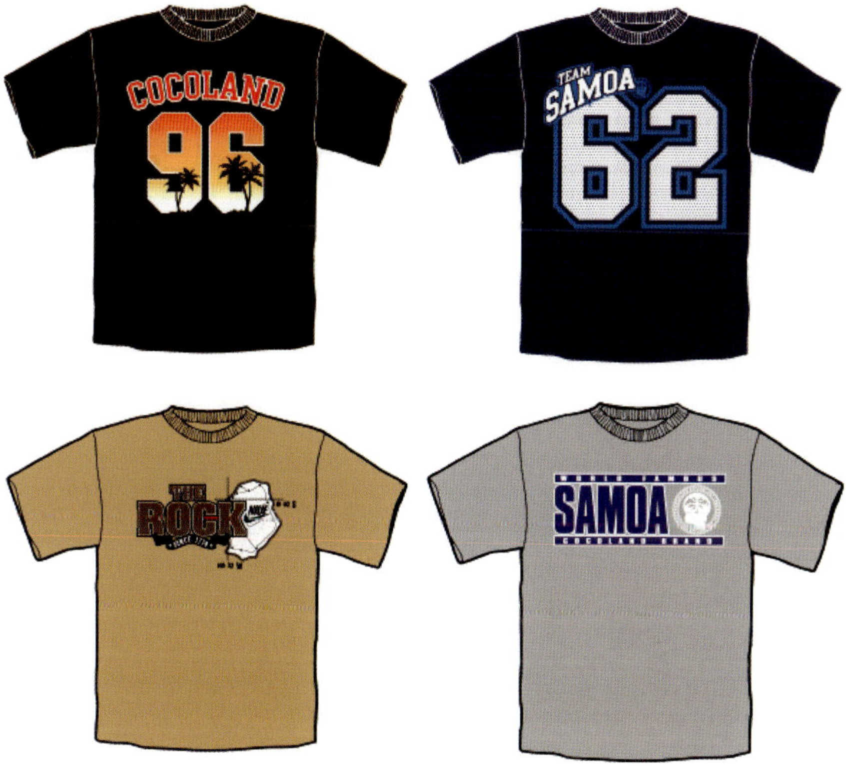

Music provided a platform from which a positive image of the Pacific could be created. Brother D, with Andy Murnane, created Dawn Raid Entertainment in 1999.[15] One of the ways that this was financed was through the development and sale of T-shirts at the Otara Market. The Cocoland label was created **[figure 6.8]**. Owning the stereotype, Cocoland incorporated international styles and logos into their T-shirts. The label became one arm of a conglomerate business that financially supported the fledgling Pacific music industry. Brother D (quoted in Shute 2004: 91) stated 'we just wanted to put out hip hop, that's what the aim has always been. If I can't put out my own I'm gonna back some young crews and get their work out there'.

Pacific hip hop in New Zealand was not just a sound, it was also an attitude, a look, a way of being Pacific. It created the possibility of creating and owning one's image. Beginning with Gifted and Brown, the Pacifikan Descendants, Sisters Underground and OMC, Pacific hip hop groups continue to lend their stories to the global music industry.

Hip hop is neither the only music genre to be colonised by Pacific peoples, nor was it the first. Bill Sevesi crowded the dance halls in the 1940s and 1950s, bringing steel guitar and the sounds of the islands to Auckland. In the 1970s, the Yandall Sisters popularised Pacific R & B, from which a number of singers emerged, especially in the 1990s. More easily appreciated (by an older, more traditional generation) than hip hop are Annie Crummer, Lole, Ma-V-Elle, Jamoa Jam and Ardijah, who all offered a Pacific take on the "softer" music that has always been appreciated in the Pacific. The Hawaiian song genre of the early 20th century—a genre that speaks of island breezes and romance—has been owned by every island, each offering their own distinctive stories. The band Te Vaka **[figure 6.9]** draws on this tradition, utilising indigenous language and drums, yet offering a contemporary take with an energised beat. All these artists not only provide a foundation for Pacific music, but maintain Pacific stories and traditions in contemporary New Zealand.

Thus, music—in conjunction with fashion—gave a voice to both a younger and an older generation. Pasifika generated stories—stories from home, stories of migration, stories of survival in a new land, stories voiced in new media. Popular culture—the street, youth magazines, music and music videos—was the next extension. The blend of fashion and the visual arts was also seen in the creation of artistic fashion T-shirts. Shigeyuki Kihara was one of the first to employ global marketing

Figure 6.9 › Te Vaka. Photograph courtesy of Julie Foa'i. www.tevaka.com

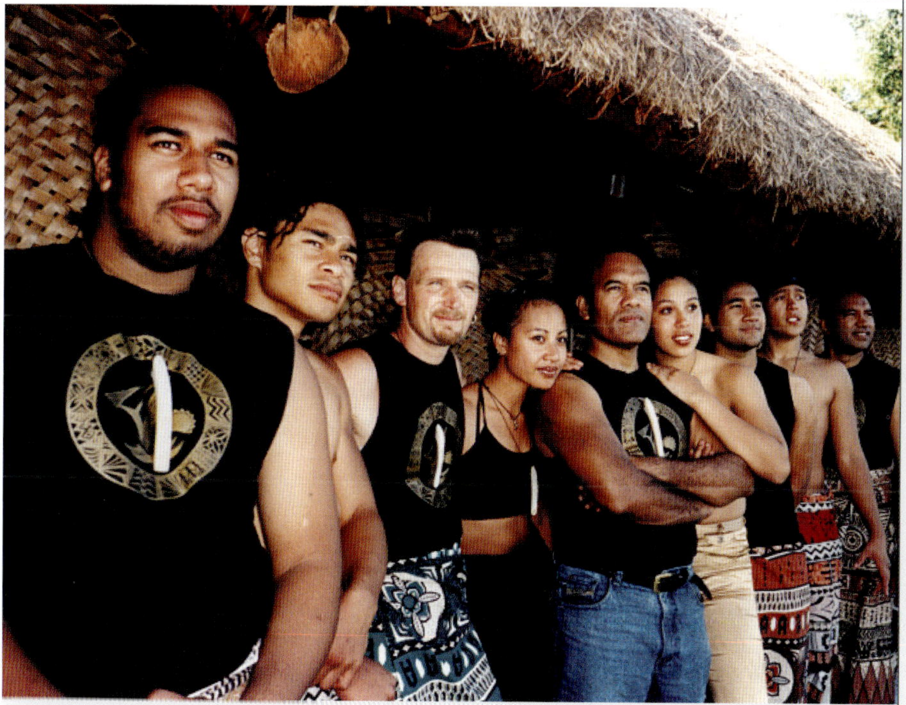

strategies to make statements about the cultural realities of Pacific Islanders in New Zealand. *Teuanoa'i (Adorn to Excess)*—a collection of twenty-eight T-shirts—is a work 'about an "Urban Pacific" identity at street level—a social commentary, indeed reality, reflected in the medium of clothing as art' (Kihara 2002: 101). Kihara's *Fobie* **[figure 6.10]**, a pink T-shirt with the head of a generic Pacific doll, moves beyond the Barbie stereotype it references, as she not only calls into question the whiteness of beauty, but also its hypocrisy, given that women of colour have been the objects of lust for centuries. These shirts also talk of community, of Otara and South Auckland, thereby owning the stereotype. T-shirts have 'been appropriated and indigenised by a new generation of Pacific Island designers. Racist words and phrases, together with slogans and brand names of multinational companies, have been reworked to speak to and reaffirm Pacific peoples' identity' (Mallon & Pereira 2002: 10).

The hybrid has been Pacified in the process of Pacific peoples choosing what aspects of their global reality to take on. Moving beyond the islands and the urban, between the local and the global market, Pacific Islanders have created an arts practice that embraces their myriad realities and interests. One aspect of this is the creation of a language and the metaphors that that language posits. Raymond's *La'a La'a Luga Le Fanua o Le Mata (A Walk in My Eyelands)* plays with words, as does the costume *G'nang G'near*. Not only does Raymond acknowledge the influence of gang life on Pacific youth, she notes:

> The 'Mongrel Mob' would patch their jeans in leather and getting your 'Patch' was entry into the gang . . . so issues of myself being a 'mongrel' afakasi (half caste) and also my entry into the Pacific Sisters . . . we weren't a gang but a collective concentrating on the celebration and continuum of age old traditions and finding space for them in the modern world . . . [16]

How artists position their identity in the art world becomes important, but also becomes maleable as they choose 'which break to catch'.[17] Their world has witnessed a Polynisation—Auckland has become a Polynesian city. Reflecting Auckland's status as the largest Polynesian city, Sheyne Tuffery's practice has envisioned it as a Pacific utopia. A futuristic blend of the island and the urban, Tuffery's utopia reinvents Samoan architecture by overlaying a futuristic, 'Jetsons', cartoon aesthetic. *New Samoan Confederate 1* **[figure 6.11]** draws on the past to create the future as

Figure 6.10 › Shigeyuki Kihara, *Fobie* from *Teuanoa'I — Adorn to Excess*, screen print, 1999. Photograph courtesy of Shigeyuki Kihara/Museum of New Zealand Te Papa Tongarewa (2001-0037-1/23).

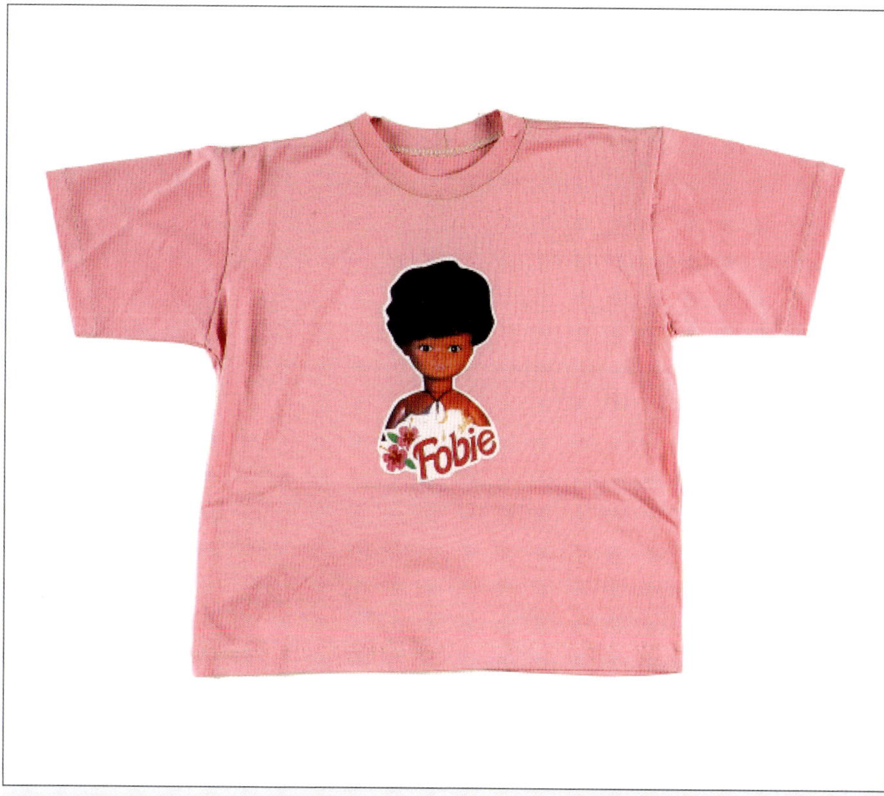

Samoan fale morph into skyscrapers. The imagery reflects key objects of Samoan material culture but also the architectual avant garde. Westernising traditional art forms, as well as indigenising Western art forms, Tuffery creates a Pacific vision for Auckland—one where the Pacific can not only become infused with the urban, but a place that urban Pacific peoples can call their own.

Greg Semu also looks to the city environment for inspiration, but his depiction is not of a utopia: it is rather of a place based in his own urban reality. The grit and graffitti of the day-to-day was the focus of his work in *Bottled Ocean* and Semu's photography conveys a strong sense of place, offering Pacific Islanders an ownership of Auckland. He also played an important role in the fashion industry, his photography being seen in numerous magazines. Semu was also a 'Pacific Sister'. Whether documenting the acquisition of tatau **[figure 2.4]** or providing a social context that is South Auckland, Semu addresses Pacific identities as they negotiate a new home.

The negotiation of two cultures underlies the practice of a number of Pacific artists—artists whose identity is a foundation for their work. This blending is not hybrid—those involved do not position themselves in that dialogue. Afakasi, a Samoan term for half-caste, is often used. It enables the assertion of an identity in tandem with the option of drawing upon various traditions. Greg Semu noted 'being born in New Zealand, of Samoan heritage, I often find myself alienated from both societies' (Brown 1996: 40–41). This is reiterated by Sheyne Tuffery, who explains, 'my work celebrates the afakasi, the halfcast—that confusion of not fitting into either side so you invent you own culture in art' (Tuffery quoted in Herrick 2002). In *Exit* **[figure 6.12]** Tuffery uses the coconut as a symbol of both Pacific Islanders and the afakasi (brown on the outside, white on the inside), thereby asserting a complex identity. The work, which is in black and white, does not scream Pacific; however, references to Samoan textiles are present. These contrasting ideas both reflect and establish the afakasi reality.

Interracial marriage, with its concomitant blending of cultures, language and traditions, is not a fantasy but the reality for many Pacific peoples. The reality of this genetic fusion is one addressed by Nanette Lela'ulu. Much of her early work is based on photographs, re-mixed and with a different take, so that they blend environments, thereby capturing and documenting the afakasi experience. Lela'ulu

Figure 6.11 › Sheyne Tuffery, *New Samoan Confederate 1*, woodblock print, 2000. Photograph courtesy of the artist.

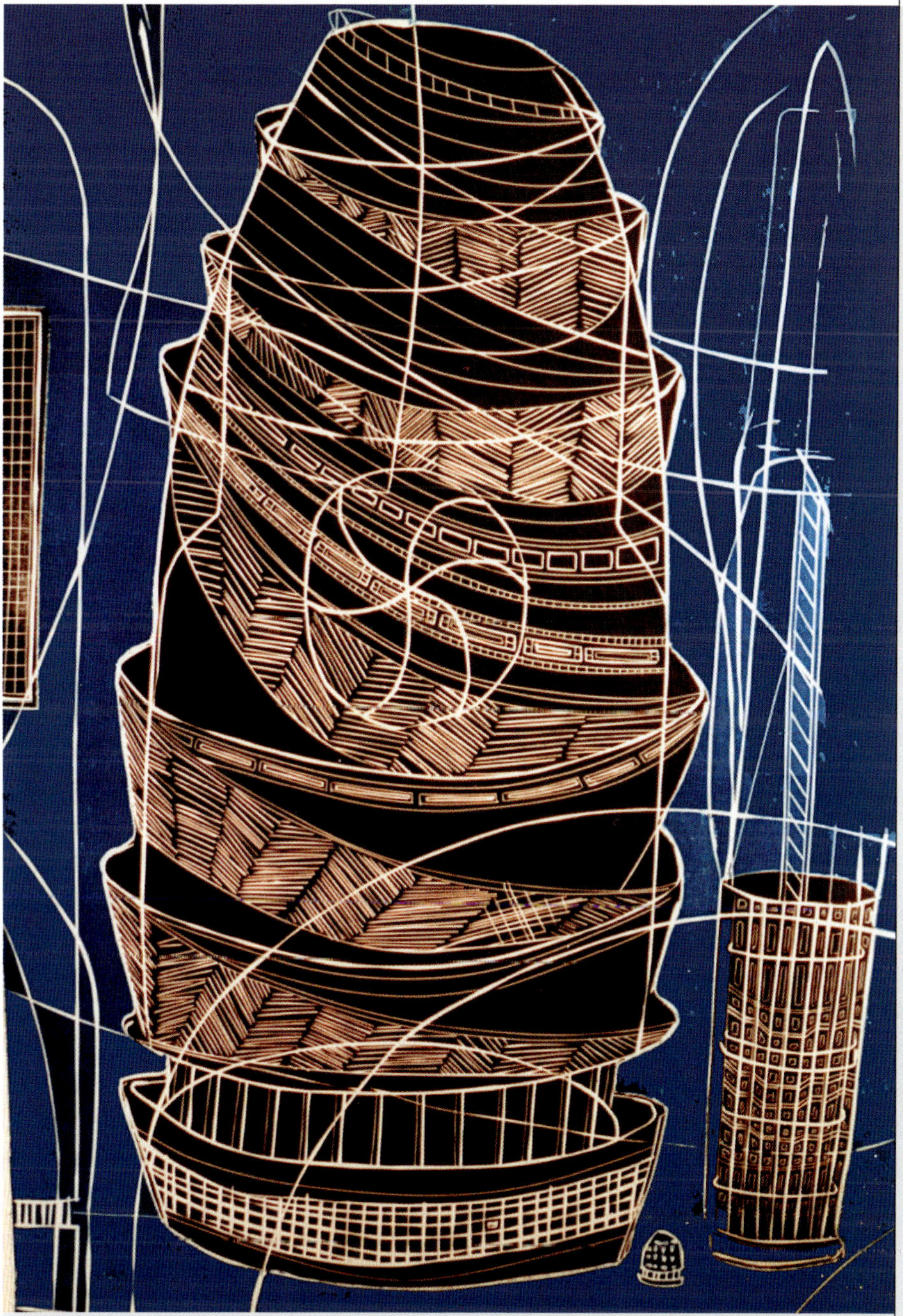

(quoted in Mallon 2002: 128) commented that 'through placing them together on one painting they become entwined and begin to represent a coming together of a new culture of people, namely the afakasi'.

Lela'ulu's practice creates the space for Pacific peoples to question who they are—to negotiate between the island and the urban. *Afakasi in Spanish Dress* **[figure 6.13]** problematises this issue, addressing the idea of mimicry, of becoming other. Lela'ula suggests not only a dressing up or drawing upon, but a choosing of one's identity.

The afakasi label can be problematic, however, since each person who embraces the label does so for different reasons. The question at heart is what is the difference between an afakasi growing up in Auckland and an afakasi growing up in Samoa? As Greg Semu (quoted in Brown 1996: 40) stated 'I feel like a tourist in my own home'. It is not only a question about nature versus nurture, it is a question of language and cultural knowledge; of not being torn by two conflicting agendas. This has been an underlying issue for contemporary Pacific artists. Asserting a Pacific identity creates a strong position in New Zealand, but also reflects islands, often not theirs. In Samoa, afakasi is a derogatory term, yet many artists like Sheyne Tuffery and Pauline Hoeft-Coker (who have both used coconuts in their work) embrace its negativity. Owning the label, they make strong assertions about their Pacific identity.

The importance of ownership is key—it is the underlying tenet of the Pasifika movement—a movement that caused tension, as Raymond (2002: 98) indicates when she said 'recognising that something powerful was happening, the elders resisted'. By 2000, however, this tension had eased. Time created understanding. In the early 1990s the audience for Pacific arts were not Pacific peoples. But times have changed and an older generation has embraced and supported these new voices. Elders have become "role models of possibility". As Anton Carter (2002: 153) noted, 'it is a voice of immigrant peoples, discovering new ways to speak taking on the responsibility, whether they realise it or not, of creating a new Pacific identity within New Zealand theatre and in a broader context the world'.

And so we find that fashion, music, theatre and dance have added to the contemporary Pacific arts in New Zealand. One could call them hybrid activities—one could also assert the Pacific's indigenisation of Western art forms. However, it is a blending

Figure 6.12 › Sheyne Tuffery, *Exit*, woodblock print, 1995. Photograph courtesy of the artist.

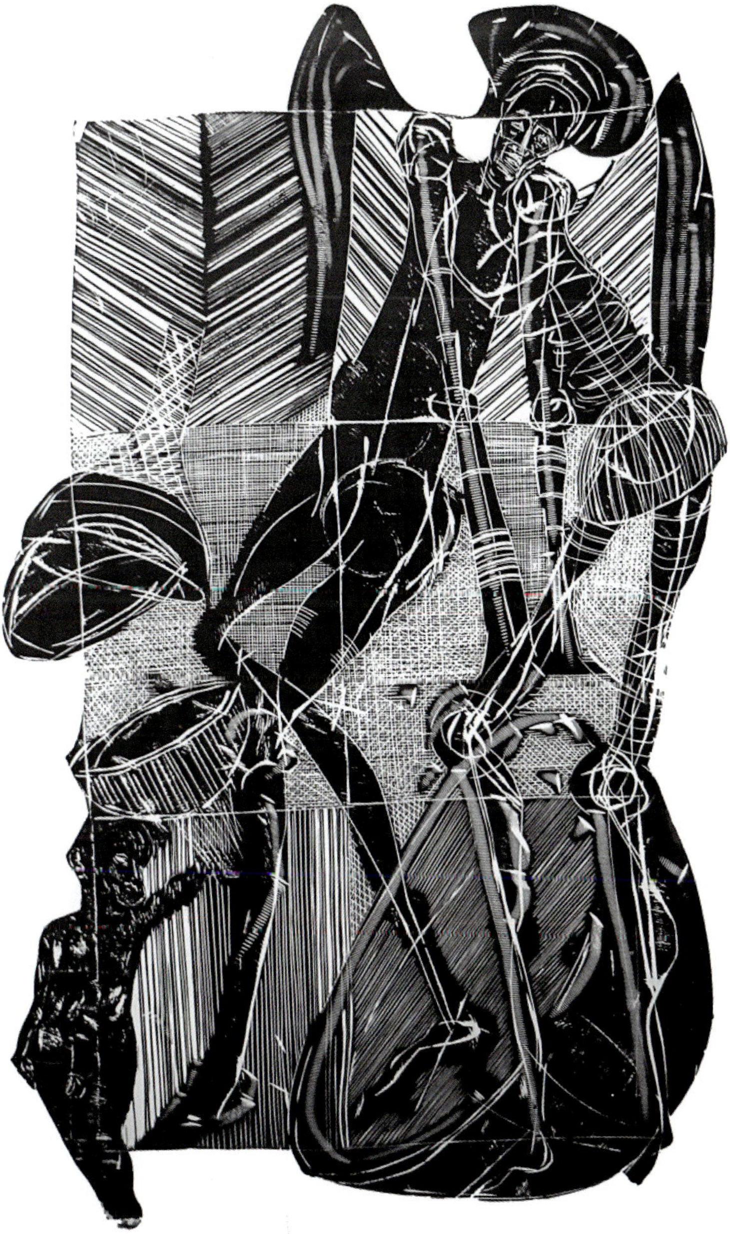

Figure 6.13 › Nanette Lela'ulu, *Afakasi in Spanish Dress*, 2000. Photograph courtesy of the artist.

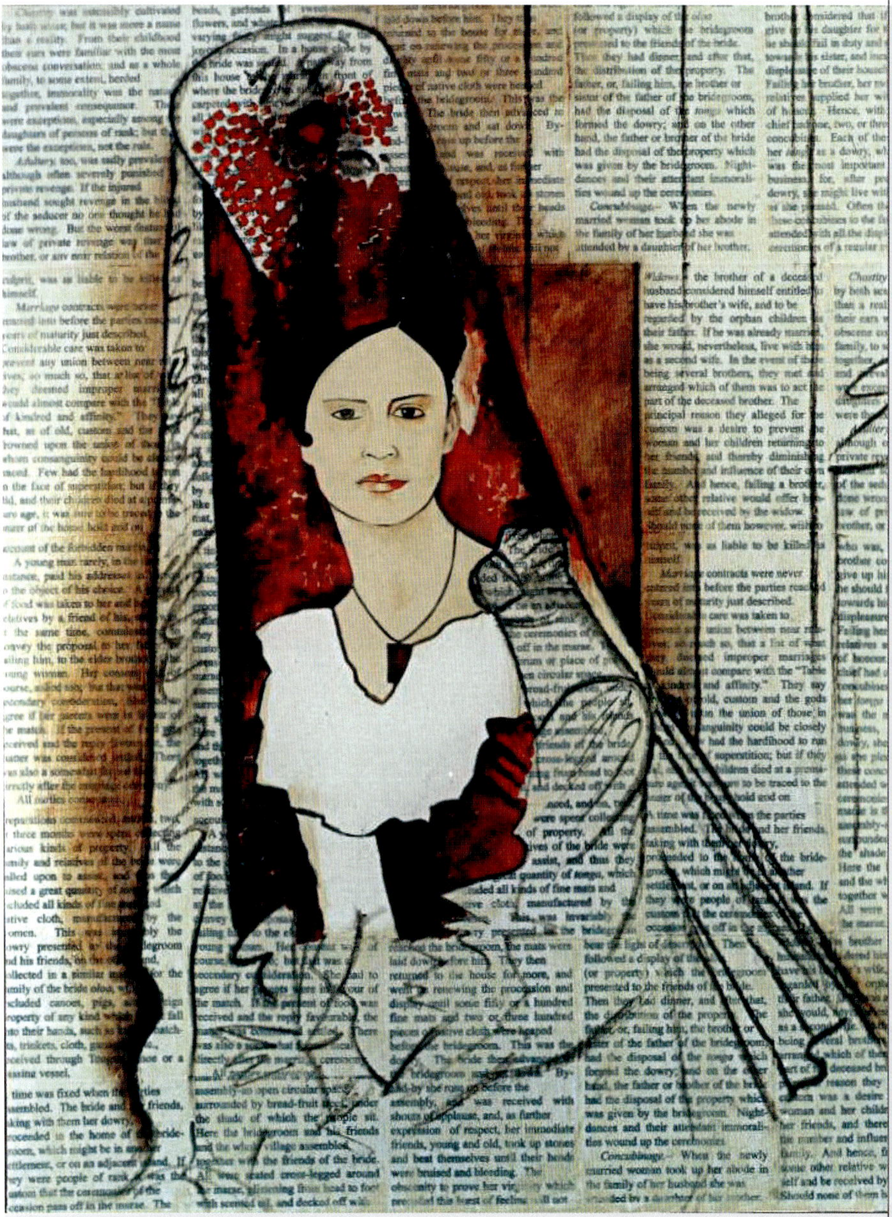

Figure 6.14 › Michael Tucker, *Polifusion. Loop* (November 2000). www.loop.co.nz. This was the cover image on *Loop* magazine, November 2000. It hearalded Pasifika and the new language of urban Pacific youth.

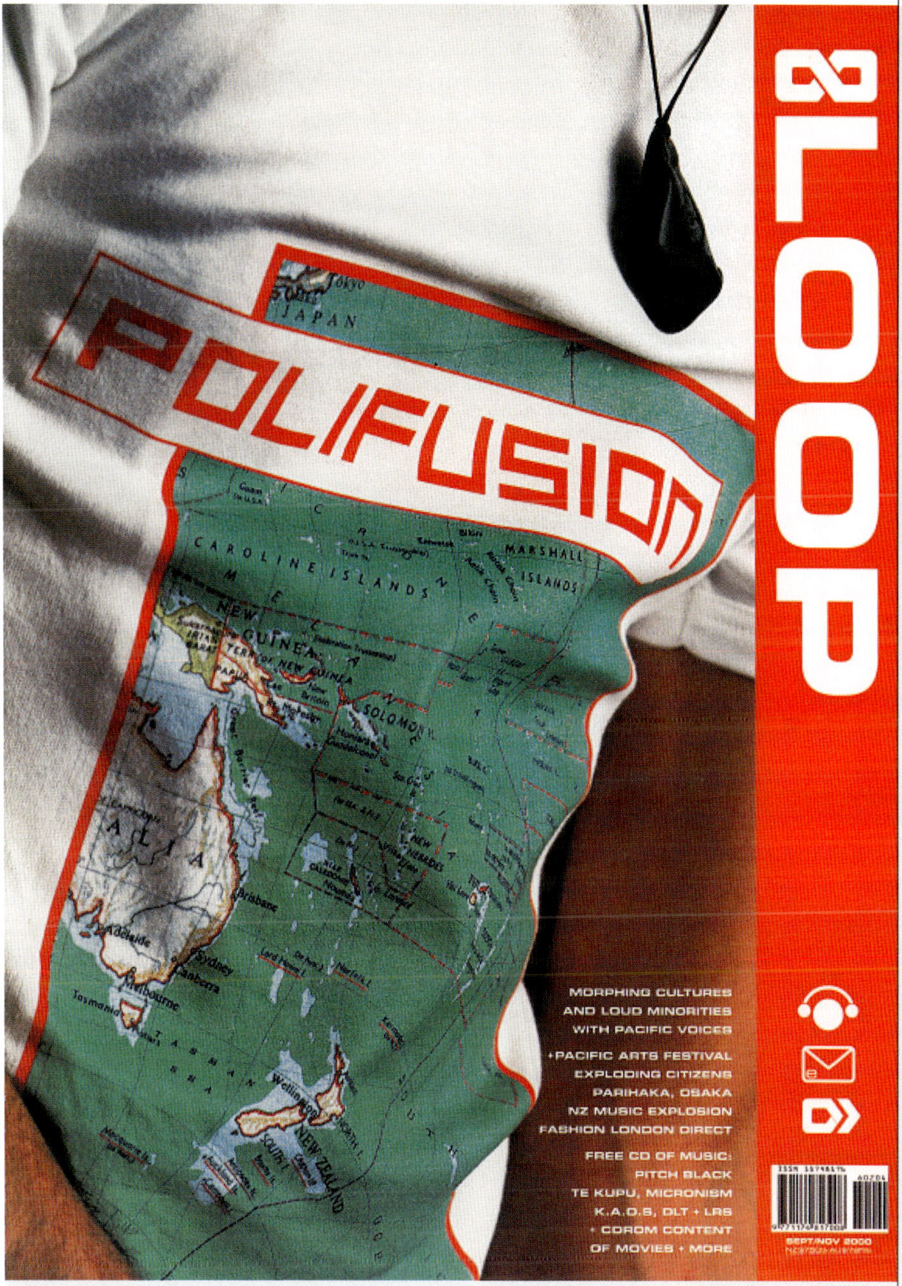

of these worlds—or the acknowledging of access to infinite possibilities—that energises these art forms. What becomes Pacific is the artist's position as a Pacific person—one whose voice, whose stories, whose histories are now being told. The interface between genres reinforces a new language.

A new Pacific reality is being posited. Within the academic world Pasifika epitomises the hybrid debate; but these young artists are not hybrid—they demand new terms that address their situation. No longer willing to embrace labels from the outside, they create their own. Polyafied, polifusion, polynisation **[figure 6.14]**—these words exemplify the synergies inherent in the visual and performing arts. Artists are creating new languages, moving beyond issues of identity, asserting a position here in New Zealand. The urban is not the island—but it is very much New Zealand spacifik.

APPENDIX 1
A Pacific Bibliography, 1985–2000

Amery, M. 1997. O'Neill makes herself at Rita's home. *Sunday Star Times*, 13 April, F14.

Amoamo, J. 1996. 'Outside In, Inside Out', in *Art New Zealand*, vol. 81, 82–83.

Anonymous. 1988a. Blending styles to produce unique art. *Manakau Courier*, 23 August, 22.

—— 1988b. Exploring Tradition in a New Way: Fatu Feu'u—Samoan Artist. *Accent*, September, 25–27.

—— 1989. Artist Contributes to Pathfinder Mural. *Central Leader*, 18 April, 12.

—— 1990. 3 Polynesian Artists: Fatu Feu'u, Ioane Ioane, Michel Tuffery. McDougall Art Annex, Christchurch.

—— 1992. The new wave, Pacific's palette. *New Zealand Herald*, 13 August, Section 3, 1.

—— 1993. Asia-Pacific triennial of art. *The Press*, 22 December, 14.

—— 1995a. Arts and culture: Paintings stir community. *Manu-Samoa International Weekly*, 16 May, 21.

—— 1995b. Touchy issue canvassed. *Manukau Courier*, 6 June, 1.

—— 1996. Samoan artist-in-residence starts. *The Chronicle*, 2 May, 1–2.

—— 1997a. 'Bulls of Fire', in *New Zealand Education Review*, 18 June, 1.

—— 1997b. Artist entwines culture and conservation in ocean work. *The Press*, 22 November, 2.

—— 1997c. 'Art in the Round', in *Pacific Wave*, November, 47.

—— 1998a. Te Aua Tiare. Fisher Gallery, Pakuranga.

—— 1998b. 'Artist fuses poetry and painting', in *Chronicle*, vol. 33, no. 17, 6.

—— 1998c. Creating Pacific Fashions. *Achievers '98*. Pacific Islands Business Development Trust, 6.

—— 1998d. Whanau, the inspiration for much of artist's work. *Kokiri Paetae*, February, 20–21.

—— 1999a. 'Renaissance', in *Te Tupu Ake*. Noumea: Centre Culturelle Tjibaou.

—— 1999b. Romantic Notions.

—— 1999c. 'Telling Stories', in *Art News*, Autumn, 29.

—— 1999d. 'Offshore Currents, Pacific Art Heats Up', in *Art News*, Autumn, 30–33.

—— 1999e Paintings to squirm to. *The Press*, 18 August, 17.

—— 2000. 'SCA joins the Olympic spirit with exhibition', in *Campus Review*. 13–19 September, 44.

Bagnall, D. 1995. South Pacific Chic. *The Bulletin*, 28 March, 95.

Baysting, A. 1999. 'Pacific Vision, Fashion's New Wave', in *Pacific Wave*, July, 8–11.

Brown, H. 1996. 'Cultural nomad: Greg Semu, photographer, looks to be in the right place at the right time', in *New Zealand Listener and TV Times*, 7 December, 40–41.

Brownson, R. 1998. 'Andy Lelei. Conversation at the Dead Mango Studio with Ron Brownson', in *Art New Zealand*, Winter, vol. 87, 38–40, 77.

Cartwright, G. 1986. 'New Stone Age', in *New Zealand Listener and TV Times*, 6 December, 56–58.

—— 1987. Artist's dream is now reality. *New Zealand Herald*, 26 November, 3.

—— 1988a. 'Fatu Feu'u', in *Pacific Way*, May, 65–66.

—— 1988b. 'Tapping Tapa', in *Metro*, July, 220–221.

—— 1989.'Visual Arts', in *More,* April, 159–161.

Chamberlain, J. 1996. 'Paint for Me Dreamer', in *North & South*, July, 12–13.

Chiu, M. 1998. *Pasifika*. Canberra: Contemporary Art Space.

Clarke, J. 1999. Jewellery to get under the skin. *Sunday Star Times*, 28 November, F3.

Cochrane, S. 1995. 'Art in the Contemporary Pacific', in *Art and AsiaPacific*, vol 2, no. 4, 50–59.

—— 1996a. 'Pacific Stories from New Caledonia', in *Artlink*, Pacific Issue, vol. 16, no. 4, 52–53.

—— 1996b. 'Pacific Peoples: Papua New Guinea, New Caledonia, Vanuatu, Torres Straight, Indigenous Australia', in the *Second Asia-Pacific Triennial of Contemporary Art*. Brisbane: Queensland Art Gallery.

—— 1997. 'All Natural: Pacific Art in its own Environment', in *Object*, 3.

—— 1999. 'Pacific-ness' in *Beyond the Future, the Third Asia-Pacific Triennial of Contemporary Art*, Queensland Art Gallery, Brisbane.

—— 2000a. *Shrines for the Next Millennium*. Sydney Olympics, Art Festival.

—— 2000b. 'Arts Today in the Pacific (recent and contemporary art)', in B. Lal et al (eds.) *The Pacific Islands, an Encyclopaedia*. Canberra : Australian National University.

Courtney, B. 1997. Cook Islands sewing circle inspires artist. *The Dominion*, 19 July, 27.

Cross, M. 1993 'Liku and the New Hiapo of John Pule', in *Art New Zealand*, Autumn, 43–45.

Dale, R. 1990. A foot in each culture. *New Zealand Herald*, 25 January, Section 3, 12.

—— 1995. 'Theatre de Poche', in *Art New Zealand*, vol. 77, 60–63.

Davis, Z. 1998. 'Pacific Sisters, Celebrating the heart of Polynesia', in *New Zealand Fashion Quarterly*, Summer, 127.

Dunbar, A. 1999. Pacific jewel. *The Press*, 27 October, 33.

Dunn, M. 1993. 'National Identities: The First Asia-Pacific Triennial of Contemporary Art', in *Art New Zealand*, vol. 69, 34–37.

Ewington, J. 1996. 'Ani O'Neill on the Town', in *Midwest Nine*, 19–21.

Feu'u, F. 1995. 'Samoan Artists in Samoa and New Zealand', in *Art and AsiaPacific*, vol. 2, no. 4, 60–67.

Findlay, K. 1991. 'I Explore these Motifs to Remember Our Past as Samoans', in *New Zealand Listener*, 24 June, 52–53.

——. 1992. 'Hands-on Art', in *New Zealand Listener and TV Times*, May, 47.

French, Br. 1997. *'inei/konei: The Pacific in photo art from Aotearoa*. Sydney: Australian Centre for Photography.

Gallagher, K. 1999. *Dagmar Vaikalafi Dyck Works*. Auckland: Dagmar Dyck.

Gardiner, S. 1996. 'Tapa for Today', in *Pacific Way*, October, 37.

Giakoumi, D. 1999. 'Centre Culturel Tjibaou, A New Meeting Place in the Pacific', in *Art AsiaPacific*, vol. 21, 27–29.

Gibbs, P. 1991. 'Fibre Art Symposium in Wanganui', in *New Zealand Listener and TV Times*, 18 February, 65–66.

Gregg, S. 1990. 'Fatu Feu'u', in *More*, February, 40.

Griffin, J. 1992. 'Southern Presence: Meetings with Five Pacific Artists', in *Art New Zealand*, vol. 64, 87.

Gunn, M. 1989. 'Michel Tuffery', in *FRAME*, 8–9.

Haldane, V. 1995. 'Having Fun in Fashion', in *Mana*, vol. 8, 29–31.

Hastings-McFall, N. 1997. *Past Pacific*.

Henderson, I. 1998. 'Sum Niu Mahi', in *CANTA*, vol. 24, 8.

Hunter, S. 1997. 'New Form from Old', in *Pacific Wave*, June, no. 106, 45.

Iosefa, S. 1997a. Return to paradise. *The Press*, 30 July, 13.

—— 1997b.The artist as dabbler. *The Press*, 13 August, 13.

Johnson, M. 1991. 'Te Mata Alea', in *Greenstone Paunamu*, vol. 1, 10–11, 13.

Kirker, A. 1993. 'Michel Tuffery', in the *First Asia-Pacific Triennial of Contemporary Art*. Brisbane: Queensland Art Gallery.

Knight, S. 1998. 'Untitled', in *Polynesia*, September/November, 5.

Laird, T. 1998. 'An art less ordinary', in *New Zealand Listener*, 31 October, 38–39.

Lay, G. 1996. *Pacific New Zealand*. (Photographs by Evotia Tamua.) Auckland: David Ling Publications.

Leilua, J. 1998. 'Pasifika Fashion', in *Southern Skies*, June, 36–37.

Losche, D. 1997. 'Nervous Culture', in *Art AsiaPacific*, vol. 15, 34–35

Mallon, S., & Pereira, P. F. 1998. *Speaking in Colour*. Wellington: Te Papa Tongarewa.

Mane-Wheoki, J. 1995a. 'Robyn Kahukiwa: My Ancestors are with Me Always', in *Art New Zealand*, vol. 75, 60–63. Reprinted in *Toi Ata-Robyn Kahukiwa: Works from 1985–1995*. Wellington: Bowen Galleries.

—— 1995b. 'The Resurgence of Maori Art: Conflicts and Continuities in the Eighties', in *The Contemporary Pacific*, vol. 7, no. 1, 1–19.

—— 1996. 'A Recentered World: Post European/Pro-Indigenous Art from Aotearoa/New Zealand and Te Moana-a-Kiwa/The South Pacific', in the *Second Asia-Pacific Triennial of Contemporary Art*. Brisbane: Queensland Art Gallery.

McAloon, William. 1992. CSA exhibition on Pacific Islands. *The Press*, 26 March, 19.

—— 1994. 'Kia Ora Tolls Here', in *Art New Zealand*, vol. 70, 46–48.

McCarthy, A. 1990. 'Adding Colour to Life in Rarotonga', in *Pacific Islands Monthly*, May, vol. 60, no. 5, 21–22.

McNamara, T. J. 1992. Youth upstages installation. *New Zealand Herald*, 28 May Section 2, 2.

Meduna, V. 1996. NZ Polynesian art features at triennial. *The Press*, 18 September, 14.

Meredith, K. 1988. Struggling artist no longer. *The Auckland Sun*, 1 July, 9.

Naigulevu, M. 1995. 'Beyond Proud/One Culture', in *Planet*.

Neale, M. 1996a. 'A Pacific Story, Screw the Rim: We Live in the Basin', in the *Second Asia-Pacific Triennial*. Brisbane: Queensland Art Gallery.

—— 1996b. 'The Waka and the Cattle Truck', in *Artlink*, Pacific Issue, vol. 16, no. 4, 18–21.

—— 1999. 'Pacific Crossings', in *Beyond the Future, the Third Asia-Pacific Triennial of Contemporary Art*. Brisbane: Queensland Art Gallery.

Nelson, R. 1999. Is jewellery useless? It's a lei-down misere. *Melbourne Age*, 19 December, D10.

Newth, K. 1999. Sculptors making it big with millennium grants. *Sunday Star Times*, 10 October, A5.

Page, M. 1997. 'Treasure Trove', in *Art AsiaPacific*, vol. 14, 26–27.

Pain, C. 1988. 'Half-caste' artist unifies cultures. *Otago Daily Times*, 10 November, 20.

Panoho, R. 1990. *Te Moemoea no Iotefa, The Dream of Joseph: A Celebration of Pacific Art and Taonga*. Wanganui: Sarjeant Gallery.

—— 1992. 'Maori: At the Centre, On the Margins', in M.Barr (ed.) *Headlands: Thinking Through New Zealand Art*. Sydney: The Museum of New South Wales.

Paton, J. 1995. Dissident and gleeful Polynesian exhibition. *The Press*, 27 September, 16.

—— 1996. 'Travel Agency: Exporting New Zealand Art', in the *Second*

Asia-Pacific Triennial. Brisbane: Queensland Art Gallery.

—— 1997. Snapshots of Auckland on a good day. *New Zealand Herald*, 14 February, B5.

Peoples, J. D. 1993. 'Exhibitions, Auckland', in *Art New Zealand*, vol. 68, 40–41.

Peterson, G. 1998. *Fireworks: Art of Pacific Age*. Auckland: Author.

—— 1999. *Ring of Fire*. Auckland: Author.

Pule, J., & Tekela Smith, S. 1999. 'Polynesian Holiday', in *Log*, vol. viii, 32–33.

Rabbe, E. 1995. 'Modernism or Folk Art: The Reception of Pacific Art in Europe', in *Art and AsiaPacific*, vol. 2, no. 4, 96–103.

Rae, B. 1995. Escapade into culture. *The New Zealand Herald*, 14 June, 1.

Refiti, A. 1996. 'Migrating Bodies: Contemporary Art Practices in New Zealand', in the *Second Asia-Pacific Triennial*. Brisbane: Queensland Art Gallery.

—— 2000. 'The Death of a God: a Performance over Time and Space', in *John Pule, People Get Ready*. Auckland: Auckland Art Gallery.

Rewi, A. 1996. Residency boosts Pacific art. *The Press*, 10 July, 15.

—— 1997a. A crafty way with furniture. *Sunday Star Times*, 19 October, F8.

—— 1997b. A new perspective on turning turtle. *Sunday Star Times*, 7 December, 12.

—— 1997c. Pacific art empowers the people. *Sunday Star Times*, 21 December, F2.

—— 1998. Pule's poetry and passion. *The Press*, 11 October, F8.

Ross, T. 1997.'Rubbish Problem Inspires Corned Beef Tin Bulls', in *The Chronicle*, vol. 32, no. 15, 4.

Sayle, J. 1992. Splashes of colour amid winter's gloom. *The Dominion*, 14 May, 22.

Schaer, C. 1998. Pasifika. *Sunday Star Times*, 8 March, 5–6.

Schamroth, H. 1998. *100 New Zealand Craft Artists*. Auckland: Godwit Press.

—— 1999. *HeadHandsHeart*. Christchurch: Centre of Contemporary Art.

Sharp, I. 1988. 'John Pule', in *Pacific Way*, vol. 12, 46, 51.

—— 1997. 'Heart of Stone', in *Pacific Way*, vol. 105, 50.

Shaw, P. 1989. 'Lively Arts Confronting the Modern World', in *Metro*, February, 152–153.

Shennan, J. 'Pacific Panoply', in *New Zealand Listener*, 26 October, 40–41.

Shopland, A. R. 1992. 'Dream Patterns', in *New Zealand Listener and TV Times*, 17 October, 50.

Simpson, E. 1999. 'Dusky Maiden', in *New Zealand House & Garden*, July, 105–108.

Simpson, Peter. 1998. Niue at heart of artist's work. *Sunday Star Times*, 19 July: F3.

Smith, A. 1995. 'What Shall We Do With Our Walls?', in *Art New Zealand*, vol. 74, 42–45.

—— 1997. Creation from a base of pain. *Sunday Star Times*, 6 April, F2.

Smith, J. 1994/5. 'Art for the Young, Muka Studio's Youth Prints', in *Art New Zealand*, vol. 73, 42–44.

Stacey, G. 1988a. 'Tautai and the Art of the South Pacific', in *Art New Zealand*, Spring, 87–89.

—— 1988b. 'The Art of Fatu Feu'u', in *Art New Zealand*, Summer, 48–51.

Stevenson, K. 1996a. 'Polynesian Tattoo', in *Artlink*, Pacific Issue, vol. 16, no. 4, 32–33.

—— 1996b. 'Art and Identity: Contemporary Pacific Artists in New Zealand', in *Bulletin of New Zealand Art History*, vol. 17, 59–68.

—— 1997a. 'Picturing Paradise', in *Art AsiaPacific*, vol 13, 28–30.

—— 1997b. 'Wicked Magic: The Seventh Pacific Festival of Arts', in *Art AsiaPacific*, vol. 14, 22–24.

—— 1997c. 'Identities', in F.Gunn (ed.) *Identikit*. Christchurch.

—— 1998a. 'Negotiating Tradition: The Art of Lily Laita and Ani O'Neill', in *Art AsiaPacific*, vol. 18, 68–73.

—— 1998b. *O's and X's, Veronica Vaevae*. Christchurch: School of Fine Arts Gallery.

—— 1998c. *Paringa Ou, Something Old Something New. Cook Islands Artists.* Cook Islands Museum and the Fiji Museum.

—— 1998d. *Sum Niu Mahi, Lily Laita.* Christchurch: School of Fine Arts Gallery.

—— 1999a. 'Creating Together/Wake Naima', in *Art AsiaPacific*, vol. 21, 29–31.

—— 1999b. 'Pacific Art: Moving Beyond the Stereotype', in *Art New Zealand*, Autumn, no. 90, 64–69.

—— 2000a. 'Po Ma Te Ao: Pacific Island Artists Creating in a Space Between', in *Biennale D'art Contemporain de Noumea*. Noumea: Agence de dévelopment de la Culture Kanak.

—— 2000b. 'Looking to the Past to Ensure the Future', in *Objects with Meaning New Directions in South Island Craft*. Christchurch: Centre of Contemporary Art.

—— 2000c. 'Another Introduced Species? Michel Tuffery, an Artist with a Conscience', in *2000 Biennial, Contemporary Visual Arts Festival*. Christchurch: Art & Industry.

Stewart, K. 1994. 'Clean, Clear and Brave; A New Exhibition Successfully Gathers Artists Rather Than Art', in *New Zealand Listener*, 2 July, 43.

—— 1996a. Craft not art. *Sunday Star Times*, 22 January, D4.

—— 1996b. A rare view of the Pacific way. *Sunday Star Times*, 24 March, F2.

—— 1997. Rushes of powerful, emotional colour. *Sunday Star Times*, 11 May, F2.

Stringer, T. 1996. Diverse group passes the screen test. *Sunday Star Times*, 11 August, F2.

Strongman, L. 1996. 'Taking it on Board', in the *Second Asia-Pacific Triennial of Contemporary Art*. Brisbane: Queensland Art Gallery.

Swain, P. 1991. Visual essays of the Pacific. *The Dominion*, 20 July, 10.

Taouma, Lisa. 1996. ' Nukututaha, A Place to Stand', in *Art New Zealand*, vol. 82, 40–43.

—— 1997 *Ani O'Neill, Cottage Industry*. Wellington: City Gallery.

—— 1999a. 'Velvet Dreams', in *Art AsiaPacific*, vol. 23, 38–39.

—— 1999b. 'Tahiono Arts Collective, Altar-ed States and the Work of the Tahiono Collective', in *Beyond the Future, the Third Asia-Pacific Triennial of Contemporary Art*. Brisbane: Queensland Art Gallery.

Thomas, Nicholas. 1994a. 'What Shall We Tell Them? Pacific Art, Politics and Culture', in *Art and AsiaPacific*, vol. 1, no. 4, 28–31.

—— 1994b 'Lost Gods: The Paintings of John Pule', in *Art and AsiaPacific*, vol.1, no. 4, 96–103.

—— 1995a. 'Bottled Ocean: Shape Shifting', in *Art and AsiaPacific*, vol. 2, no. 4, 44–45.

—— 1995b. 'Reflections on South Pacific Art', in *Art and AsiaPacific*, vol. 2, no. 4, 16–18.

—— 1995c. 'Pacific Dualities: Bottled Ocean in Wellington and Auckland', in *Art New Zealand*, vol. 74, 46–50.

—— 1995d. *Oceanic Art*. London: Thames and Hudson.

—— 1996a. 'The Dream of Joseph: Practices of Identity in Pacific Art', in *The Contemporary Pacific*, vol. 8, no. 2, 291–317.

—— 1996b. 'From Exhibit to Exhibitionism: Recent Polynesian Presentations of "Otherness"', in *The Contemporary Pacific*, vol. 8, no. 2, 319–348.

—— 1996c. 'Contemporary Art and the Limits of Globalisation', in the *Second Asia-Pacific Triennial of Contemporary Art*. Brisbane: Queensland Art Gallery.

—— 1997a. 'Marked Men', in *Art AsiaPacific*, vol. 13, 66–73.

—— 1997b. *Born in Paradise*. Auckland: Gow Langsford Gallery.

—— 1999. *Possessions: Indigenous Art/Colonial Culture*. London: Thames and Hudson.

—— 2000. 'Pulenoa: without Consent', in *John Pule, People Get Ready*. Auckland: Auckland Art Gallery.

Thompson, K. 1998. Tohi takes sculpting skills to school. *The Daily News*, 2 September, 1.

Tiatia, J. 1998. *Caught Between Cultures: a New Zealand Born Pacific Island Perspective*. Auckland: Christian Research Association.

Tiavouane, D. 1996. 'Soapstone Workshop', in *Artlink*, Pacific Issue, vol. 16, no. 4, 55.

Timms, P. 2000. Twist on traditional is nothing more. *Melbourne Age*, 19 January, B5.

Tyler, Linda. 1997. 'Badges of Courage', in *Art New Zealand*, vol. 83, 47–49.

Vaigro, W. 1995. 'Bottled Ocean: Shape Shifting', in *Art and AsiaPacific*, vol. 2, no. 4, 44–45.

Vandenberg, M. 1989. Blending Pacific and European. *The Press*, 17 May, 21.

Venning, E. 1998. Catalyst for appreciation of Pasifika. *The Press*, 5 August, 16.

Vercoe, C. 1996. 'Postcards as Signatures of Place', in *Art AsiaPacific*, vol. 3, no. 1, 84–89.

—— 1999. 'Navigating Pacific Art', in *Art AsiaPacific*, vol. 22, 34–35.

Vercoe, C., & Leonard, R. 1997. 'Pacific Sisters: Doing It for Themselves', in *Art AsiaPacific*, vol. 14, 42–45.

Vivieaere, J. 1994. *Bottled Ocean*. Wellington City Gallery.

—— 1996. 'The Island Race in Aotearoa', in *Artlink*, Pacific Issue, vol. 16, no. 4, 57.

—— 1999. 'Michel Tuffery and Patrice Kaikilekofe, a One-night Stand, in *Beyond the Future: The Third Asia-Pacific of Contemporary Art*. Brisbane: Queensland Art Gallery.

Walker, P. 1989. 'On View, Double Dugong', in *New Zealand Listener and TV Times*, 27 May, 64.

Walker, T. 1994. 'Everything is Connected: The Art of Michel Tuffery', in *Art New Zealand*, vol. 70, 64– 67.

Watson, M. 1999. Scultpor's art links cultures and times. *The Daily News*, 10 April, 17.

West, N. 1995. 'Art and the Bomb', in *Art New Zealand*, vol. 78, 40–42.

Whyte, R. 1992. 'Look for . . . ', in *New Zealand Listener and TV Times*, 14 November, 48.

Wynyard, J. 1996. Stone art hard to live with at home. *Sunday Star Times*, 11 February, A4.

Zepke, S. 1996. 'Connecting Issues, Bodies in Question', in *Art New Zealand*, vol. 78, 66–67.

APPENDIX 2
A Pacific Bibliography, 1985–2000 Continued

These references add to the published works on contemporary Pacific art from 1985–2000. Unfortunately they are each lacking a piece of information and, therefore, are not full citations. However, this information may be of use.

Anonymous. 1987. Fatu Feu'u. *Hepanui*, 2 November.

—— 1988. Fa'a Samoa. *Capital Times*, 9–16 February.

—— 1989. Artist contributes to Pathfinder Mural. *Central Leader*, 18 April, 12.

—— 1990. Artists reinterpret Pacific traditions. *The Press*, 25 July.

—— 1994. Where cultures combine. *New Zealand Herald*, 30 November.

—— 1995. First art exhibition shapes as stepping stone into art scene. *Manu-Samoa International Weekly*, 2 May.

—— 1996a. Pacific views. *The Star*, 6 November, 9.

—— 1996b. Fatu Feu'u. *The Star*, 11 May, 1.

—— 1997a. The future face of dynamic NZ. *Manukau Courier*, 25 September, 11.

—— 1997b. Exhibition on the move. *Manukau Courier*, 4 November.

—— 1998a. Artists work draws controversy. *Manukau Courier*, 3 December.

—— 1998b. Pacific wave 98 launched at Bondi. *Community Arts Express*, December 1–3.

Bilbrough, M. Island Vision.

Burton, D. 1995. Sculptors carve out new NZ identity. *The Press*, 1 February.

Cain, S. 1992. Works have a chilling edge. *The Evening Post*, 25 June.

Carroll, P. 1996. Guardians at the gates of culture. *The New Zealand Herald*, 31 July.

—— 1997. Seventies child navigates a voyage around his people. *The New Zealand Herald*, 29 September.

Cartwright, G. Cultural Crossover. *Auckland Star*, 12 February.

Christian, D. 1996. Artist honoured by request. *Manukau Courier*, 1.

Clayton, P. 1989. Shed 11 houses powerful art. *Contact*, 3 March.

Duke, T. 1995. Bi-cultural theme extended. *Manukau Courier*, 19 May.

Fusco, C. 1995. Samoan splendours. *The Press*, 8 March.

Gregg, S. . . . for a 'brown consciousness'. *Sunday Star Times*.

Hansby, B. 1998. Mangere artist off to Sydney. *Manukau Courier*.

Harper, P. 1991. Arts. *Contact* 11 July.

Houlahan, M. 1991. Pacific culture explored. *The Dominion*, 9 July.

Johnstone, J. 1999. Capturing passion on canvas. *The Star*, 30 June.

Mayston, B. 1995. Weaving in plastic. *The Otago Daily Times*, 14 June.

McNamara, T. J. 1988. Finely feminine. *New Zealand Herald*, 17 March.

—— 1991. The real meaning of angst. *New Zealand Herald*, 16, May.

—— 1992a. Campbell cuts a bold message. *New Zealand Herald*, 2 April.

—— 1992b. Youth upstages installation. *New Zealand Herald*, 28 May, 2.

—— 1992c. Something for all along the trail. *New Zealand Herald*, 26 November.

—— 1993. Esoteric imagery from old Spain. *New Zealand Herald*, 6 May.

—— 1995. Raw energy in awards show. *New Zealand Herald*, 25 October Section Three, 9.

Melhop, S. 1990. Island colour, imagery. *The Star*, Christchurch, 16 August.

Meredith, K. 1988. Struggling artist no longer. *Auckland Sun*, 1 July, 9.

Mitchell, M. Bold and furious. *Liverpool Leader*.

Orme, P. 1993. Works by Feu'u. *The Press*, 7 April.

Raphael, M. Visa Gold Art Award, 42.

Schamroth, H. 1990a. Dark dream theme is entrancing work. *New Zealand Herald*, 1 March.

—— 1990b. Magnificent masks. *New Zealand Herald*, 26 April.

Taouma, L. 1988. Inspired by local art. *Manukau Courier*, 21 July.

Taylor, R. 1989. Grand opportunity to view a wide sweep of art history. *The Dominion*, 8 March.

Thompson, A. 1991. Pacific arts mix old and new. *The Dominion*, 24 July.

Ussher, R. A feast of prints to savour. *The Press.*

Wedde, I. 1988. Tapa of the Pacific—beautiful and durable. *The Evening Post*, 18 February.

—— 1990. Painting as camouflage. 8 February.

Notes

INTRODUCTION

1 I use the generic term "barkcloth" as each Pacific language has its own word for this material product. Also, Pacific words, such as tivaevae, are not set within quotation marks as they are not foreign to Pacific speakers. This text does, however, provide a glossary for Polynesian words. *Shortland Street* is a popular New Zealand soap opera, and Annie Crummer, Sulata and Lole are Pacific vocal artists.

2 The scholars and the volumes that they have written are too numerous to elaborate upon here. See Appendices 1 and 2 for an example of the scope of this debate.

3 Self-governing status was attained by the Cook Islands (1965), Nauru (1968), Fiji (1970), Niue (1974), Papua New Guinea (1975), the Solomon Islands and Tuvalu (1978), and Kiribati (1979).

4 In 1981, a series of rugby matches between South Africa's Springboks and New Zealand's All Blacks became know as the Springbok Tour. At that time many countries had ceased sporting activities with South Africa due to its apartheid policies. However, in New Zealand, sport overtook politics and the tour took place—against vociferous protest. Protestors, many of whom had a stake in New Zealand's sovereignty politics, wanted to demonstrate their condemnation of apartheid policies. A major result was that New Zealand positioned itself as an anti-apartheid government.

5 At the time of writing, Young is back in New Zealand. Both Jessop and Tangaroa continue to create work; however, their practice is not highly visible in New Zealand.

6 This core—Fatu Feu'u, Niki Hastings-McFall, Ioane Ioane, Lily Laita, Iosefa Leo, Ani O'Neill, Johnny Penisula, John Pule, Filipe Tohi, Michel Tuffery and Jim Vivieaere—continued to work and to be key players in the contemporary Pacific art movement over this fifteen-year period. Some artists have joined their ranks; others have exited from the spotlight.

7 Unfortunately, it took academics interested in the Pacific more than a decade to address sovereignty and civil rights issues in their work. Anthropologists remained ensconced in "salvage anthropology", and style area analysis was the only Pacific art history that was being studied.

8 This issue was complicated for art historians as the authenticity/tourist-art debate blurred their ability to acknowledge contemporary art production as Pacific art.

9 Exceptions to this are the Museums of New Zealand and the Bishop Museum of Honolulu.

10 In the 1980s and 1990s, there was lively debate concerning authenticity and the traditional. Some of the main scholars involved were Linnekin & Poyer, Kaeppler, and Keesing & Tonkinson. For further information, see the Appendices section.

11 New Zealand's need for a stronger labour force was one of the main reasons for immigration from the Pacific. In the early 1960s, Samoans and Tongans were permitted three-month working visas, which were not policed. In 1967 the New Zealand government put annual quotas into place. Other island groups, however, were not affected by this quota system. Subsequently, in the early 1970s, a decline in the economy led many to believe that Pacific Islanders were becoming a burden on New Zealand's social services. This led to what were called the dawn raids, a period when Pacific households were raided in order to find people who had overstayed their visas. This period led to a questioning of all islanders, as well as Māori, reinforcing ethnic tensions.

12 Pasifika was a label that they could use to represent themselves. It became fashion, street culture and hip hop. It is also interesting that PACIFICA is an acronym for a woman's group PACIFICA Inc. stands for Pacific Allied (Women's) Council Inspires Faith Ideals Concerning All—a national organisation established in 1976 as part of a movement to bridge the gap between the island and the urban. It provides support for Pacific women and also lobbies on issues of concern to them.

13 As the contemporary Pacific art movement is still in its infancy, the number of scholars interested in this field is limited. However, this does not mean that little has been written. Appendices 1 and 2 represent an attempt at a compilation of everything that was written about contemporary Pacific art between 1985 and 2000. Unfortunately, as many of these pieces were in newspapers, full citations are not available for all texts.

14 These include Herda, Hereniko, Keesing, Linnekin, Teilhet/Teilhet-Fisk and Tiatia.

15 I use the phrase to emphasise the stereotype. None of these terms are pan-Pacific. However, their generic use by the West may suggest that they are.

16 In 2000, Andy Lelei changed his name to Andy Leleisi'uao. Andy's father had shortened the name to facilitate bureaucratic matters (as did many Polynesian immigrants). Andy was unaware of this until 2000, at which time he took back his family name. My first reference to him is as Lelei, the name he used at that time. However, I refer to him as Leleisi'uao subsequently, as that is his correct name.

CHAPTER 1

1 *Te Maori*, an exhibition of Māori art, toured the United States between 1984 and 1986. Opening at the Metropolitan Museum of Art (September 1984), it then travelled to the Saint Louis Museum of Art (February 1985), the H. M. de Young Museum (San Francisco, August 1985) and finally the Field Museum in Chicago (March 1986). *Te Hokinga Mai* opened at the National Museum (Wellington, August 1986), followed by Dunedin (November 1986), Christchurch (March 1987) and Auckland (June 1987). It is interesting to note that three of the four venues in the United States were art galleries, whereas three of the four venues in New Zealand were museums.

2 This quote, by Stacy Gregg of *More* magazine (1990: 27–46), offers a perspective of New Zealand in 1990—the 150th anniversary of the signing of the Treaty of Waitangi and the time for an opportunity to move forward the ideology of a bicultural nation. This quote suggests the uneasiness the status created for many Pākehā, who much preferred to re-situate themselves as a non-threatening Pacific nation.

3 The bibliography on contemporary indigenous arts is too large to cite here. There are many books and exhibition catalogues that focus on individual artists, and yet few authors have endeavoured to write broadly and address the issues surrounding contemporary indigenous art practice. Those who have include W. Jackson Rushing, Janet C. Berlo, Ruth Phillips, Howard Morphy and Susan Cochrane.

4 Key galleries during this early period (1985–1994) were ASA Gallery, Muka Studio, Maota Samoa Tautai, RKS Gallery, the Lane Gallery in Auckland, and 33 1/3 in Wellington. The National Art Gallery and The Dowse Art Museum, Wellington; the Govett-Brewster Gallery, New Plymouth; the McDougall Contemporary Art Annex, Christchurch; and the Fisher Galleries also held Pacific exhibitions during this period.

5 See Mead, Mane-Wheoki and Panoho.

6 In essence, the exhibition introduced New Zealand to Fatu Feu'u, Ioane Ioane, Sale Jessop, Lily Laita, Iosefa Leo, Johnny Penisula, John Pule, Filipe Tohi, Michel Tuffery and Jim Vivieaere.

7 At the time, Robin White positioned herself as a Pākehā living in Kiribati. Since then Robin has acknowledged her Māori heritage.

8 This type of reflection was also demonstrated in *5 New Artists* at the National Art Gallery and Dominion Museum, which included Lily Laita and Māori artist Ralph Hotere.

9 The exhibition was held at City Gallery Wellington; the Auckland City Gallery; the Waikato Art Gallery, Hamilton; Te Manawatu, Palmerston North; and the McDougall Contemporary Art Annex, Christchurch.

10 The core twenty-three included Fatu Feu'u, William Furneaux, Patriq Futialo, Bruce George, Niki Hastings-McFall, Ioane Ioane, Lily Laita, Iosefa Leo, Simmie Nichols, Ani O'Neill, Johnny Penisula, Lyle Penisula, Laugutu Poloai, John Pule, Albert Refiti, Toegamau Tom Sefo, Greg Semu, Tania Short, Filipe Tohi, Michel Tuffery, Lape Fakalaga Tulisi, Veronica Vaevae and Loretta Young. The following are some of the artists that were added along the way: Luana Asiata, Grace, Sale Jessop, Sasha Kronfeld, Sheyne Tuffery, Evotia Tamua and Glenda Vilisoni.

11 Michel Tuffery, who is dyslexic, is known to misspell words in the titles of his works. Tiangi is not a Samoan word. However, tianigi is the word for pain (personal communication, F. Pereira, 2007). Clearly the association with the excruciating pain of acquiring a pe'a, as well as the pain endured in the crucifixion, was the relationship Tuffery was positing with this image.

12 These include: *Te Kare Mowhiti—Romance of the Mask 1998; Heart of the Niu, 1998; Fireworks: Art of the Pacific Age, 1998; Ring of Fire, 1999;* and *Island Crossings, 2000.*

13 These include *Fresh off the Boat* (1994), *Tatau* (1996), *Romeo and Tusi* (1997) and *Dawn Raids* (1997).

14 *The Semisis*, created by Dave Armstrong and Danny Mulheron, was a television series aired in New Zealand in 1998. Its core cast comprised Dave Fane, Hori Ahipene, Robbie Magasiva, Jackie Clark and Lyndee-Jane Rutherford. It provided the opportunity for Pacific actors and writers—Eteuati Ete, Sima Urale, Ivan Tanuvasa, Erolia Ifopo and Oscar Kightley amongst others.

15 In New Zealand, the creation of arts trusts allowed various orqanisations to access government funds; a large percentage of these funds came from the Pacific Arts Committee of Creative New Zealand, which was established in 1994. Many of these trusts were community based; others, like the Tautai Contemporary Pacific Arts Trust, are national organisations. The Pacific Business Trust, which supports the Pacific Art Awards, receives funding from the Ministry of Pacific Island Affairs.

16 The development of a new vocabulary allowed Pacific artists to own what they were doing. This idea is further developed in Chapter 6.

CHAPTER 2

1 For further information about the use of cultural symbols in the creation of a national identity see Keesing & Tonkinson 1982 and Rosi 1991.

2 Often contemporary political boundaries have nothing to do with the cultures now bound by them. This complicates both the need for, and the process of, creating national identities.

3 For further information see Hereniko 1994, Mane-Wheoki 1995b, Nero 1992 and Thomas 1995b.

4 Stephanie Taylor & Margaret Wetherell (1995: 69–84) made this distinction quite clear when they wrote 'a claim to national identity . . . can be merely a description of one's official citizenship, a reference to the type of passport one carries. However, these can also be references with a psychological significance, the points where personal history is seen as intersecting with social history'.

5 Personal communication, Ioane Ioane, March 1997.

6 Tangata whenua is a Māori term meaning 'people of the land'. Its use addresses the reality of Māori as the indigenous people of New Zealand, a status that Pacific peoples clearly do not have.

7 Key scholars involved in this debate were Linnekin & Poyer, Kaeppler and Keesing & Tonkinson.

8 Personal communication, John Pule, May 1996.

9 Personal communication, Ani O'Neill, June 1996.

10 Personal communication, Ani O'Neill, June 1996.

11 Personal communication, Ani O'Neill, June 1996.

12 Personal communication, Lily Laita, June 1996.

13 Personal communication, Michel Tuffery, June 1996.

CHAPTER 3

1 According to the *Random House Dictionary of the English Language* (1979: 6), abstraction is 'a. of or pertaining to the formal aspect of art, emphasising lines, colours, generalised or geometric forms, etc., esp. with reference to their relationship to one another. b. (often cap.) pertaining to the non-representational art styles of the 20th century'.

2 Recent theoretical forays into the concept of va or space within a Polynesian context has clearly demonstrated the complex theoretical foundations of Pacific thought and action. For further information see Mahina, Wendt and Refiti.

3 Jocelyn Linnekin reviews this literature in Linnekin & Poyer 1990.

4 The belief that art production was a communal activity derives from the practice of groups of men and women working and creating while talking. Conversing while doing repetitive activities and/or utilising groups for large-scale projects (for example barkcloth production) is labelled communal. This practice enabled the passing of cultural knowledge, via story telling and/or both contextualising and reinforcing the knowledge and skills necessary for that activity.

5 In the past, most sculpture from the Pacific was perceived to be representative images of the gods.

6 As weaving and tivaevae are rarely considered part of New Zealand's contemporary art traditions, there is a distinct lack of information about key artists. Emma Kesha (Samoa) and Matafetu Smith (Niue) are well-known traditional weavers. Those individuals involved with the innovation and utilisation of plastics in weaving are not named. For further information see Pereira in Mallon & Pereira, 2002.

7 Personal communication, Ani O'Neill, September 1998.

8 Personal communication, Filipe Tohi, September 2000.

9 The fibre used to lash these works together is flax, referencing Cooper's Māori ancestry as well.

CHAPTER 4

1 This chapter does not refer to the fusion of the island and the urban with the term "hybrid" (as it is often labelled). Bhabha's hybrid (and that debate) does not lead to an understanding of this art movement, nor does it provide Pacific artists with a voice. The hybrid issue is, however, acknowledged and addressed in Chapter 6.

2 Tony Fomison was a key player in New Zealand's art world in the 1980s. He took an interest in Feu'u's work, and his encouragement had a significant influence on Feu'u's practice.

3 Personal communication, John Pule, 1996.

CHAPTER 5

1 In other writings I titled this work *Samoan Born Ministers are Wankers*, as this is written across the work. Andy Leleisi'uao recently corrected my mistake.

2 Polynesians historically used humour as a means of critique. The faleaitu in Samoa (Sinavaiana), the arioi in Tahiti (Oliver) and clowning in Rotuma (Hereniko) are all examples of institutions that enable political and social criticism.

3 Pacific Underground was formed in 1992 by Oscar Kightley, Erolia Ifopo, Mishelle Muagututi'a, Michael Hodgson and Simon Small. They enlisted the support of other friends (Pos Mavaega, Tanya Muagututi'a), and over time their company grew to include (from time to time) Joy Vaele, Dave Fane, Anton Carter, Sara-Lia Tamati, Dallas Tamaira, Shimpal Lelisi and Mario Gaoa. They wrote, directed and produced *Fresh off the Boat* (Oscar Kightley and Simon Small, 1993), *Romeo and Tusi* (Erolia Ifopo and Oscar Kightley, 1996), *Tatau* (Erolia Ifopo and Oscar Kightley, 1996), *When the Frigate Bird Sings* (Oscar Kightley and Dave Fane, 1996) and *Dawn Raids* (Oscar Kightley, 1997). Pacific Underground also played a key role in the community, taking their 'School Play' productions into secondary schools.

4 As I am not a literary critic, I have not elaborated on the body of literature produced by Albert Wendt, John Kneubuhl, Alistair Campbell, Epeli Hau'ofa and Sia Figel. Their works have added greatly to the re-presentation of Pacific identities, not only in New Zealand, but also across the Pacific.

5 The 1930s and 1940s were the years when Dashiell Hammett's Sam Spade character (The Maltese Falcon, 1931) came to prominence. It was also the period when McPhee (and his mentor, Leeteg) were in Tahiti.

6 Personal communication, Michel Tuffery, 1997.

CHAPTER 6

1 In the 1970s and 1980s Pacific Islanders were asserting a cultural voice. Many academics refuted the "traditional" or "authentic" nature of what was perceived to be re-invented traditions. Key voices in this debate were Kessing & Tonkinson, Linnekin & Poyer and Wendt.

2 Pacific histories and stories have not played a prominent position in the New Zealand education system. Pacific Underground, Linda Smith, Albert Wendt, as well as other writers, artists and musicians, are all rectifying this by using these stories and themes as a basis for their work.

3 This chapter looks at a variety of art forms that flourished during this period. As this text attempted to utilise only images that had not previously been published, I direct the reader to Mallon & Pereira 2002 for discussions around the themes of this chapter and the photographs associated with them.

4 Makerita Urale made this comment at *Tatau/Tattoo: Embodied Art and Cultural Exchange c1760–2000*, held at Victoria University 21–23 August 2003.

5 Stacy Gregg, *More*, 'Pacifica' issue, 1990: 27.

6 Other categories included: three-piece collection, wearable arts and Pasifika menswear. In 1998 three new categories were introduced: Pasifika body art (painted only), parent and child, and fa'afafine Pasifika glamour. See Raymond 2002, p. 97.

7 There were two "camps": those working from a more traditional base, including Daphne Coles, Paddy Walker, Paula Chan-Cheuk, Mi'i Quarter and Frances Palu; and those focused on streetwear, such as Louis Fesola'i, Mere Naigulevu, Pacific Sisters, Sofia Tekela-Smith, Ani O'Neill and Shigeyuki Kihara. For more information see Raymond 2002, pp. 91–102.

8 Personal communication, Rosanna Raymond, 2007.

9 Personal communication, Rosanna Raymond, 2007.

10 The core group of 'Sisters' included Suzanne Tamaki, Rosanna Raymond, Ani O'Neill, Lisa Reihana, Niwhai Tupaea, Fiona Wall, Selina Forsyth, Toni Symons, Karlos Quartez and Greg Semu. Both Mika and Henry Ah-Foo Taripo contributed to performances. For further discussion on Pacific Sisters, see Stevenson 1997, Vercoe 1999 and Vercoe & Leonard 1997.

11 Personal communication, Rosanna Raymond, 2007.

12 Personal communication, Rosanna Raymond, 2007.

13 The foundations of hip hop were laid in the 1990s, but clearly the popularity of this music genre has not waned; in fact, it has continued to grow. This has led Gareth Shute to comment (2004: 145), 'By 2003 the hip hop scene had reached a size where it was difficult to keep track'. Some of the key players post-2000 are Che Fu, King Kapisi, Savage, Scribe, Nesian Mystik, Ladi6, Footsouljahs, Ill Semantics and Deceptikonz. For further information see Mitchell 2001, Shute 2004 and Zemke-White 2002.

14 I utilise this current (2007) instance of cover art as an example of the names and the play on words used by hip hop artists.

15 Dawn Raid Entertainment continues to be a huge player in both New Zealand music and fashion. Two key compilation CDs—*Southside Story* 1999 and *Southside Story 2* 2001—cemented Dawn Raid Entertainment's place in the music industry. They continue to produce Ill Semantics, Deceptikonz, Footsouljahs and Mareko. Dawn Raid Entertainment also produces a line of clothing, including T-shirts. King Kapisi, too, created a line of clothing—under the label Overstayer—for this specific youth market.

16 Personal communication, Rosanna Raymond, 2007.

17 Personal communication, Andy Leleisi'uao, March 2006.

Glossary

'afakasi	part-European
arioi	a fraternity of travelling 'players'
aumakua	family or personal god
fa'afafine	effeminate man. (Today, this could also be a trans-gendered person. The role of fa'afafine, traditionally, was quite important in Polynesian societies. Most labour tasks were divided by gender (not sexuality). If a family did not have a daughter (or enough daughters) to complete all of the women's tasks, a son would be used; in essence he would be raised as a girl.
fa'aSamoa	characteristic of or belonging to Samoa. (It is utilised when making comment about traditions or activities that are both inherently Samoan and/or define Samoan-ness.)
fale	house
faleaitu	comedy, clowning
heliaki	speak ironically, to say one thing and mean another
hiapo	barkcloth in Niuean

kapkap	a suspended breast ornament (found in both the Solomon Islands as well as the Marquesas)
kete	a basket
koloa	property, wealth
lalava	to bind
Lapita	Lapita is the name associated with a group of people who were also termed the proto-Polynesians. It is believed that it is from this group of people that Polynesians descend.
lavalava	clothes
lei	head or neck ornaments
mana	power, spiritual essence
ngatu	barkcloth in Tongan
Pākehā	non-Māori, European
palangi	white, European
pareu	garment worn around the loins of both sexes
pe'a	tattoo
siapo	barkcloth in Samoan
siva	dance
tangata whenua	local people, aborigines, natives
taonga	property, treasure
tatau	tattoo
taulima	a feature characteristic of or denoting the upper arm (arm adornment). A taulima (today) is a tattoo that signals a relationship (ideally a cultural heritage) with Samoa.

taupou	a title/position held, according to Samoan custom by a virgin singled out for her charm, looks and manners.
tifaifai	to patch (an appliqué quilt in Tahiti)
tiki	an image, statue, neck ornament
tivaevae	to patch (an appliqué quilt in the Cook Islands)
tivaevae ta'orei	piecework
tuiga	ceremonial headdress
umu	stone underground oven
upeti	tablet or board used in applying designs on barkcloth
va'a/vaka	canoe
waka	canoe

Artists

ARTISTS WITH ILLUSTRATIONS

Tai Mulitalo

Shigeyuki Kihara

Evotia Tamua

Nanette Lela'ulu

Sheyne Tuffery

Anderson Leleisi'uao

Sima Urale

Lonnie Hutchinson

Rosanna Raymond

Laugutu Poloai

Ani O'Neill

Greg Semu

Misa Tupou

Fatu Feu'u

Johnny Penisula

John Pule

Filipe Tohi

Jim Vivieaere

Ioane Ioane

Lily Laita

Lyle Penisula

Michel Tuffery

Veronica Vaevae

Dagmar Dyck

Ian George

Iosefa Leo

Richard Shortland Cooper

Frances Palu

Loretta Young

Niki Hastings-McFall

Riki Tangaroa

Graham Fletcher

Pacific Sisters

Dawn Raid Entertainment

Pacific Underground

ARTISTS MENTIONED/NO IMAGES

Visual artists

Robin White

Chris Charteris

Simmie Nichols

Sofia Tekela-Smith

Luana Asiata

Sasha Kronfeld

Glenda Vilisoni

Grace

Charlie McPhee

Matafetu Smith

Emma Kesha

Tania Short

Patriq Futialo

Bruce George

Sale Jessop

Toegamau Sefo

William Furneaux

Pauline Hoeft-Cocker

Fashion

Paula Chan-Cheuk

Janine Clarkson

Louis Fesola'i

Daphne Coles

Paddy Walker

Mere Naigulevu

Theatre

Paul and Justine Simei-Barton

Nathaniel Lees

Makerita Urale

Victor Rodger

Ioa Fraser

Hori Ahipene

Robbie Magasiva

Jackie Clark

Eteuati Ete

Ivan Tanuvasa

ARTISTS MENTIONED/NO IMAGES

Writers

Albert Wendt

John Kneubuhl

Alistair Campbell

Epeli Hau'ofa

Sia Figel

Musicians

Phil Fuemana

K.O.S.

Pacifikan Descendants

Jamoa Jam

Ardijah

Te Vaka

Che Fu

King Kapisi

Scribe

Nesian Mystik

Ladi6

Footsouljahs

OMC

Sisters Underground

Dei Hamo

AKA Brown

Moizna

Lost Tribe

Bobby Owen

The Pasifikans

Dei Hamo

Dam Native

Gifted and Brown

Overstayers

Token Village

King Kapisi

Yandall Sisters

Annie Crummer

Lole

Sulata

Ma-V-Elle

COLLECTIVES

Dawn Raid Entertainment (music):

Brother D

Andy Murnane

Ill Semantics

Deceptikonz

Savage

Pacific Underground (theatre/music):

Oscar Kightley

Erolia Ifopo

Dave Fane

Sara-lia Tamati

Dallas Tamaira

Shimpal Lelisi

Mario Gaoa

Mishelle Muagututi'a

Michael Hodgson

Simon Small

Dianna Fuemana

Pos Mavaega

Tanya Muagututi'a

Joy Vaele

Pacific Sisters (fashion/performance):

Suzanne Tamaki

Lisa Reihana

Niwhai Tupaea

Fiona Wall

Selina Forysth

Toni Symons

Karlos Quartez

Mika

Henry Ah-Foo Taripo

Rosanna Raymond

Ani O'Neill

COLLECTIVES

Dance:

Black Grace—Neil Ieremia

Mau—Lemi Ponifasio

Exhibitions and Festivals mentioned:

Te Maori

Te Hokinga Mai

Whatu Aho Rua: A Weaving Together of Traditional and Contemporary Pieces of Taonga

Te Moemoea no Iotefa

Bottled Ocean

Asia-Pacific Triennial of Contemporary Art

Emerging into the Light

Pacific Dragons: Art of Protest and Promise from Fifteen Nations of the Rim.

Island Crossings

5 New Artists

Pasifika Festival

Pasifika Fashion Week

Curators:

Jim Vivieaere

Rangihiroa Panoho

Giles Peterson

Jonathan Mane-Wheoki

Margo Neale

Key Scholars:

Adrienne Kaeppler

Keesing & Tonkinson

Linnekin & Poyer

Anton Carter

Albert Refiti

Nicholas Thomas

Sean Mallon

Fulimalo Pandora Pereira

Justin Paton

Kristen Zemke-White

Index

Page numbers in italics are those of illustrations.

I

J

K

L

P

Q

R

S

T

U

V

W

Y